The
BIBLE
Puzzle & Quiz Book

This edition printed in 2010 by
CHARTWELL BOOKS, INC.
A Division of **BOOK SALES, INC.**
276 Fifth Avenue Suite 206
New York, New York 10001 USA

Copyright © 2010 Arcturus Publishing Limited
26/27 Bickels Yard, 151–153 Bermondsey Street,
London SE1 3HA

Puzzles copyright © 2009 Puzzle Press Ltd

ISBN-13: 978-0-7858-2608-8
ISBN-10: 0-7858-2608-4
AD001253EN

Printed in India

The BIBLE

Puzzle & Quiz Book

OVER 500 PUZZLES AND QUESTIONS
WITH A BIBLICAL THEME

CHARTWELL
BOOKS, INC.

CONTENTS

INTRODUCTION

The puzzles and quizzes presented in the *Bible Puzzle and Quiz Book* have been specially devised to present an entertaining variety of puzzles with a Biblical flavor.

Whatever your taste in puzzles and quizzes, we are sure you will find this selection challenging and fun.

Solutions to all of the puzzles can be found at the back of the book, but try not to peek!

Jacob's Ladder

Change one letter at a time (but not the position of any letter) to make a new word – and move from the word at the top of each ladder to the word at the bottom, using the exact number of rungs provided.

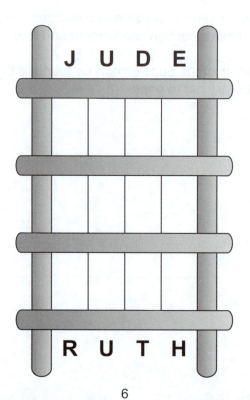

J U D E

R U T H

Bible Codeword

Every letter in this crossword has been replaced by a number, the number remaining the same for that letter wherever it occurs. Can you substitute numbers for letters and complete the crossword? The letters either side of the grid and the reference box showing which numbers have been decoded can also aid solving.
One word has already been entered into the grid, to help you on your way.
When finished, use the code to spell out a quotation from the Bible.

Left labels: A B C D E F G H I J K L M
Right labels: N O P Q R S T U V W X Y Z

20	7	4	9	17 (S)	19	■	17	24	9	5	15	19	16	22
7	■	9	■	5 (T)	■	■	9	■	16	■	16	■	6	
17	7	13	22	7 (A)	14	■	15	14	9	2	11	9	13	25
5	■	25	■	4 (R)	■	17	■	22	■	20	■	4	■	
7	17	17	7	17 (S)	17	9	13	■	26	8	4	16	17	5
■	18	■	20	■	■	2	■	5	■	4	■	17	■	19
1	9	22	16	8	■	9	■	4	■	7	9	17	14	16
9	■	■	■	17	8	14	22	9	16	4	■	■	■	26
17	23	6	7	5	■	7	■	6	■	10	7	15	19	5
5	■	5	■	4	■	4	■	2	■	■	9	■	16	■
7	15	5	6	7	14	■	7	20	8	20	14	16	3	10
■	16	■	15	■	17	■	19	■	16	■	12	■	16	
15	8	4	4	9	22	8	4	■	15	7	2	16	4	7
6	■	14	■	21	■	4	■	■	4	■	15	■	4	
20	7	10	2	16	13	5	17	■	25	14	6	5	16	13

Reference Box

1	2	3	4	5	6	7	8	9	10	11	12	13
			R	T		A						

14	15	16	17	18	19	20	21	22	23	24	25	26
			S									

Quotation

14	16	5	13	8	5	5	19	16	17	6	13	25	8	22	8
24	13	6	20	8	13	10	8	6	4	24	4	7	5	19	

S Bend

3

Place the letters of each word, one per cell, so that every word flows in a clockwise direction around a number. Where the hexagons of one word overlap with those of another, the letter in each cell is common to both.

When finished, rearrange the letters in the pale gray hexagons to form the name of a character from the Bible.

ARCHED

BEMUSE

CAMERA

HUMANE

JESTER

PLASMA

REPAIR

SERIAL

SLOPPY

SNAPPY

WALLET

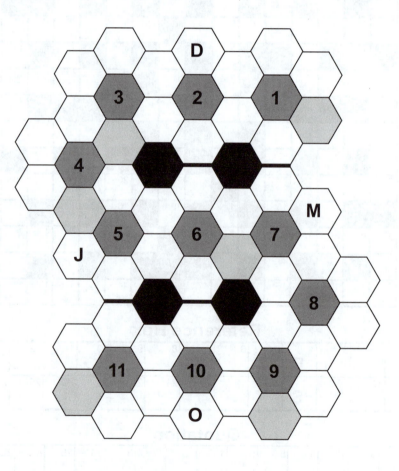

The name is: _____

Phone-etics

Use the telephone dial in order to spell out the Bible quotation.

4 9 2 3 3   6 6 8 ,   1 6 2   0 3   8 4 1 5 5   6 6 8   1 3

4 9 2 3 3 2 :   2 6 6 2 3 5 6   6 6 8 ,   1 6 2   0 3   8 4 1 5 5

6 6 8   1 3   2 6 6 2 3 5 6 3 2 :   3 6 7 3 4 9 3 ,   1 6 2   0 3

8 4 1 5 5   1 3   3 6 7 3 4 9 3 6 .

Wordwheel

How many words of three or more letters can you make from those in the wheel, without using plurals, abbreviations or proper nouns?

The central letter must appear once in every word and no letter in a section of the wheel may be used more than once.

There is at least one nine-letter word in the wheel, which is a proper noun: the name of a book in the Bible.

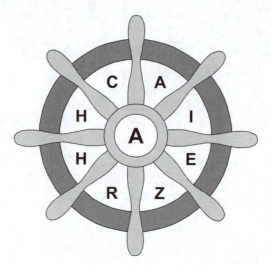

_____

_____

_____

_____

_____

_____

_____

_____

_____

The nine-letter word is: _____

Into the Ark

Can you discover the way through this maze, and thus help these animals to find their way into Noah's Ark at the center?

Christening Conundrum

Mr & Mrs Wordsmith are having a hard time choosing a name for their baby son, who is due to be baptized next Wednesday morning. They have, however, narrowed the choice down to 21 possible names (some of them rather uncommon!). See if you can find them all hidden in the grid below.

Words may run forwards or backwards, either horizontally, diagonally or vertically, but always in a straight, uninterrupted line.

```
Q L Q Y W C Z D L D F L G
D I D D P T X E E W P R S
D C Q D B W R A R N A J U
K E I T L F N E R L N X I
H C H R I S T O P H E R L
K Z A X S L O H N U H U E
N T R R A S D B J D R Y N
S A O T B H O A O J V J R
E R L F F T N R R C M E O
T Q D Y S I L A S R A E C
W U J Q D T O Q Y R E J P
Q I F S T U Z W E R D N A
Y N O T L S I S A A C W Z
```

ANDREW	DYLAN	RAOUL
BASIL	HAROLD	ROSS
CECIL	ISAAC	RUPERT
CHRISTOPHER	JACOB	RYAN
CORNELIUS	RALPH	SILAS
DARREN		TARQUIN
DEAN		TITUS
DICK		TONY

Keyword Crossword

8

Solve the crossword puzzle in the usual way, then rearrange the letters in the shaded squares to spell out a keyword, which is the name of place (it might be a country, region, river, garden, hill, mountain, town or city) that appears in the Bible.

Across
1 Funniness (6)
4 Extreme (6)
9 Rouse, stir up (7)
10 Keyboard instrument (5)
11 In that place (5)
12 Language used by Jews from central and eastern Europe (7)
13 Fairly large, significant (11)
18 Localized ulcer or sore (7)
20 Rascal (5)
22 Changes direction (5)
23 Greed (7)
24 Intelligent (6)
25 Popular drink (6)

Down
1 Pure (6)
2 Indian corn (5)
3 Boxlike containers in a piece of furniture (7)
5 Lukewarm (5)
6 Egg-shaped and flute-like musical instrument (7)
7 Token of victory (6)
8 First of January (3,5,3)
14 Rapid rise (7)
15 Windstorm characterized by a funnel-shaped cloud (7)
16 Plan for attaining a particular goal (6)
17 Become more distant (6)
19 Result from (5)
21 Great unhappiness (5)

Bible Passage Storyword

Some of the words in the Bible passage below have been replaced with clue numbers. The missing words all fit into the grid opposite. For example, if the phrase is "Seek and ye 18A find", this indicates that the solution to 18 Across is 'SHALL', which can then be written into the grid.

Don't worry if you can't discover the precise word required at first glance – when more words are filled into the grid, the letters which intersect with others will help you discover further words.

This passage is taken from Matthew, Chapter 8.

5: And 36A Jesus was 34D into Capernaum, there came 18D him a centurion, 31A him.

6: And 17D, Lord, my servant lieth at 5D 23D of the 16D, 22A 15A.

7: And 12D saith unto him, I will come and heal him.

8: The centurion 33A and said, Lord, I am not 6A that thou shouldest come under my 40A: but 14D the 2D only, and my servant shall be healed.

9: For I am a man under 1D, having 21D under me: and I say to this man, Go, and he 32D; and to another, Come, and he 35A; and to my servant, Do this, and he 10A it.

10: When Jesus 9A it, he 25D, and said to them that 28D, Verily I say unto you, I have not found so 26A 4D, no, not in 19A.

11: And I say unto you, That 37A shall come from the 13A and 36D, and shall sit 38D with 29D, and 27A, and Jacob, in the kingdom of 24D.

12: But the 3D of the kingdom shall be 8D out into 30D 20A: there shall be weeping and 22D of 42A.

13: And Jesus said unto the centurion, Go thy 39D; and as 7A hast believed, so be it 43A unto thee. And his servant was 9D in the 41A 11A.

Bible Passage Storyword

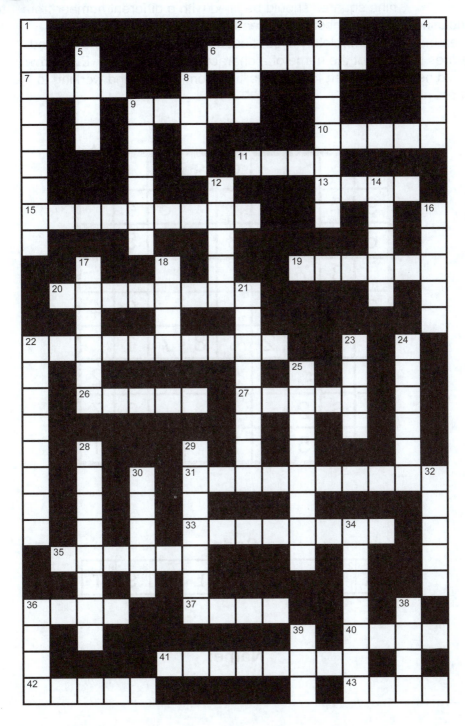

Bible Sudoku

Every row, every column and each of the nine smaller boxes of nine squares should be filled with a different number from 1 to 9 inclusive. Some numbers are already in place.

When the grid is completely filled, decode the numbers in the shaded squares to spell out the name of a character from the Bible. Every row should be read from left to right, starting from the top and working to the bottom of the grid.

1				9	3	2		8
9	7					3	4	
6				8			5	
	3	7	4		9			
2	1						8	4
			2		8	7	1	
	8			5				2
	6	2					9	7
4		5	3	7				1

Code

1	2	3	4	5	6	7	8	9
A	D	E	H	I	L	O	S	T

Name:

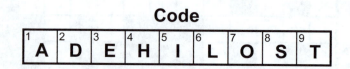

Scripture Knowledge

How's your knowledge of the scriptures? See if you can answer the questions below…

1 Although not specifically named in the New Testament, what was the name of the wife of Pontius Pilate?

_____

2 What is the ninth of the Ten Commandments?

_____

3 Which relative of Jesus lived on locusts and wild honey?

_____

4 Who was the father of the apostles James and John?

_____

5 What is the first word in Genesis, the first book of the Bible?

_____

6 Which book of the Bible follows Deuteronomy?

_____

7 How many books are in the New Testament: 17, 27, 37 or 47?

_____

8 The 12 tribes of Israel were named after the 12 sons of whom?

_____

Shape-up

Every row and column in this grid originally contained one cross, one loaf, one fish, one star and two blank squares, although not necessarily in that order. Every symbol with a black arrow refers to the first of the four symbols encountered when traveling in the direction of the arrow. Every symbol with a white arrow refers to the second of the four symbols encountered in the direction of the arrow. Can you complete the original grid?

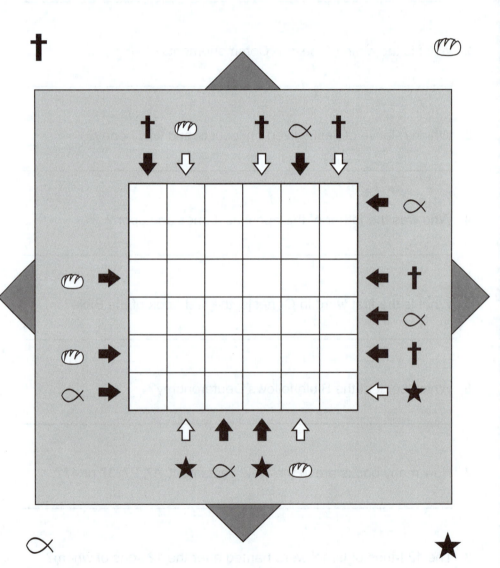

Paul's Pathfinder

The object of this puzzle is to trace a single path from the top left square to the bottom right square of the grid, traveling through all of the cells in either a horizontal, vertical or diagonal direction. Every cell must be entered once only and your path should take you through the letters in the sequence P-A-U-L-P-A-U-L, etc. Can you find the logical way through?

P	A	L	P	A	L	U	A
A	U	A	U	L	U	P	L
U	P	L	P	U	P	U	P
A	L	L	A	P	L	A	A
P	U	A	U	L	A	U	L
A	U	L	P	U	P	A	P
P	A	L	L	A	P	L	U
L	U	P	U	P	A	U	L

Simon's Squares

Fit the letters S, I, M, O and N into the grid in such a way that each horizontal row, each vertical column and each of the heavily outlined sections of five squares each contains a different letter. Some letters are already in place.

M			O	
	I			
			S	
		S		O
N				

The Bottom Line

Can you fill each square in the bottom line with the correct symbol? Every square in the solution contains a symbol from each of the lines above, although two or more squares in the solution may contain the same symbol.

At the end of every row is a score, which shows:

a the number of symbols placed in the correct finishing position on the bottom line, as indicated by a tick; and

b the number of symbols which appear on the bottom line, but in a different position, as indicated by a cross.

SCORE

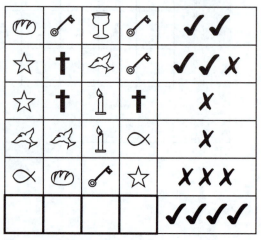

20

Round Dozen

First solve the clues. All of the solutions end with the letter in the center of the circle, and in every word an additional letter is in place. When the puzzle is complete, you can then go on to discover the two names reading clockwise around the outermost ring of letters.

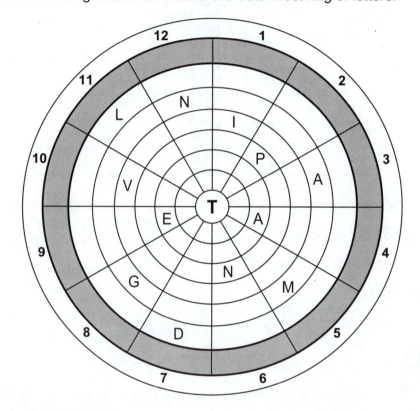

1 Someone opposed to violence or war
2 Resident of a particular place
3 Member of an order of monks noted for austerity and a vow of silence
4 Uneducated
5 Small paperback book, brochure
6 Pleasure-seeking person
7 Next to, alongside
8 Army unit smaller than a division
9 Franz ____, Austrian composer (1797-1828)
10 Most weighty
11 Animal and US Republican Party symbol
12 Structure erected to commemorate persons or events

The names are:

_____ and _____

Pyracross

Solve the clues on each level of the pyramid and reveal the word in the central column of bricks.

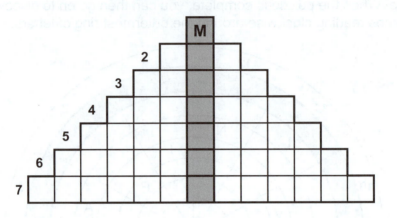

2 Domestic swine

3 Hoarder of money

4 Comical or entertaining

5 Custom

6 Female US sharpshooter who featured in Buffalo Bill's Wild West Show (5,6)

7 Contentious, quarrelsome

Spelling Test

18

Which is the only one of the following to be correctly spelled?

a. **NEBUCHADNEZZAR**

b. **NEBBUCHADNEZAR**

c. **NEBBUCADNEZAR**

d. **NEBUCADNEZZAR**

Bookmark

Answer the clues by using the groups of letters in the lower box, crossing them out as you go. When finished, rearrange the remaining letters to make the name of a book of the Bible.

1 Scandalous, bringing shame
2 Country, capital Vilnius
3 Group of people inhabiting a territory
4 Knowledge acquired through study or experience
5 Having an inferior or less favorable position
6 Country sharing a border with Italy and France
7 State in the north central US
8 Diplomatic building where ambassadors work
9 Fraction, half of a half
10 Reference work containing articles on various topics

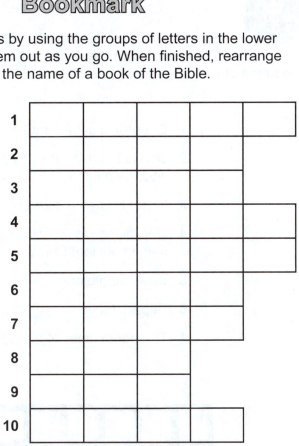

UL	ER	FO	SC	VAN	SY	POP	ON	QUA
UL	IC	HU	DIS	AT	SWI	AC	TA	RMA
ON	GED	YCL	ION	DIA	LE	IA	BAS	RT
SIN	AN	VIT	WI	TI	EM	ERL	EF	TZ
OPE	AD	IN	AND	US	LIT	ENC	DIS	GR

Book: _____

Character Assignation

Fill in the Across clues in this crossword in the normal way.
Then read down the diagonal line of seven squares, to reveal
the name of a character from the Bible.

1 Country, capital Tirana

2 Dense and elaborate trap
   spun by a spider

3 Water lily held sacred by the Egyptians

4 One-piece cloak worn by
   men in ancient Rome

5 Every single one

6 Depart, leave

7 Thirteenth letter of the alphabet

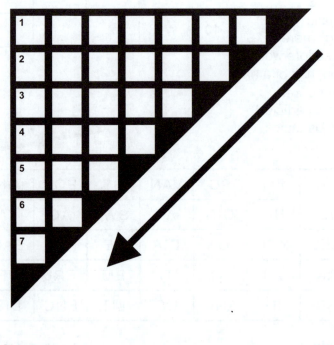

Character: ___ ___ ___ ___ ___ ___ ___

21

What's It Worth?

Each symbol stands for a different number. In order to reach the correct total at the end of each row and column, what is the value of the cross, dove, key and star?

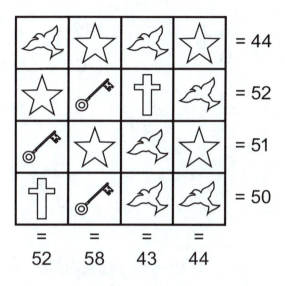

22

Pharaoh's Pyramid

Every brick in this pyramid contains a number which is the sum of the two numbers below it, so that F=A+B, etc. Just work out the missing numbers!

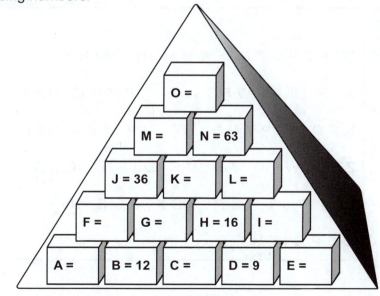

Jigsaw Puzzle

23

Which four pieces (two black and two white) fit together to make a copy of the bell shown here? Any piece may be rotated, but none may be flipped over.

A

B

C

D

E

F

G

H

I

J

Cryptography

24

Each letter of the alphabet in the scroll below has been replaced by another. Can you decipher the code to reveal the quotation, which is taken from Matthew 7:12?

UIFSFGPSF BMM UIJOHT

XIBUTPFWFS ZF XPVME UIBU

NFO TIPVME EP UP ZPV, EP

ZF FWFO TP UP UIFN: GPS

UIJT JT UIF MBX BOE UIF

QSPQIFUT.

The True Path

The chart gives directions to the church in the central square in the grid. Move the indicated number of spaces north, south, east and west (eg 4N means four squares north) stopping at each square once only to arrive there. At which square should you start?

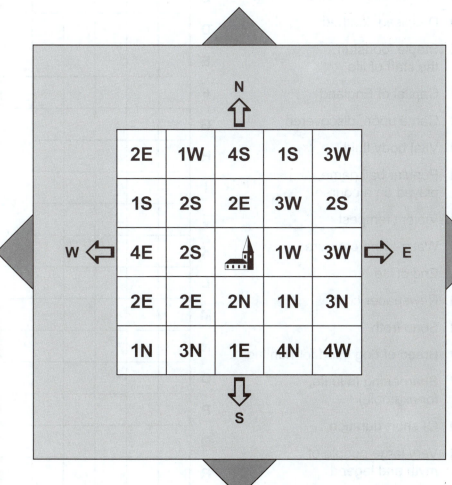

Acrostic

Solve the clues and enter the answers into the grid below.
Then cross-reference the letters to their indicated positions in the grid on the opposite page to reveal a verse from the Bible.

A Warmth

B Mammal used in desert regions

C Intrude upon, overrun

D Despised, loathed

E Staple foodstuff, the staff of life

F Capital of England

G Came upon, discovered

H Vital body fluid

I Popular ball game, played on a course

J Violent tempest

K Water-living creatures

L End of life

M Newspaper chief

N Soap froth

O Breed of dog used for hunting

P Sharpening (a knife, for example)

Q Of short duration

R Very large people of myth and legend

S Season of the year

T Flesh out, make plump

	1	2	3	4	5	6
A						
B						
C						
D						
E						
F						
G						
H						
I						
J						
K						
L						
M						
N						
O						
P						
Q						
R						
S						
T						

Acrostic

C4	P5	M2		D3	L5	T5		B5	M5	E2	L1		I1	G2
O5		T1	H4	Q2	S4	A2	H5		S3	B2	F3		J3	I4
	J2	N4	B4 .		E5	O3	S1	M4		O2	G1		T4	K4
S5		R1	J4	H3	S2	C2	D5	,		T2	P3	C5		H1
M6	Q4	D2	L4	A1	E3	F4		P4	G4	N3	F2		P1	C1
R6		T6	P2	J1	A4	S6	M3	I3	K3		T3	O1	M1	
E1	N6	L2	R3	R5	D1		F5	Q5		F1	R2	K1	C6	;
	N2	R4	G5		B3	L3	O4		Q1	N5	B1	A3	J5	D4
	E4		H2	Q3	C3	K2	F6	P6		J1	I2	G3	N1	.

Shape Spotter

Which is the only shape to appear twice in exactly the same shading (black, white or gray) in the box below? You'll need a keen eye for this one, as some shapes overlap others!

Riddle-Me-Ree

28

Find one letter per line, following the clues given in the verse below. For example, 'My first is in houses, but never in homes' gives the letter U as the first letter. When you have finished, the letters will spell a name.

My first is in LEMON, and also in LIME,

My second's in MOMENT, but never in TIME,

My third is in LEISURE, as well as in HASTE,

My fourth's not in FASHION, but is found in TASTE,

My fifth is in TREASURE, as well as in CASKET,

My name? Think of bulrushes, also of basket!

1st	2nd	3rd	4th	5th

Stop Gaps

29

Certain words from the text below have been removed and are listed to the right, in alphabetical order. Can you replace them in their correct positions?

Revelation 1:1 The Revelation of _____ Christ, which God gave unto him, to shew unto his _____ things which must _____ come to _____; and he sent and _____ it by his _____ unto his servant John:

Revelation 1:2 Who bare _____ of the word of God, and of the _____ of Jesus Christ, and of all _____ that he _____.

ANGEL
JESUS
PASS
RECORD
SAW
SERVANTS
SHORTLY
SIGNIFIED
TESTIMONY
THINGS

Scripture Knowledge

How's your knowledge of the scriptures? See if you can answer the questions below…

1 In which river did John the Baptist carry out his baptisms of repentant Jews?

_____

2 Which city came to be known as 'David's City'?

_____

3 What kinds of food did John the Baptist find to sustain him in the desert?

_____

4 Saint Paul experienced his conversion whilst on the road to which city?

_____

5 What is the more common title for the Decalogue?

_____

6 Why did King David kill Uriah?

_____

7 What was the fate of Naboth, so that his vineyard could be taken?

_____

8 In Matthew 24, according to Jesus, of what future event are the angels unable to tell?

_____

Jacob's Ladder

31

Change one letter at a time (but not the position of any letter) to make a new word – and move from the word at the top of each ladder to the word at the bottom, using the exact number of rungs provided.

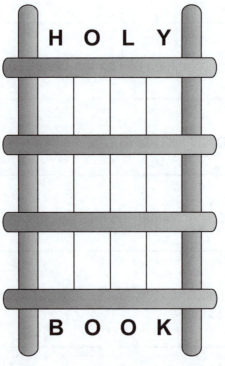

H O L Y

B O O K

Bible Codeword

32

Every letter in this crossword has been replaced by a number, the number remaining the same for that letter wherever it occurs. Can you substitute numbers for letters and complete the crossword? The letters either side of the grid and the reference box showing which numbers have been decoded can also aid solving.
One word has already been entered into the grid, to help you on your way.
When finished, use the code to spell out a quotation from the Bible.

Left side labels (top to bottom): A B C D E F G H I J K L M

Right side labels (top to bottom): N O P Q R S T U V W X Y Z

12	15	5	18	7	26			19	15	1	9	8	25	9	16
7			13		7				1		4		7		7
10	12	20	6	22	22	24	13	8		6		26			26
9			22		22		9	17	12	7	2	7	26	9
10	9	13	22		9	13	22			13					20
	20		9		26		26	7	17	24		18			10
10	7	1	25	18	7	11		2		3	24	13	12	19
4		9		7		7	11	15		9		9			9
6	1	12	6	26		1		16	24	25	15	16	9	25
9		23		19	15	11	10		5		20		23	
7			20			7	10	14		12(C)	19(H)	9(E)	22(F)
5	7	20	21	15	20	7	5		20		19			15
24		9		15		11	9	1	9	20	7	26	15	20
10		9		5		9			10		20			12
19	24	13	13	10	24	25	9		10	7	25	25	13	9

Reference Box

1	2	3	4	5	6	7	8	9 (E)	10	11	12 (C)	13
14	15	16	17	18	19 (H)	20	21	22 (F)	23	24	25	26

Quotation

6	1	26	15	26	19	9	14	6	20	9	7	13	13
26	19	24	1	11	10	7	20	9	14	6	20	9	

33

S Bend

33

Place the letters of each word, one per cell, so that every word flows in a clockwise direction around a number. Where the hexagons of one word overlap with those of another, the letter in each cell is common to both.

When finished, rearrange the letters in the pale gray hexagons to form the name of a character from the Bible.

BUTLER
COSINE
DIFFER
FIESTA

HUBRIS
ITSELF
MARTEN

OCTANE
RELIEF
SENTRY
SUPPLE

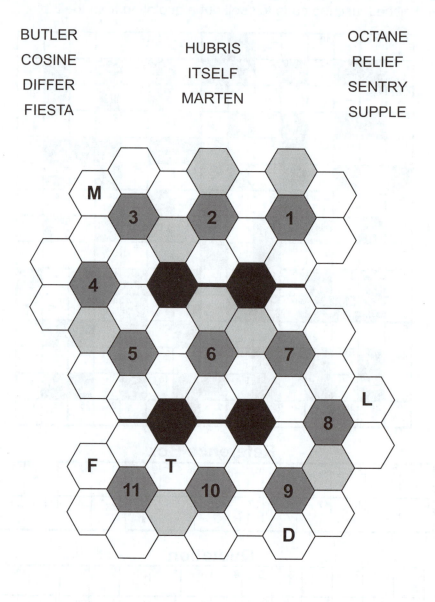

The name is: _____

Use the telephone dial in order to spell out the Bible quotation.

162 843 31784 918 9484698 3675,

162 9642; 162 21746388 918 9666

843 3123 63 843 2336. 162 843

864748 63 362 56932 9666 843

3123 63 843 918378.

Wordwheel

How many words of three or more letters can you make from those in the wheel, without using plurals, abbreviations or proper nouns?

The central letter must appear once in every word and no letter in a section of the wheel may be used more than once.

There is at least one nine-letter word in the wheel, which is a proper noun: the name of a person in the Bible.

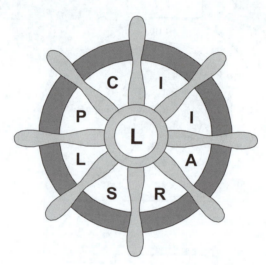

_____

_____

_____

_____

_____

_____

_____

_____

_____

_____

_____

The nine-letter word is: _____

Into the Ark

Can you discover the way through this maze, and thus help these animals to find their way into Noah's Ark at the center?

Books of the Bible

Can you find the listed books of the Bible, which are all hidden in the grid below?

Words may run forwards or backwards, either horizontally, diagonally or vertically, but always in a straight, uninterrupted line.

```
N M S G H U V T H S S Q G
K O E L V A J I L T L W H
M E M S U T I T Y E U A S
X K A E A F Z M O Y C R R
E G J M L S I J E I J N E
X Q O O R I M S M R S S B
O S J Z V J H L A N E U M
D D J U H V G P A I F J U
U F O O D X T M M S A V N
S K S K I E O B Z D P H A
X E H A I R A H C E Z C H
A E U S U C I T I V E L U
B G A L A T I A N S D U M
```

AMOS	JOSHUA	NAHUM
EXODUS	JUDE	NUMBERS
GALATIANS	LEVITICUS	PHILEMON
HOSEA	MICAH	PSALMS
ISAIAH		ROMANS
JAMES		RUTH
JEREMIAH		TITUS
JOEL		ZECHARIAH

Keyword Crossword

Solve the crossword puzzle in the usual way, then rearrange the letters in the shaded squares to spell out a keyword, which is the name of place (it might be a country, region, river, garden, hill, mountain, town or city) that appears in the Bible.

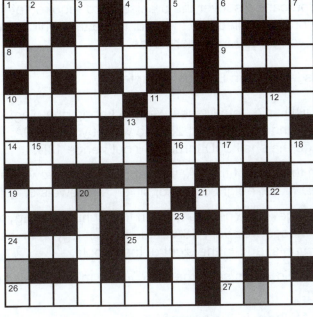

Across

- **1** Entanglement (4)
- **4** Stimulating (8)
- **8** Upright (8)
- **9** Misplace (4)
- **10** Hair on the chin (5)
- **11** The suffering of Jesus at the Crucifixion (7)
- **14** Eight-legged creature (6)
- **16** Not subject to change (6)
- **19** Letter carrier's pouch (7)
- **21** Wild animal (5)
- **24** No longer showing signs of life (4)
- **25** Diminished in strength or quality (8)
- **26** Motion (8)
- **27** Movable barrier in a fence or wall (4)

Down

- **2** Daughter of one's brother (5)
- **3** Schooled (7)
- **4** Every one (4)
- **5** Fall down, as in a heap (8)
- **6** Tall stories (5)
- **7** Color of the rainbow (5)
- **10** Public transport vehicle (3)
- **12** Not easily explained (3)
- **13** Plan and direct (a complex undertaking) (8)
- **15** Small vegetable (3)
- **17** Latter part of the day (7)
- **18** Hitherto (3)
- **19** Device used to connect computers by a phone line (5)
- **20** Narrow shelf (5)
- **22** Aroma (5)
- **23** Catch sight of (4)

Bible Passage Storyword

Some of the words in the Bible passage below have been replaced with clue numbers. The missing words all fit into the grid opposite. For example, if the phrase is "Seek and ye 18A find", this indicates that the solution to 18 Across is 'SHALL', which can then be written into the grid.

Don't worry if you can't discover the precise word required at first glance – when more words are filled into the grid, the letters which intersect with others will help you discover further words.

This passage is taken from Exodus, Chapter 11.

1: And the LORD said unto Moses, Yet will I bring one plague more upon Pharaoh, and upon Egypt; 23D he will let you go 29A: when he shall let 32A go, he shall 30D thrust you out hence 13D.

2: 21D now in the ears of the 9A, and let 5D man borrow of his neighbor, and every 19D of her neighbor, 6D of silver, and jewels of 18D.

3: And the 26D gave the people favor in the sight of the Egyptians. 14D the man Moses was very 18A in the land of Egypt, in the sight of Pharaoh's servants, and in the sight of the people.

4: And Moses said, Thus saith the LORD, 11D midnight will I go out into the 7A of Egypt:

5: And all the firstborn in the land of Egypt shall die, from the firstborn of 16A that 8D upon his 31A, even unto the firstborn of the 7D that is behind the 15A; and all the firstborn of beasts.

6: And there shall be a great 37A throughout all the land of Egypt, such as there was 4A like it, nor shall be 27A it any more.

7: But against any of the children of Israel shall not a 17A move his tongue, 11A man or beast: that ye may 36A how that the LORD doth put a 10D 25D the Egyptians and Israel.

8: And all 38A thy servants shall come down unto me, and 33A down 20A unto me, saying, Get thee out, and all the people that 12A thee: and after that I will go out. And he 34D out from Pharaoh in a great 35A.

9: And the LORD said unto Moses, Pharaoh shall not 2A unto you; that my 19A may be multiplied in the land of 28D.

10: And Moses and 22A did all these wonders 3A Pharaoh: and the LORD 24A Pharaoh's 2D, so that he 1D not let the children of Israel go out of his 27D.

Bible Passage Storyword

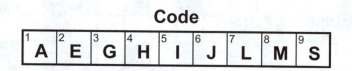

Bible Sudoku

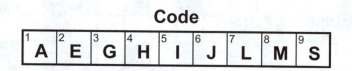

40

Every row, every column and each of the nine smaller boxes of nine squares should be filled with a different number from 1 to 9 inclusive. Some numbers are already in place.

When the grid is completely filled, decode the numbers in the shaded squares to spell out the name of a character from the Bible. Every row should be read from left to right, starting from the top and working to the bottom of the grid.

		9	2			1		7
			3					6
			4	7		3	2	
				1		4	7	
		5				8		
	3	6		4				
	6	1		3	4			
5					8			
9		4			2	7		

Code

1	2	3	4	5	6	7	8	9
A	E	G	H	I	J	L	M	S

Name:

Scripture Knowledge

How's your knowledge of the scriptures? See if you can answer the questions below...

1 In the Sermon on the Mount, the road to destruction is said to be "broad and with a wide ___" what?

_____

2 Who became Moses' wife after their first meeting by a well?

_____

3 What is the name given to the first five books of the Bible?

_____

4 What is Elijah's prediction which he makes in his first appearance in the Bible?

_____

5 Who wrote that Jesus was "a lamb without blemish or defect"?

_____

6 At the time of his resurrection, what did Jesus eat to show that he was real and not a spirit?

_____

7 Jesus said that a man who marries a divorced woman commits what?

_____

8 At his crucifixion, what four-letter inscription appeared at the head of Jesus' cross?

_____

Shape-up

42

Every row and column in this grid originally contained one cross, one loaf, one fish, one star and two blank squares, although not necessarily in that order. Every symbol with a black arrow refers to the first of the four symbols encountered when traveling in the direction of the arrow. Every symbol with a white arrow refers to the second of the four symbols encountered in the direction of the arrow. Can you complete the original grid?

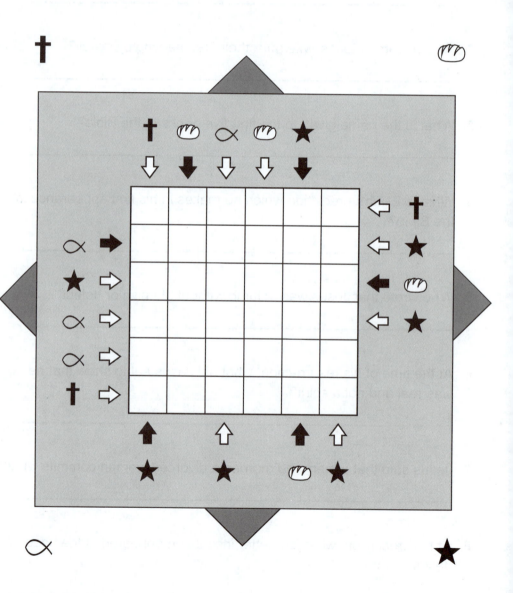

Paul's Pathfinder

The object of this puzzle is to trace a single path from the top left square to the bottom right square of the grid, traveling through all of the cells in either a horizontal, vertical or diagonal direction. Every cell must be entered once only and your path should take you through the letters in the sequence P-A-U-L-P-A-U-L, etc. Can you find the logical way through?

P	U	A	P	U	A	U	A
L	A	U	L	P	L	P	P
A	P	L	P	L	U	A	L
U	A	A	L	P	U	P	U
U	L	P	U	U	A	L	A
A	L	U	A	L	L	P	A
U	P	A	L	P	L	U	U
L	P	P	A	U	A	P	L

Simon's Squares

Fit the letters S, I, M, O and N into the grid in such a way that each horizontal row, each vertical column and each of the heavily outlined sections of five squares each contains a different letter. Some letters are already in place.

I			M	
N				
		O		
			N	I
	S			

45

The Bottom Line

Can you fill each square in the bottom line with the correct symbol? Every square in the solution contains a symbol from each of the lines above, although two or more squares in the solution may contain the same symbol.

At the end of every row is a score, which shows:

a the number of symbols placed in the correct finishing position on the bottom line, as indicated by a tick; and

b the number of symbols which appear on the bottom line, but in a different position, as indicated by a cross.

				SCORE
🕯	🫓	†	🏺	✗ ✗
🫓	🏺	🕊	🗝	✗ ✗
🏺	🕊	☆	∝	✗ ✗
🫓	🕯	∝	☆	✗
∝	🫓	🕯	🗝	✓ ✗
				✓✓✓✓

Round Dozen

First solve the clues. All of the solutions end with the letter in the center of the circle, and in every word an additional letter is in place. When the puzzle is complete, you can then go on to discover the two names reading clockwise around the outermost ring of letters.

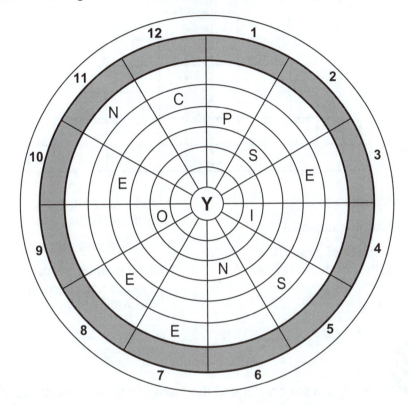

1 Endangerment

2 Envoy, representative

3 Depository for money, etc

4 All mankind

5 Pungent herb much used in cooking

6 Lacking special distinction

7 Month of the year

8 Time without end

9 Gustav Mahler's *Resurrection*, for example

10 Hymn of mourning

11 Wobbly

12 Part of a church where sacred vessels are kept

The names are:

_____   and   _____

Pyracross

Solve the clues on each level of the pyramid and reveal the word in the central column of bricks.

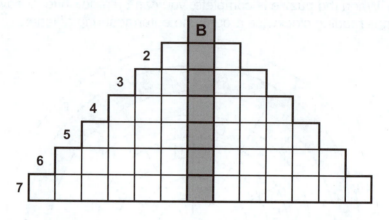

2 Automobile

3 Country, capital Tokyo

4 Disciple of Jesus, the author of the first Gospel

5 Area such as Asia, Europe, Africa, etc

6 Indiscriminately, at random

7 First woman aviator to fly solo non-stop across the Atlantic (6,7)

Spelling Test

Which is the only one of the following to be correctly spelled?

a. THESALONIANS

b. THESALLONIANS

c. THESSALONIANS

d. THESSOLONIANS

Bookmark

Answer the clues by using the groups of letters in the lower box, crossing them out as you go. When finished, rearrange the remaining letters to make the name of a book of the Bible.

49

1 Book of words and their meanings

2 Roman emperor who succeeded Augustus Caesar

3 Former US president, Dwight ___

4 Country, capital Lahore

5 Point to which one travels

6 Percussion instrument

7 Citrus fruit, also a shade of orange

8 Long-legged bird with white or pink plumage

9 Western state of the USA

10 Popular fruit associated with summer

1					
2					
3					
4					
5					
6					
7					
8					
9					
10					

TI	NE	LA	NIA	FL	ST	UM	UK	GE
GO	TLE	EI	RI	ST	BA	DI	ION	AM
KK	CAL	WB	DR	OR	GU	HO	DES	LI
ION	ER	IN	HA	PA	ARY	CA	KET	CT
SEN	KI	RA	NAT	RY	WER	TAN	AN	IF

Book: _____

Character Assignation

Fill in the Across clues in this crossword in the normal way. Then read down the diagonal line of seven squares, to reveal the name of a character from the Bible.

1 Italian composer of *The Four Seasons*

2 Seventh book of the Old Testament

3 Body of the Jewish sacred writings

4 Biblical first man

5 Large constrictor snake

6 Chemical symbol for iron

7 Penultimate letter of the first half of the alphabet

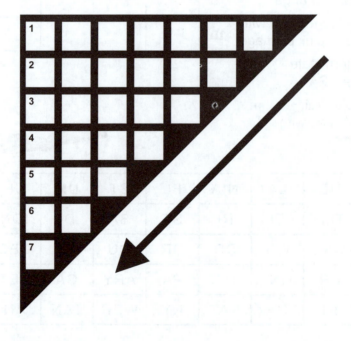

Character: ___ ___ ___ ___ ___ ___ ___

51

What's It Worth?

Each symbol stands for a different number. In order to reach the correct total at the end of each row and column, what is the value of the cross, dove, key and star?

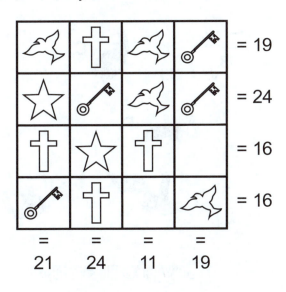

Pharaoh's Pyramid

Every brick in this pyramid contains a number which is the sum of the two numbers below it, so that F=A+B, etc. Just work out the missing numbers!

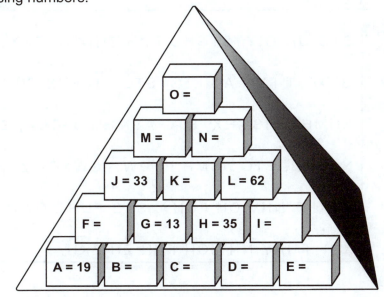

Jigsaw Puzzle

53

Which four pieces (two black and two white) fit together to make a copy of the fish shown here? Any piece may be rotated, but none may be flipped over.

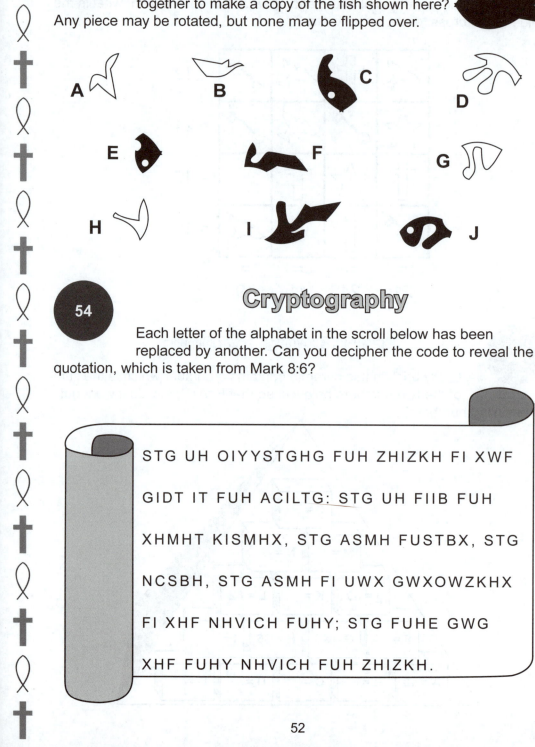

A

B

C

D

E

F

G

H

I

J

Cryptography

54

Each letter of the alphabet in the scroll below has been replaced by another. Can you decipher the code to reveal the quotation, which is taken from Mark 8:6?

STG UH OIYYSTGHG FUH ZHIZKH FI XWF

GIDT IT FUH ACILTG: STG UH FIIB FUH

XHMHT KISMHX, STG ASMH FUSTBX, STG

NCSBH, STG ASMH FI UWX GWXOWZKHX

FI XHF NHVICH FUHY; STG FUHE GWG

XHF FUHY NHVICH FUH ZHIZKH.

The True Path

The chart gives directions to the church in the central square in the grid. Move the indicated number of spaces north, south, east and west (eg 4N means four squares north) stopping at each square once only to arrive there. At which square should you start?

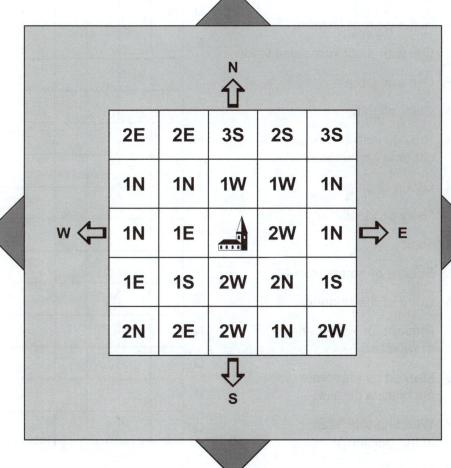

Acrostic

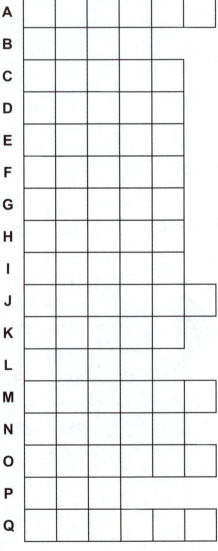

Solve the clues and enter the answers into the grid below. Then cross-reference the letters to their indicated positions in the grid on the opposite page to reveal a verse from the Bible.

A Natural body of running water flowing on or under the earth

B Light drawn around the head of a saint

C Cooked in oil

D Acute pain or torment

E Eye with malicious satisfaction

F Use one's brain

G Color slightly

H Provide with a special gift or entertainment

I Group of singers

J Dairy product

K Topic

L Source of nourishment

M Color of the rainbow

N Present for acceptance or rejection

O Marked by elaborate decorative details

P Weeding tool used in the garden

Q Quantity

56

Acrostic

G2	E5		M4	A1		G5	A5	J5	I4	K3	C2		N2	D3
H2		Q1		I1	H4	Q2	K5	B3		G1	B4		M5	I3
	H5	J2	A3	E3	Q4	G4	B1		F1	K2	J6		J4	D5
C4		L3	N3		D1		F4	N4	O6	M3	E2	P3	,	
H1	P1	O4	O3		C1	L2	I5		B2		N5	M1	J1	I2
	A6	E4	G3		K1	P2		J3	Q5	A2	H3	O2		F3
D4	Q6	M6		O5	F2	A4		F5	C3	M2	D2	L4	O1	K4
	N1	L1		E1	Q3	C5	.							

Shape Spotter

Which is the only shape to appear twice in exactly the same shading (black, white or gray) in the box below? You'll need a keen eye for this one, as some shapes overlap others!

Riddle-Me-Ree

58

Find one letter per line, following the clues given in the verse below. For example, 'My first is in houses, but never in homes' gives the letter U as the first letter. When you have finished, the letters will spell a name.

My first is in TEETH, and also in CHEW,

My second's in FALSE, as well as in TRUE,

My third is in UNDER, but not in BENEATH,

My fourth is in FLOWER, but not found in LEAF,

My fifth is in WINDOW, as well as in DOOR.

My whole is a king: one you've heard of, I'm sure!

1st	2nd	3rd	4th	5th

Stop Gaps

59

Certain words from the text below have been removed and are listed to the right, in alphabetical order. Can you replace them in their correct positions?

Psalm 121:1 I will lift up mine eyes unto the hills, from whence _____ my help.

Psalm 121:2 My help cometh from the _____, which made _____ and _____.

Psalm 121:3 He will not _____ thy _____ to be moved: he that keepeth thee will not _____.

Psalm 121:4 _____, he that _____ Israel shall neither slumber nor _____.

BEHOLD
COMETH
EARTH
FOOT
HEAVEN
KEEPETH
LORD
SLEEP
SLUMBER
SUFFER

Scripture Knowledge

How's your knowledge of the scriptures? See if you can answer the questions below…

1 When David slew Goliath, where did the stone from David's sling strike Goliath?

_____

2 With 176 verses, which of the Psalms has the longest chapter in the whole of the Bible?

_____

3 At his resurrection, who mistook Jesus for a gardener?

_____

4 In Genesis, whose dream shows him sheaves of corn?

_____

5 How did an angel first appear to Moses?

_____

6 "Daughter your faith has healed you" was said to a woman Jesus had just healed from twelve years of suffering what?

_____

7 In the Old Testament, which prophet said "I will pour out my spirit on all people"?

_____

8 Which king's hand shriveled up after he ordered a holy man to be seized at Bethel?

_____

Holy Bible

Jacob's Ladder

Change one letter at a time (but not the position of any letter) to make a new word – and move from the word at the top of each ladder to the word at the bottom, using the exact number of rungs provided.

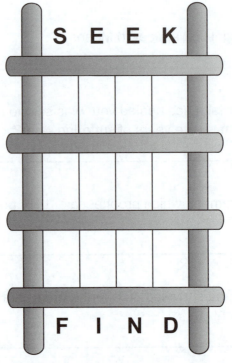

S E E K

F I N D

Bible Codeword

Every letter in this crossword has been replaced by a number, the number remaining the same for that letter wherever it occurs. Can you substitute numbers for letters and complete the crossword? The letters either side of the grid and the reference box showing which numbers have been decoded can also aid solving.
One word has already been entered into the grid, to help you on your way.
When finished, use the code to spell out a quotation from the Bible.

Left column: A B C D E F G H I J K L M
Right column: N O P Q R S T U V W X Y Z

Grid:

7	19	9	17	8	17	23	25	16		23	10	13	25	7
2		17		10		10		10		25		26		13
26	25	22	25	26		15	19	5	10	5	4	10		17
20		25		25		19		18		16		5		5
15	10	8	2	25	9	19	26		21	25	26	18	17	5
		3		5			18		26					25
23	10	8	18		17	5	23	25	26	9	19	13	25	26
2		9		14		20		13		3		25		25
17	5	25	14	20	10	9	17	23	3		7 (S)	13 (P)	19 (O)	23 (T)
26				17		9				17		13		
23	12	25	9	1	25		25	24	24	7	2	25	9	9
17		6		25		13		20		19		26		20
25		13	25	26	22	20	11	25		15	9	19	19	11
23		25		25		11		7		10		5		13
2	19	9	25	16		13	10	23	25	26	5	17	23	3

Reference Box

1	2	3	4	5	6	7 S	8	9	10	11	12	13 P
14	15	16	17	18	19 O	20	21	22	23 T	24	25	26

Quotation

22	19	26	2	25	23	2	10	23	17	7	16	25	10	16
17	7	22	26	25	25	16	22	26	19	11	7	17	5	

S Bend

Place the letters of each word, one per cell, so that every word flows in a clockwise direction around a number. Where the hexagons of one word overlap with those of another, the letter in each cell is common to both.

When finished, rearrange the letters in the pale gray hexagons to form the name of a character from the Bible.

BEHOLD

BYLINE

FONDLY

GARLIC

HAGGLE

HEREOF

LOAVES

NATURE

REVEAL

SLEEVE

TEETHE

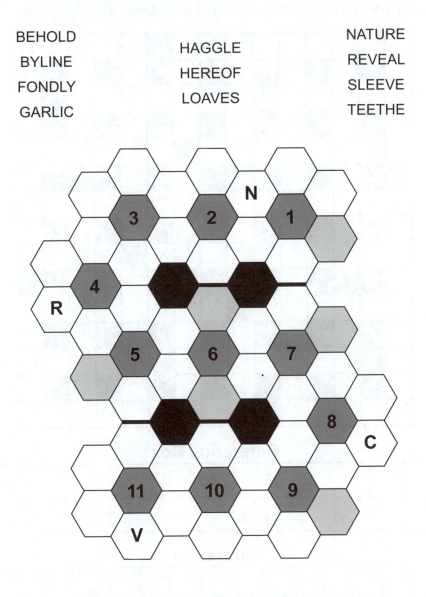

The name is: _____

Phone-etics

Use the telephone dial in order to spell out the Bible quotation.

162 9436 843 26952 668 566337

4423 445, 843 8664 367 445 16 174

63 195798438, 162 219132 48 9484

85453 162 9484 64824, 162 698 843

24452 8437346; 162 843 5142 48 46

843 35138 10 843 74937'8 17464.

Wordwheel

How many words of three or more letters can you make from those in the wheel, without using plurals, abbreviations or proper nouns?

The central letter must appear once in every word and no letter in a section of the wheel may be used more than once.

There is at least one nine-letter word in the wheel, which is a proper noun: the name of a person in the Bible.

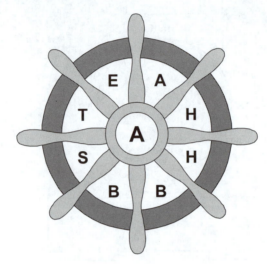

_____

_____

_____

_____

_____

_____

_____

_____

_____

The nine-letter word is: _____

Into the Ark

Can you discover the way through this maze, and thus help these animals to find their way into Noah's Ark at the center?

Saints' Names

Can you find all of the 21 listed names of saints hidden in the grid below?

Words may run forwards or backwards, either horizontally, diagonally or vertically, but always in a straight, uninterrupted line.

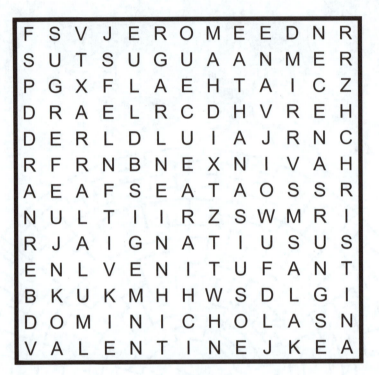

```
F S V J E R O M E E D N R
S U T S U G U A A N M E R
P G X F L A E H T A I C Z
D R A E L R C D H V R E H
D E R L D L U I A J R N C
R F R N B N E X N I V A H
A E A F S E A T A O S S R
N U L T I I R Z S W M R I
R J A I G N A T I U S U S
E N L V E N I T U F A N T
B K U K M H H W S D L G I
D O M I N I C H O L A S N
V A L E N T I N E J K E A
```

ALBERT	DUNSTAN	MONICA
ANDREA	FERGUS	NAZAIRE
ATHANASIUS	HEILER	NICHOLAS
AUGUSTUS	IGNATIUS	SWITHIN
AUSTELL	JEROME	URSANE
BERNARD		VALENTINE
CHRISTINA		WINIFRED
DOMINIC		XAVIER

Keyword Crossword

Solve the crossword puzzle in the usual way, then rearrange
the letters in the shaded squares to spell out a keyword,
which is the name of place (it might be a country, region, river, garden, hill,
mountain, town or city) that appears in the Bible.

Across

3 Having no definite form (9)
8 Country once called Persia (4)
9 White wine flavored with
   aromatic herbs (8)
10 Come into view (6)
13 Propel through the air (5)
14 Large heavy knife used
   for cutting vegetation (7)
15 Hand over money (3)
16 Applauded (7)
17 Theatrical entertainment (5)
21 Compound capable of
   turning litmus blue (6)
22 Salutation, especially
   on meeting (8)
23 Creature said to live in
   the Himalayas (4)
24 Crucial (9)

Down

1 Farm animals, generally (9)
2 Cosmetic product used
   to soften the skin (4,5)
4 Be suspended in the air (5)
5 Depict (7)
6 King of beasts (4)
7 Third son of Adam and Eve (4)
11 Split up (9)
12 Infectious liver disease (9)
14 Crazy (3)
15 Persevere, endure (7)
18 Molten rock in the
   Earth's crust (5)
19 Sword lily (4)
20 Unit of heredity (4)

Bible Passage Storyword

Some of the words in the Bible passage below have been replaced with clue numbers. The missing words all fit into the grid opposite. For example, if the phrase is "Seek and ye 18A find", this indicates that the solution to 18 Across is 'SHALL', which can then be written into the grid.

Don't worry if you can't discover the precise word required at first glance – when more words are filled into the grid, the letters which intersect with others will help you discover further words.

This passage is taken from Luke, Chapter 8.

4: And when much people were gathered 36D, and were come to him out of every city, he 1D by a parable:

5: A 8A went out to sow his seed: and as he sowed, some fell by the 16A side; and it was 38D 10D, and the 24A of the 26A devoured it.

6: And some fell upon a 46A; and as 25A as it was sprung up, it withered away, because it 23D 6D.

7: And 2D fell among thorns; and the thorns sprang up with it, and 42A it.

8: And other fell on good ground, and 34A up, and 3D fruit an 48A. And when he had said these things, he 43D, He that hath 45A to hear, let him hear.

9: And his 21D 40D him, saying, What might this parable be?

10: And he 44D, Unto you it is 28D to know the 20D of the 18A of God: but to 13A in parables; that 1A they might not see, and 14A they 27A not understand.

11: Now the 7A is this: The seed is the word of 15D.

12: Those by the way 9A are they that hear; then cometh the 21A, and taketh away the word out of their hearts, 41A they should believe and be 31A.

13: They on the rock are they, which, when they hear, 11A the word with joy; and these have no 4A, which for a while believe, and in time of 37A 22A 17D.

14: And that which fell among 5D are they, which, when they have 47A, go forth, and are choked with 39A and 32A and 35D of this life, and bring no fruit to 7D.

15: But that on the 19D ground are they, which in an honest and good 33D, having heard the word, 29A it, and bring forth 12D with 30D.

Bible Passage Storyword

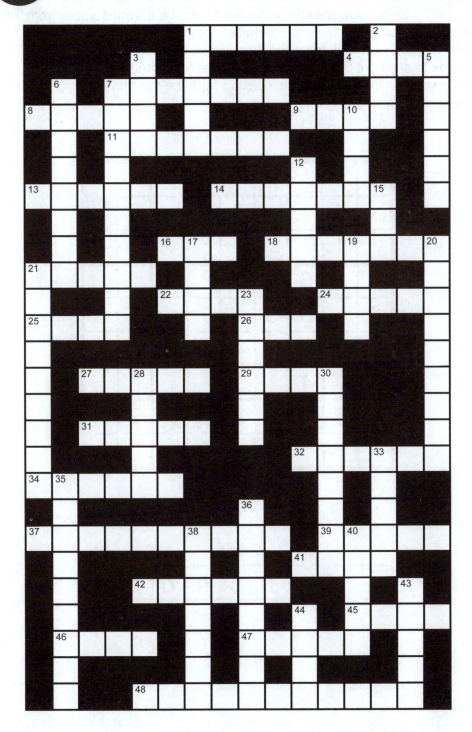

Bible Sudoku

Every row, every column and each of the nine smaller boxes of nine squares should be filled with a different number from 1 to 9 inclusive. Some numbers are already in place.

When the grid is completely filled, decode the numbers in the shaded squares to spell out the name of a character from the Bible. Every row should be read from left to right, starting from the top and working to the bottom of the grid.

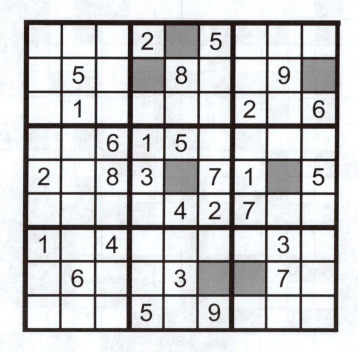

Code

1	2	3	4	5	6	7	8	9
A	C	E	I	G	N	O	S	T

Name:

Scripture Knowledge

How's your knowledge of the scriptures? See if you can answer the questions below…

1 What was the name of Abraham before God changed it?

_____

2 What name was given to the place where Abraham swore an oath with Abimelech?

_____

3 On which mountain did Elijah fight and defeat 450 false prophets devoted to Baal?

_____

4 In Exodus, what foodstuff did God send down to the Israelites as they wandered in the desert?

_____

5 Which close friend of David was killed in a battle with the Philistines?

_____

6 Whose prophesy warned of a time when God would "sweep away the birds of air and the fish of the sea"?

_____

7 On which day did God create the sky?

_____

8 In Genesis, what is inflicted upon the men of the city of Sodom?

_____

Shape-up

72

Every row and column in this grid originally contained one cross, one loaf, one fish, one star and two blank squares, although not necessarily in that order. Every symbol with a black arrow refers to the first of the four symbols encountered when traveling in the direction of the arrow. Every symbol with a white arrow refers to the second of the four symbols encountered in the direction of the arrow. Can you complete the original grid?

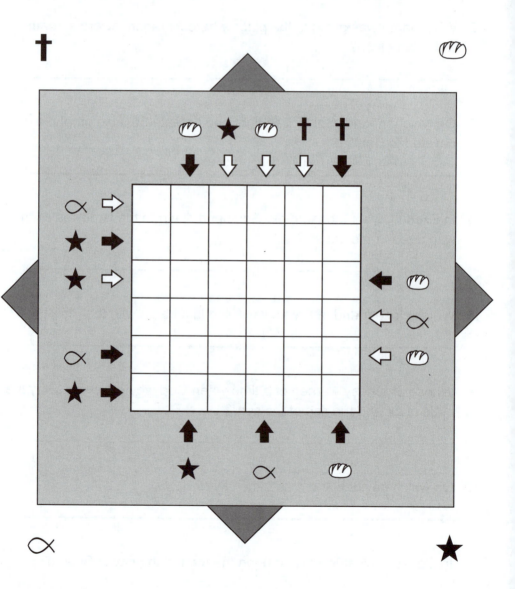

Paul's Pathfinder

The object of this puzzle is to trace a single path from the top left square to the bottom right square of the grid, traveling through all of the cells in either a horizontal, vertical or diagonal direction. Every cell must be entered once only and your path should take you through the letters in the sequence P-A-U-L-P-A-U-L, etc. Can you find the logical way through?

P	A	L	A	P	A	P	L
A	P	U	L	U	L	U	P
U	L	U	L	P	P	A	U
P	A	U	A	A	U	L	A
P	L	L	U	L	P	L	P
A	P	U	A	P	U	A	A
P	U	A	L	U	A	U	P
L	A	U	L	P	U	L	L

Simon's Squares

74

Fit the letters S, I, M, O and N into the grid in such a way that each horizontal row, each vertical column and each of the heavily outlined sections of five squares each contains a different letter. Some letters are already in place.

I				M
	O			
		I		
	S			
M		N		

The Bottom Line

75

Can you fill each square in the bottom line with the correct symbol? Every square in the solution contains a symbol from each of the lines above, although two or more squares in the solution may contain the same symbol.

At the end of every row is a score, which shows:

a the number of symbols placed in the correct finishing position on the bottom line, as indicated by a tick; and

b the number of symbols which appear on the bottom line, but in a different position, as indicated by a cross.

SCORE

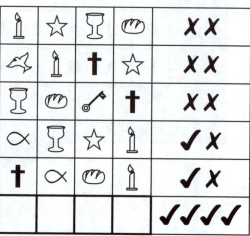

72

Round Dozen

First solve the clues. All of the solutions end with the letter in the center of the circle, and in every word an additional letter is in place. When the puzzle is complete, you can then go on to discover the two names reading clockwise around the outermost ring of letters.

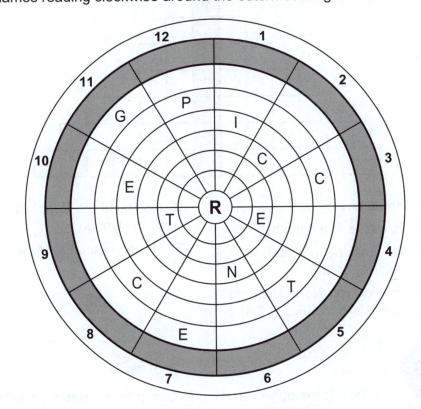

1 Go-between

2 Kidnapper

3 Instrument also known as a 'fipple-flute'

4 Shakespearean tragic monarch (4,4)

5 Figure of speech

6 Wrongdoer

7 Caribou

8 Month of the year with the shortest day-length

9 Teacher

10 Headland in south-eastern North Carolina (4,4)

11 Person who stirs up trouble

12 Person who passes himself off as another

The names are:

_____ and _____

Pyracross

Solve the clues on each level of the pyramid and reveal the word in the central column of bricks.

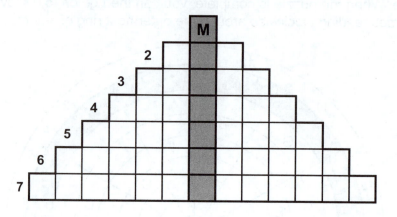

2 Adult males

3 Passage in a church

4 Mediterranean island, capital Ajaccio

5 President of North Vietnam from 1945 to 1969 (2,3,4)

6 Capital of the Republic of the Congo

7 Rolling out, unbending

Spelling Test

Which is the only one of the following to be correctly spelled?

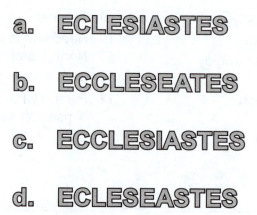

a. ECLESIASTES

b. ECCLESEATES

c. ECCLESIASTES

d. ECLESEASTES

Bookmark

Answer the clues by using the groups of letters in the lower box, crossing them out as you go. When finished, rearrange the remaining letters to make the name of a book of the Bible.

1 Portable form of protection against rain

2 North American great lake

3 Wallchart showing months, dates and holidays

4 Form of water transport

5 Outerwear garment worn in cold weather

6 Color, a mixture of blue and green

7 Gift brought to the infant Jesus

8 Divide, part

9 Maker and seller of hats

10 Last book of the New Testament

1				
2				
3				
4				
5				
6				
7				
8				
9				
10				

CO	ON	LA	EA	RQU	ANK	ND	RA	RI
OR	AI	SE	MI	OV	SE	OI	HA	RE
SE	ER	CA	FR	UM	OAT	IN	AT	MB
EL	ST	LL	PA	EN	ER	SU	LA	INC
BR	TE	TU	PE	VE	AR	TI	GG	LE

Book: _____

Character Assignation

Fill in the Across clues in this crossword in the normal way. Then read down the diagonal line of seven squares, to reveal the name of a character from the Bible.

1 Avid enthusiasts of a cause

2 Six-winged angel of the first order

3 Australian eucalyptus tree-dwelling marsupial

4 Former name of Thailand

5 Porcine animal, hog

6 Abbreviation for US state of Virginia

7 Mathematical symbol for radius

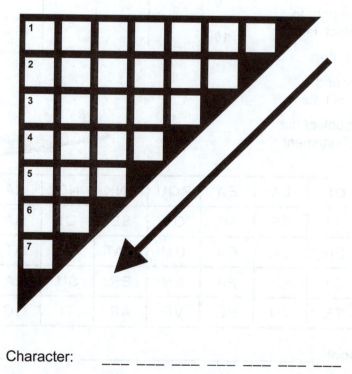

Character: ___ ___ ___ ___ ___ ___ ___

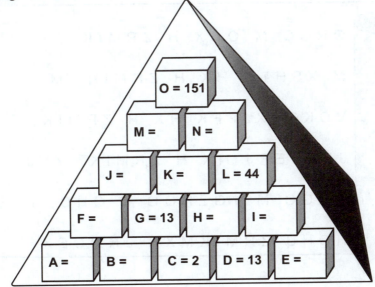

81

What's It Worth?

Each symbol stands for a different number. In order to reach the correct total at the end of each row and column, what is the value of the cross, dove, key and star?

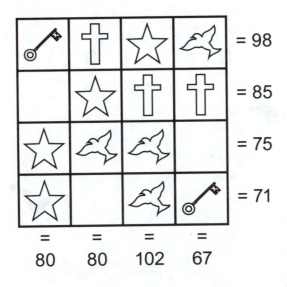

82

Pharaoh's Pyramid

Every brick in this pyramid contains a number which is the sum of the two numbers below it, so that F=A+B, etc. Just work out the missing numbers!

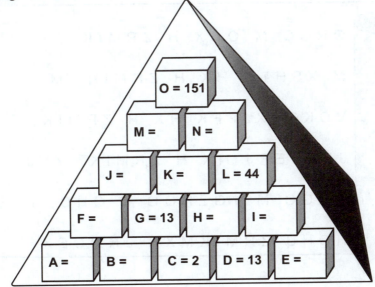

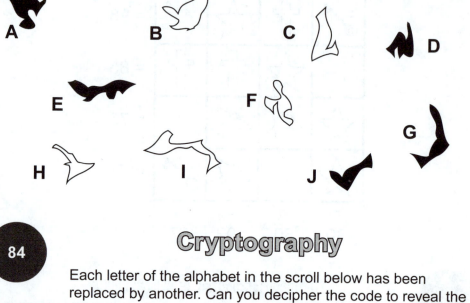

Jigsaw Puzzle

83

Which four pieces (two black and two white) fit together to make a copy of the dove shown here? Any piece may be rotated, but none may be flipped over.

A

B

C

D

E

F

G

H

I

J

Cryptography

84

Each letter of the alphabet in the scroll below has been replaced by another. Can you decipher the code to reveal the quotation, which is taken from 1 Corinthians 13:11?

ORGC M OHX H ZRMIK,

M XSHTG HX H ZRMIK, M

VCKGPXJFFK HX H ZRMIK, M

JRFVERJ HX H ZRMIK: YVJ

ORGC M YGZHQG H QHC, M SVJ

HOHU ZRMIKMXR JRMCEX.

The True Path

The chart gives directions to the church in the central square in the grid. Move the indicated number of spaces north, south, east and west (eg 4N means four squares north) stopping at each square once only to arrive there. At which square should you start?

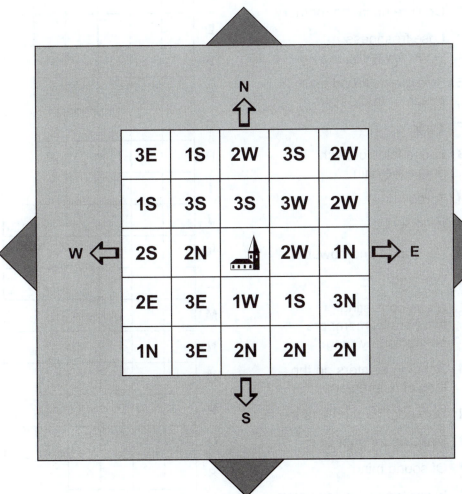

N

3E	1S	2W	3S	2W
1S	3S	3S	3W	2W
2S	2N	⛪	2W	1N
2E	3E	1W	1S	3N
1N	3E	2N	2N	2N

W

E

S

Acrostic

86

Solve the clues and enter the answers into the grid below.
Then cross-reference the letters to their indicated positions in
the grid on the opposite page to reveal a verse from the Bible.

A Heap or mound of snow formed by the wind

B Utterance expressing disapproval or despair

C Conjure up in the memory

D Lose freshness, vigor or vitality

E Fine grains found on a beach or in a desert

F Topic

G Loose folds of flesh under the chin

H Torso

I Bonnet

J Very large and powerful

K Warmed

L Steps consisting of two parallel members connected by rungs

M Rotating pointers on the face of a timepiece

N Between the third and the fifth

O Make up for past sins

P Of sound mind

Q In existence, having being

R Finished, over

	1	2	3	4	5	6
A						
B						
C						
D						
E						
F						
G						
H						
I						
J						
K						
L						
M						
N						
O						
P						
Q						
R						

Acrostic

E2	M3	A1		G3	I1	P2	J5	P1	H2	D5	C2	L5	B2	
H4	F5		L4	N2		J2	B5		D1	G2	N4	K6		I3
L6		M4	C5	O5	L3	,		E4	B3		O1	L1	Q1	
Q4	R3		K4	D4	F3		P3	M2	J1	C1		I2	A4	
A5	J4	R4		G4	R2	A2	R1		G1	K5	E1	N3	G5	,
	B1	A3	Q3	D2	O4	J3		D3	N6	L2	Q5	C4	M5	
N5	O3		Q6	C3	I4		K3	E3	H3		F1	K1	P4	
N1	B4	O2	F2	K2	D6		H1	J6		M1	Q2	F4	.	

Shape Spotter

Which is the only shape to appear twice in exactly the same shading (black, white or gray) in the box below? You'll need a keen eye for this one, as some shapes overlap others!

Riddle-Me-Ree

88

Find one letter per line, following the clues given in the verse below. For example, 'My first is in houses, but never in homes' gives the letter U as the first letter. When you have finished, the letters will spell a name.

My first is in JOSHUA, also in JOHN,

My second's not in WENT, though it is seen in GONE,

My third is in WONDERFUL, also in NICE,

My fourth is in CINNAMON, never in SPICE,

My fifth's not in RAIN, though it does fall in HAIL,

My whole was once swallowed up by a great whale!

1st	2nd	3rd	4th	5th

Stop Gaps

89

Certain words from the text below have been removed and are listed to the right, in alphabetical order. Can you replace them in their correct positions?

Revelation 10:1 And I saw _____ mighty

_____ come down from _____, clothed

with a _____: and a _____ was upon

his head, and his _____ was as it were the

_____, and his feet as _____ of fire:

Revelation 10:2 and he had in his _____ a

little _____ open: and he set his right foot

upon the sea, and his left foot on the _____.

ANGEL

ANOTHER

BOOK

CLOUD

EARTH

FACE

HAND

HEAVEN

PILLARS

RAINBOW

SUN

Scripture Knowledge

How's your knowledge of the scriptures? See if you can answer the questions below...

1 Who in the Bible is the first man to be called a prophet?

_____

2 In Genesis 41, Pharaoh has a dream in which 'ears of corn' are scorched by what?

_____

3 Which Old Testament name is said to mean 'God is my judge'?

_____

4 In John 6:19, Jesus is said to have walked upon the water of which lake?

_____

5 Which gospel begins with the words "In the beginning was the Word..."?

_____

6 To whom did God say "Two nations are within your womb"?

_____

7 In the Great Flood, how many humans were on board Noah's Ark?

_____

8 In The Creation, on which day did God create man?

_____

Holy Bible

Jacob's Ladder

Change one letter at a time (but not the position of any letter) to make a new word – and move from the word at the top of each ladder to the word at the bottom, using the exact number of rungs provided.

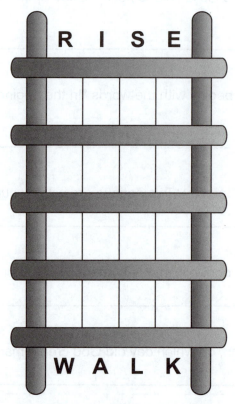

R I S E

W A L K

Bible Codeword

Every letter in this crossword has been replaced by a number, the number remaining the same for that letter wherever it occurs. Can you substitute numbers for letters and complete the crossword? The letters either side of the grid and the reference box showing which numbers have been decoded can also aid solving. One word has already been entered into the grid, to help you on your way. When finished, use the code to spell out a quotation from the Bible.

A B C D E F G H I J K L M

5	21	20	18	4	5	5	23	18	■	18	■	12	■	12
21	■	■	20	■	4	■	21	■	18	26	13	21	12	18
13	25	20	9	18	20	9	18	22	■	5	■	23	■	15
8	■	■	25	■	22	■	■	1	8	1	23	18	23	18
4	13	3	1	21	18	12	13	18	■	20	■	20	■	20
26	■	■	15	■	7	■	25	■	■	2	■	13	■	21
■	2	15	4	22	21	18	20	9	■	18	17	18	20	9
20	■	■	2	■	13	■	24	■	4	■	18	■	■	19
25 O	20 N	12 S	18 E	9 T	■	2	1	20	11	21	2	6	9	■
9	■	7	■	15	■	■	15	■	11	■	18	■	■	4
18	■	25	■	4	■	15	18	13	18	5	9	21	25	20
13	4	23	19	5	12	25	■	■	13	■	4	■	■	19
4	■	22	■	18	■	22	18	4	9	6	14	23	25	10
12	20	18	18	16	18	■	2	■	18	■	23	■	■	4
18	■	15	■	18	■	12	25	23	22	21	18	15	23	19

N O P Q R S T U V W X Y Z

Reference Box

1	2	3	4	5	6	7	8	9 T	10	11	12 S	13
14	15	16	17	18 E	19	20 N	21	22	23	24	25 O	26

Quotation

6	18	9	6	4	9	6	4	9	6	18	4	15	12	9
25	6	18	4	15	23	18	9	6	21	7	6	18	4	15

S Bend

Place the letters of each word, one per cell, so that every word flows in a clockwise direction around a number. Where the hexagons of one word overlap with those of another, the letter in each cell is common to both.

When finished, rearrange the letters in the pale gray hexagons to form the name of a character from the Bible.

CANARY

CATNIP

CYCLED

GRASSY

MENACE

MOROSE

OYSTER

RECENT

REGARD

SMUDGE

UPHELD

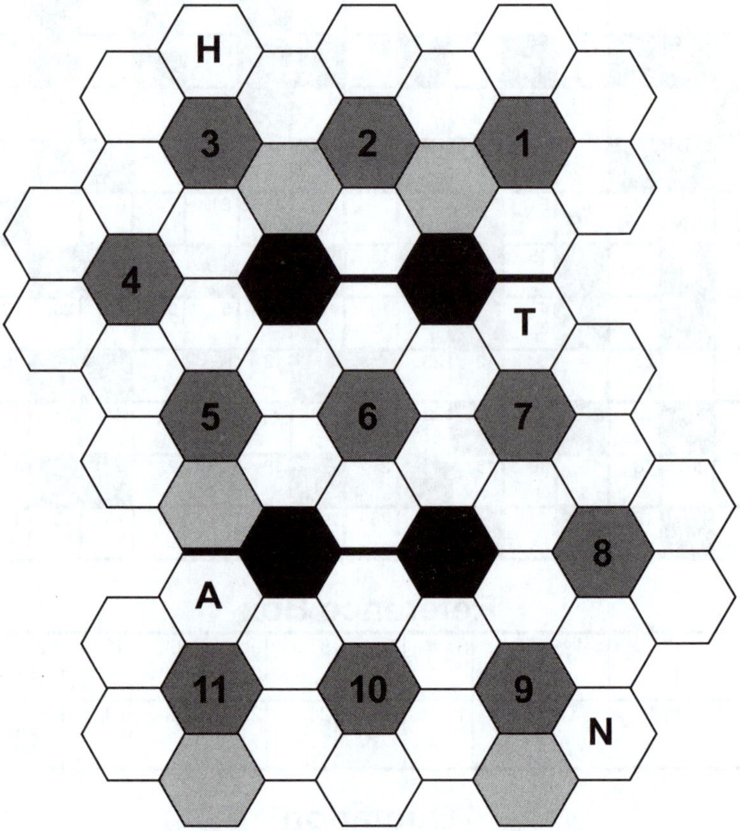

The name is: _____

Phone-etics

Use the telephone dial in order to spell out the Bible quotation.

846934 8469 30158. 8408353 18

843 31353, 162 846934 8469

838 840 6388 15663 843 88178,

843623 9455 4 17463 8433 2696,

81484 843 5672.

Wordwheel

How many words of three or more letters can you make from those in the wheel, without using plurals, abbreviations or proper nouns?

The central letter must appear once in every word and no letter in a section of the wheel may be used more than once.

There is at least one nine-letter word in the wheel, which is a proper noun: the name of a book in the Bible.

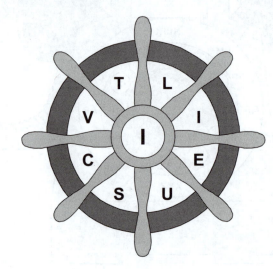

_____

_____

_____

_____

_____

_____

_____

_____

_____

_____

The nine-letter word is: _____

Into the Ark

Can you discover the way through this maze, and thus help these animals to find their way into Noah's Ark at the center?

Christening Conundrum

97

Mr & Mrs Wordsmith are having a hard time choosing a name for their baby daughter, who is due to be baptized next Wednesday morning. They have, however, narrowed the choice down to 21 possible names (some of them rather uncommon!). See if you can find them all hidden in the grid below.

Words may run forwards or backwards, either horizontally, diagonally or vertically, but always in a straight, uninterrupted line.

```
T F J V E R I T Y Q K X N
R I J G O A E V F E M C T
E Y F A S C O B Z I E V R
F E E I C N X E M D H A E
I M L R N Q A T V A O F I
N M I E I N U H O S N R N
N A C O I E R E R M E I A
E N I T N E M E L C Y R H
J U T J W Y Y L L I D L P
F L Y P A G R H A U N U E
H L F K D O A U P R E E T
G E C N A T S N O C W W S
K B K T A L L E B A S I D
```

AMBER	HONEY	MYRA
BETH	ISABELLA	OPAL
CLEMENTINE	JACQUELINE	SADIE
CONSTANCE	JENNIFER	STEPHANIE
DAWN	LISA	TINA
DORA		VERITY
EMMA		WENDY
FELICITY		YVONNE

Keyword Crossword

Solve the crossword puzzle in the usual way, then rearrange the letters in the shaded squares to spell out a keyword, which is the name of place (it might be a country, region, river, garden, hill, mountain, town or city) that appears in the Bible.

Across

1 Morbid fear of open spaces (11)
9 Line on a map connecting points of equal height (7)
10 US state in the Rocky Mountains (5)
11 Crop (4)
12 Most shadowy or vague (8)
14 Having existence (5)
15 Country, capital Tokyo (5)
20 Festival marked by merrymaking and processions (8)
22 Gives assistance (4)
24 Kingdom in the South Pacific (5)
25 Extremely cold (7)
26 Weather forecasting (11)

Down

2 Authentic (7)
3 Space for movement (4)
4 Social outcast (6)
5 Eastern (8)
6 Mental representation (5)
7 Severe and intense (5)
8 According to Mark, the number of days that Christ sojourned in the wilderness (5)
13 Point to (8)
16 Dwelling (7)
17 English explorer who reached the South Pole just a month after Amundsen (5)
18 Forest fire fighter (6)
19 Religious song (5)
21 Wash out soap (5)
23 Frozen rain (4)

Bible Passage Storyword

Some of the words in the Bible passage below have been replaced with clue numbers. The missing words all fit into the grid opposite. For example, if the phrase is "Seek and ye 18A find", this indicates that the solution to 18 Across is 'SHALL', which can then be written into the grid.

Don't worry if you can't discover the precise word required at first glance – when more words are filled into the grid, the letters which intersect with others will help you discover further words.

This passage is taken from Acts, Chapter 13.

1: Now there were in the church that was at 36D, certain prophets and teachers; as Barnabas, and Simeon that was called 28D, and Lucius of 17A, and Manaen, which had been brought up with 47A the tetrarch, and Saul.

2: As they ministered to the Lord, and fasted, the Holy Ghost said, 23D me Barnabas and Saul for the work 19D I 31D called them.

3: And when they had 11A and prayed, and laid their hands on them, they sent them 18A.

4: So they, being 25D forth by the Holy Ghost, 35A unto Seleucia; and from thence they sailed to Cyprus.

5: And when they were at Salamis, they preached the word of God in the synagogues of the 40D: and they had also John to their 26D.

6: And when they had 9A through the 22A unto 39D, they found a 14D 3D, a 43A 29D, a Jew, whose name was Bar-jesus:

7: Which was with the deputy of the country, Sergius Paulus, a prudent 10D; who called for Barnabas and Saul, and 2A to 21A the word of 9D.

8: But Elymas the sorcerer (for so is his name by 27A) 44A them, seeking to 38A away the 2D from the faith.

9: Then Saul, (who 5D is called Paul,) filled with the Holy Ghost, set his eyes on him,

10: And said, O 43D of all 8D and all mischief, thou 20A of the 16D, thou 37D of all righteousness, wilt thou not 7A to 33A the 30A 4A of the Lord?

11: And now, 12D, the hand of the 45A is upon 42A, and thou shalt be 15A, not seeing the sun for a 24D. And immediately there fell on him a mist and a darkness; and he went about seeking 6D to 34D him by the 41A.

12: Then the deputy, when he 46A what was done, 1D, being 32A at the 13A of the Lord.

Bible Passage Storyword

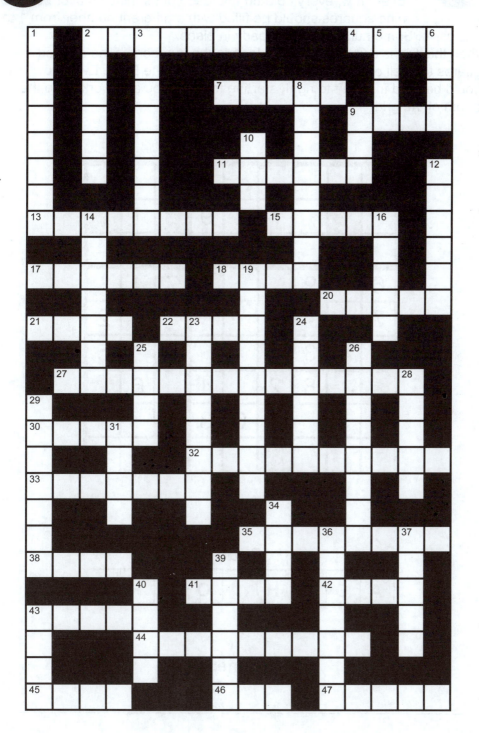

Bible Sudoku

Every row, every column and each of the nine smaller boxes of nine squares should be filled with a different number from 1 to 9 inclusive. Some numbers are already in place.

When the grid is completely filled, decode the numbers in the shaded squares to spell out the name of a character from the Bible. Every row should be read from left to right, starting from the top and working to the bottom of the grid.

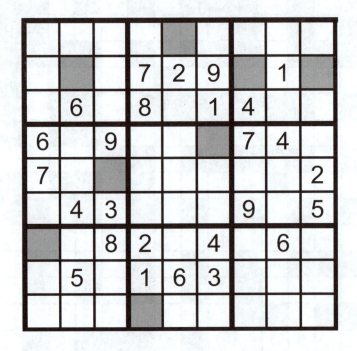

Code

1	2	3	4	5	6	7	8	9
A	D	E	H	I	O	P	R	S

Name:

Scripture Knowledge

How's your knowledge of the scriptures? See if you can answer the questions below…

1 Who directed the Magi to Bethlehem?

_____

2 Who was the barren wife of Jacob?

_____

3 Whose wife was turned into 'a pillar of salt' at the destruction of Sodom and Gomorrah?

_____

4 Moses had two sons; what were their names?

_____

5 Who told Joseph and Mary to name their son Jesus?

_____

6 Which two sisters plotted to get Lot drunk so that they could seduce him?

_____

7 According to Isaiah 2 what activity will be replaced by plowing and pruning?

_____

8 How did Elijah divide the waters of the River Jordan?

_____

Shape-up

102

Every row and column in this grid originally contained one cross, one loaf, one fish, one star and two blank squares, although not necessarily in that order. Every symbol with a black arrow refers to the first of the four symbols encountered when traveling in the direction of the arrow. Every symbol with a white arrow refers to the second of the four symbols encountered in the direction of the arrow. Can you complete the original grid?

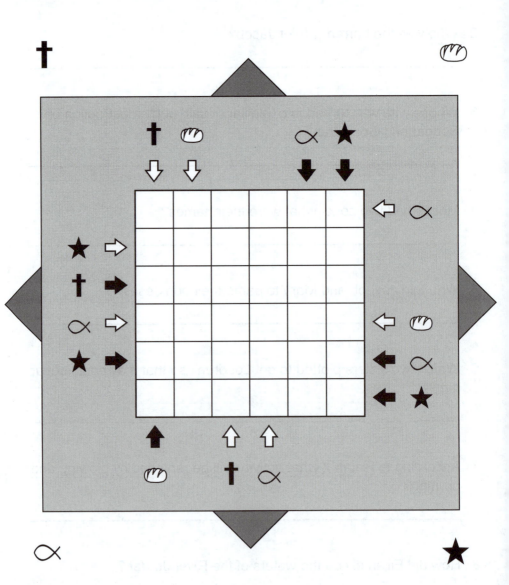

Paul's Pathfinder

The object of this puzzle is to trace a single path from the top left square to the bottom right square of the grid, traveling through all of the cells in either a horizontal, vertical or diagonal direction. Every cell must be entered once only and your path should take you through the letters in the sequence P-A-U-L-P-A-U-L, etc. Can you find the logical way through?

P	A	U	L	U	A	P	U
A	P	L	A	P	U	A	L
L	U	P	P	L	A	P	L
A	U	A	P	A	L	U	P
P	L	L	U	P	U	A	L
U	P	L	A	L	U	A	U
A	U	A	U	U	P	U	A
P	L	A	P	L	L	P	L

Simon's Squares

Fit the letters S, I, M, O and N into the grid in such a way that each horizontal row, each vertical column and each of the heavily outlined sections of five squares each contains a different letter. Some letters are already in place.

N				
			M	
O		S		
	M			I

The Bottom Line

Can you fill each square in the bottom line with the correct symbol? Every square in the solution contains a symbol from each of the lines above, although two or more squares in the solution may contain the same symbol.

At the end of every row is a score, which shows:

a the number of symbols placed in the correct finishing position on the bottom line, as indicated by a tick; and

b the number of symbols which appear on the bottom line, but in a different position, as indicated by a cross.

SCORE

🕯	🍞	✜	🍷	X X
☆	†	🗝	🕊	X
🍞	🗝	🕊	🕯	X
🍷	🍷	†	🍞	X X
✜	†	🍷	✜	X X
				✓✓✓✓

98

Round Dozen

First solve the clues. All of the solutions end with the letter in the center of the circle, and in every word an additional letter is in place. When the puzzle is complete, you can then go on to discover the two names reading clockwise around the outermost ring of letters.

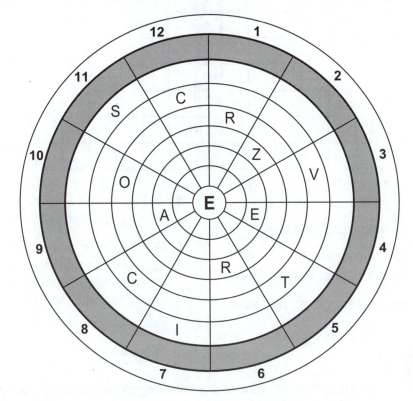

1 Atrocious, very ugly

2 Defraud

3 Early-morning bugle call

4 Outdated and no longer in use

5 Imaginary line on the Earth's surface – roughly along the 180th meridian

6 Gird

7 African country formerly called Rhodesia

8 Switch over

9 World War II Japanese suicide pilot

10 Incapable of movement

11 Thin slice of meat, usually breaded and fried

12 Ball game invented by native Americans

The names are:

_____ and _____

Pyracross

107

Solve the clues on each level of the pyramid and reveal the word in the central column of bricks.

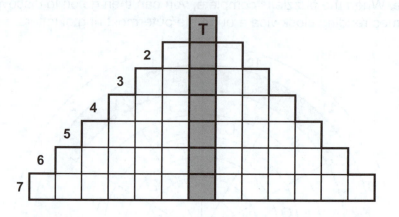

2 Attempt

3 Country, capital Beijing

4 William Jefferson ____, 42nd president of the USA

5 Inoculate (against disease)

6 Collector and student of postage stamps

7 Popular child actress who appeared in movies such as *Heidi* and *Rebecca of Sunnybrook Farm* (7,6)

Spelling Test

108

Which is the only one of the following to be correctly spelled?

a. PHILLIMON

b. PHILIMON

c. PHILLEMON

d. PHILEMON

Bookmark

109

Answer the clues by using the groups of letters in the lower box, crossing them out as you go. When finished, rearrange the remaining letters to make the name of a book of the Bible.

1 Country, capital Harare

2 Form of binding used to stop the flow of blood

3 Eating house

4 Month of the year

5 Warped, bent out of shape

6 Lucky charm

7 Tall geographical feature

8 Glowing, luminous

9 Rolls of paper filled with tobacco

10 Building where the sick and injured are treated

UR	NT	ORT	CAN	RA	VE	UN	ET	MB
RE	NO	ZI	MO	JO	TO	SM	IN	AU
IN	TAL	TA	CI	ST	ST	AB	TA	ER
WE	NAH	DES	NI	MB	HO	ES	GA	LI
DI	TT	AN	ED	NT	CE	QU	RE	SPI

Book: _____

Character Assignation

Fill in the Across clues in this crossword in the normal way. Then read down the diagonal line of seven squares, to reveal the name of a character from the Bible.

1   Awesome, mind-boggling

2   Haitian religious cult

3   Capital of South Korea

4   Major Asian desert

5   Large native New Zealand parrot

6   Computer science (inits)

7   Eighth letter of the alphabet

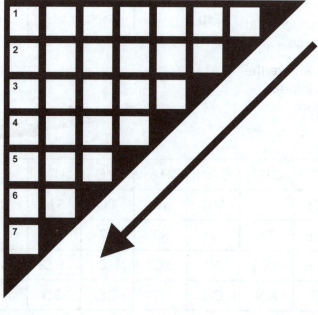

Character: ___ ___ ___ ___ ___ ___ ___

What's It Worth?

Each symbol stands for a different number. In order to reach the correct total at the end of each row and column, what is the value of the cross, dove, key and star?

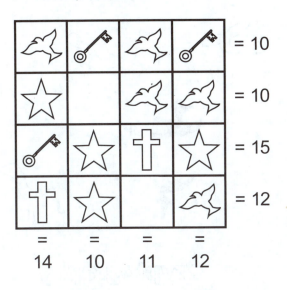

Pharaoh's Pyramid

Every brick in this pyramid contains a number which is the sum of the two numbers below it, so that F=A+B, etc. Just work out the missing numbers!

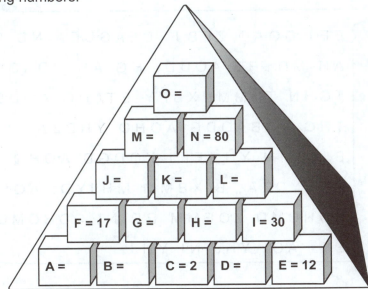

Jigsaw Puzzle

113

Which four pieces (two black and two white) fit together to make a copy of the lamb shown here? Any piece may be rotated, but none may be flipped over.

A

B

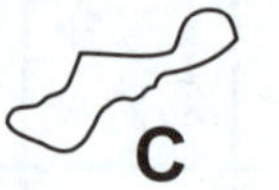

C

D

E

F

G

H

I

J

Cryptography

114

Each letter of the alphabet in the scroll below has been replaced by another. Can you decipher the code to reveal the quotation, which is taken from Ruth 1:16?

EFJ GQAO ZEBJ, DFAGDEA ND FHA
AH MDEPD AODD, HG AH GDAQGF
TGHN THMMHXBFY ETADG AODD:
THG XOBAODG AOHQ YHDZA,
B XBMM YH; EFJ XODGD AOHQ
MHJYDZA, B XBMM MHJYD: AOI
CDHCMD ZOEMM RD NI CDHCMD,
EFJ AOI YHJ NI YHJ.

The True Path

The chart gives directions to the church in the central square in the grid. Move the indicated number of spaces north, south, east and west (eg 4N means four squares north) stopping at each square once only to arrive there. At which square should you start?

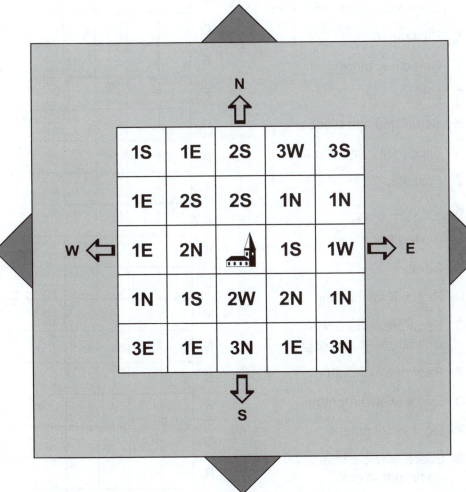

116 Acrostic

Solve the clues and enter the answers into the grid below. Then cross-reference the letters to their indicated positions in the grid on the opposite page to reveal a verse from the Bible.

A Compass point at 180 degrees
B Made of timber
C Popular French soft cheese
D Requesting, inquiring after
E Pastime
F Objective, target
G Noise
H Separated into pieces
I Slice thinly with a knife
J Possess
K Supple
L Waited upon
M Shrub
N Reach a destination
O Semi-precious stone with streaked coloring
P Rear of an aircraft
Q Every twelve months
R Light violet color
S Score of two strokes under par in golf

	1	2	3	4	5	6
A						
B						
C						
D						
E						
F						
G						
H						
I						
J						
K						
L						
M						
N						
O						
P						
Q						
R						
S						

Acrostic

M1	H5		M3	B3	E3	L5	N3			C1	Q2		R4	N4
D6	P3	Q5	S2	D5	P1			E4	K5	I1	N1	M2	L1	S5
	E5	J1	A3	I3		Q3	B4	I4	S1	N2	G1	D1	Q4	Q6
		K3	M4	C4		G5	R5	L4	K2	P4			R2	D2
	P2		L3	B2	O1	H2	D4	B6	O2		K1	F2	G2	J3
		J2	O3	S4	D3	I5	A4	E1		F1	H1	A2	R3	O4
		A1	O5	B5	H4	C3	G4	S3		B1	K4	E2	R1	
A5	N6		F3	I2	Q1		L6	L2	N5	H3	G3	C2		

Shape Spotter

Which is the only shape to appear twice in exactly the same shading (black, white or gray) in the box below? You'll need a keen eye for this one, as some shapes overlap others!

Riddle-Me-Ree

118

Find one letter per line, following the clues given in the verse below. For example, 'My first is in houses, but never in homes' gives the letter U as the first letter. When you have finished, the letters will spell a name.

My first is in BAGELS, but never in PIES,

My second's in WEEPS, but never in CRIES,

My third is in UPSET, and also in SPOILED,

My fourth's not in GREASE, but is found in OILED,

My fifth is in ICE CREAM, also in LICKED,

My whole is a fruit Eve should never have picked

1st	2nd	3rd	4th	5th

Stop Gaps

119

Certain words from the text below have been removed and are listed to the right, in alphabetical order. Can you replace them in their correct positions?

Habakkuk 2:12 Woe to him that buildeth a _____ with blood, and establisheth a _____ by _____!

Habakkuk 2:13 _____, is it not of the Lord of hosts that the people shall _____ in the very _____, and the people shall _____ themselves for very vanity?

Habakkuk 2:14 For the _____ shall be filled with the _____ of the glory of the Lord, as the _____ cover the sea.

BEHOLD

CITY

EARTH

FIRE

INIQUITY

KNOWLEDGE

LABOR

TOWN

WATERS

WEARY

Scripture Knowledge

How's your knowledge of the scriptures? See if you can answer the questions below…

1 The word 'angel' is derived from the Greek word 'angelos'. What is the actual meaning of this word?

_____

2 Who imprisoned John the Baptist?

_____

3 "Be ever hearing but never understanding" are words by which Old Testament prophet?

_____

4 Which three people survived being thrown into the fiery furnace?

_____

5 Which Old Testament prophet was thrown into a cistern?

_____

6 "Then the Lord my God will come and all the holy ones with him" are words by the prophet Zechariah. To what event does this refer?

_____

7 According to Isaiah's prophesy, which animal will feed with the bear?

_____

8 Who asked of King Herod that the head of John the Baptist should be presented to her on a plate?

_____

Jacob's Ladder

Change one letter at a time (but not the position of any letter) to make a new word – and move from the word at the top of each ladder to the word at the bottom, using the exact number of rungs provided.

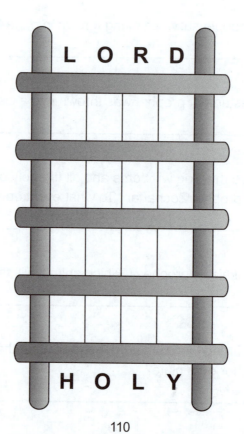

L O R D

H O L Y

122

Bible Codeword

Every letter in this crossword has been replaced by a number, the number remaining the same for that letter wherever it occurs. Can you substitute numbers for letters and complete the crossword? The letters either side of the grid and the reference box showing which numbers have been decoded can also aid solving. One word has already been entered into the grid, to help you on your way. When finished, use the code to spell out a quotation from the Bible.

A B C D E F G H I J K L M

25	■	5	■	14	■	7	23	11	23	17	12	20	13	8
13	11	11	6	11	■	13	■	■	7	■	13	■	9	■
11	■	23	■	23	11	5	2	9	7	13	17	23	18	6
22	23	5	6	16	■	23	■	■	17	■	7	■	2	■
■	■	25	■	21	■	16	13	5	13	21	21	9	14	12
5	11	13	13	7	12	■	24	■	14	■	■	16	■	6
9	■	11	■	6	■	■	22	■	■	21	23	14	9	16
16	■	3	■	11	13	26	11	13	21	2	■	13	■	8
13	1	23	17	14	■	■	6	■	■	6	■	11	■	13
24	■	5	■	■	5	■	9	■	15	4	23	10	13	11
23	19	25	19	23	11	8	17	12	■	17	■	9	■	■
■	13	■	9	■	13	■	■	6	■	8	11	13	23	8 D
5	23	16	8	9	8	23	14	4	11	13	■	19	■	11 R
■	10	■	13	■	9	■	■	16	■	11	13	13	10	13 E
11	13	19	11	9	14	9	16	18	■	21	■	11	■	19 W

N O P Q R S T U V W X Y Z

Reference Box

1	2	3	4	5	6	7	8 D	9	10	11 R	12	13 E
14	15	16	17	18	19 W	20	21	22	23	24	25	26

Quotation

9	2	23	10	13	22	13	13	16	23	21	14	11	23	16	18
13	11	9	16	23	21	14	11	23	16	18	13	17	23	16	8

S Bend

Place the letters of each word, one per cell, so that every word flows in a clockwise direction around a number. Where the hexagons of one word overlap with those of another, the letter in each cell is common to both.

When finished, rearrange the letters in the pale gray hexagons to form the name of a character from the Bible.

EXCEPT

IMPISH

LESION

PERMIT

PUFFIN

REGRET

SALLOW

SLOPED

SQUEAL

TEASEL

WOEFUL

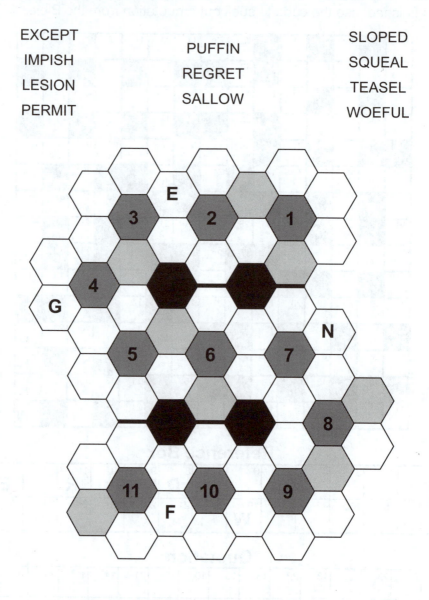

The name is: _____

Phone-etics

Use the telephone dial in order to spell out the Bible quotation.

6 5672 697 5672, 469

302355368 48 840 6153 46 155

843 31784! 946 4188 838 840

35670 11693 843 4319368.

Wordwheel

How many words of three or more letters can you make from those in the wheel, without using plurals, abbreviations or proper nouns?

The central letter must appear once in every word and no letter in a section of the wheel may be used more than once.

There is at least one nine-letter word in the wheel, which is a proper noun: the name of a person in the Bible.

_____

_____

_____

_____

_____

_____

_____

_____

_____

_____

_____

The nine-letter word is: _____

Into the Ark

Can you discover the way through this maze, and thus help these animals to find their way into Noah's Ark at the center?

Easter Wordsearch

There are 21 words relating to Easter hidden in the grid below. Can you find them all?

Words may run forwards or backwards, either horizontally, diagonally or vertically, but always in a straight, uninterrupted line.

```
C R C T N I N T H H O U R
P R E R H O V I N E G A R
C E E T U I M A N G E L S
T M L S E C E I N H N I W
H M G R U P I V S S O R C
O A D R U R D F E P T J S
R U N E S I R Z I S S T P
N S J P T H R E E X H Y E
S N K P S F U B C O I V A
E N E L A D G A M T Y O R
G O I C L R J A O S I Q N
G A W I B K S M W Z Z O A
N B A R A B B A S J Z B N
```

ANGELS	NINTH HOUR	SPEAR
BARABBAS	PETER	STONE
CROSS	RESURRECTION	THIEVES
CRUCIFIXION	RISEN	THOMAS
EMMAUS	SIMON	THORNS
JOHN		THREE
MAGDALENE		TOMB
NAILS		VINEGAR

Keyword Crossword

128

Solve the crossword puzzle in the usual way, then rearrange the letters in the shaded squares to spell out a keyword, which is the name of place (it might be a country, region, river, garden, hill, mountain, town or city) that appears in the Bible.

Across

1 Pointers (6)
4 Hydrophobia (6)
9 Nuclear plant (7)
10 Last letter of the Greek alphabet (5)
11 Fashion (5)
12 Larger than others of its kind (7)
13 Causing intense interest, stunning (11)
18 Audrey ___, Oscar-winning film actress (7)
20 Limbless reptile (5)
22 Scour vigorously (5)
23 Tell a story (7)
24 Decreased in size (6)
25 Sweet plant fluid (6)

Down

1 To the opposite side (6)
2 Prepared for action (5)
3 Spectator (7)
5 Higher up (5)
6 Motionlessness (7)
7 Set of steps (6)
8 Scary (11)
14 Male ruler (7)
15 Watch attentively (7)
16 Dissertation (6)
17 Shooting star (6)
19 Of the city (5)
21 At a distance (5)

Bible Passage Storyword

Some of the words in the Bible passage below have been replaced with clue numbers. The missing words all fit into the grid opposite. For example, if the phrase is "Seek and ye 18A find", this indicates that the solution to 18 Across is 'SHALL', which can then be written into the grid.

Don't worry if you can't discover the precise word required at first glance – when more words are filled into the grid, the letters which intersect with others will help you discover further words.

This passage is taken from Joshua, Chapter 6.

10: And Joshua had 8A the people, saying, Ye shall not shout, nor make any 12D with your 1D, neither shall 27A word proceed out of your 39D, until the day I bid you 32A; then shall ye shout.

11: So the ark of the LORD compassed the 21D, going about it once: and they came into the camp, and 28A in the camp.

12: And Joshua rose 10D in the 22D, and the priests took up the ark of the 5A.

13: And seven 35D bearing seven trumpets of 25A 30A before the ark of the LORD went on continually, and blew with the trumpets: and the armed men went before them; but the 18D came after the ark of the LORD, the priests going on, and 34D with the trumpets.

14: And the 9A day they compassed the city once, and returned into the 13D: so they did 26D days.

15: And it came to pass on the seventh day, that they rose early about the dawning of the day, and compassed the city after the same manner seven times: only on that day they compassed the city 17D times.

16: And it came to 16A at the seventh 3D, when the priests blew with the trumpets, 4D said unto the people, Shout; for the LORD 36A given you the city.

17: And the city shall be accursed, even it, and all that are therein, to the LORD: only Rahab the 6D shall live, she and all that are with her in the 29D, because she 24D the 22A that we sent.

18: And ye, in any 15A keep 19A from the accursed thing, lest ye make yourselves 42A, when ye 41D of the accursed thing, and make the camp of Israel a curse, and 37D it.

19: But all the 44A, and 33A, and 7D of 34A and 2D, are 13A unto the LORD: they shall come into the treasury of the LORD.

20: So the people shouted when the priests blew with the trumpets: and it came to pass, when the people 36D the 31D of the trumpet, and the 11D shouted with a 14A shout, that the 40A fell down 38D, so that the people went up 23A the city, every man 20D before him, and they 43A the city.

Bible Passage Storyword

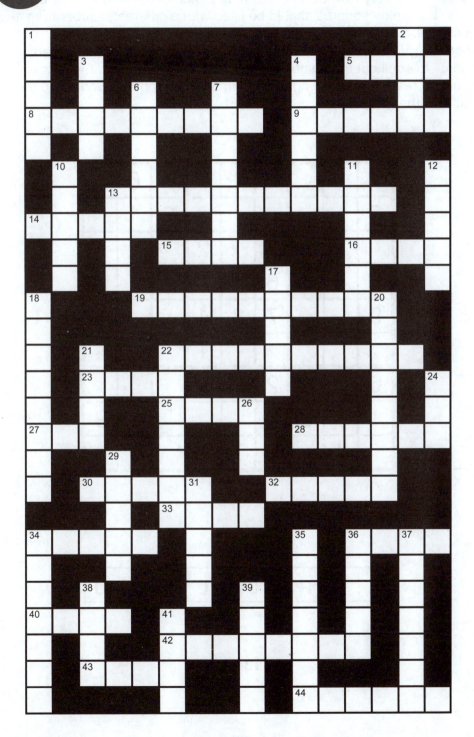

Bible Sudoku

Every row, every column and each of the nine smaller boxes of nine squares should be filled with a different number from 1 to 9 inclusive. Some numbers are already in place.

When the grid is completely filled, decode the numbers in the shaded squares to spell out the name of a character from the Bible. Every row should be read from left to right, starting from the top and working to the bottom of the grid.

				1	9		6	
3						9	1	
					2			5
5	8		6					
9			7	8	4			3
				1			9	4
6			2					
	3	8						9
	4		9	7				

Code

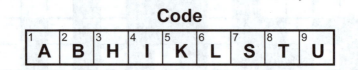

1	2	3	4	5	6	7	8	9
A	B	H	I	K	L	S	T	U

Name:

Scripture Knowledge

How's your knowledge of the scriptures? See if you can answer the questions below…

1 Which Old Testament king met his death soon after seeing a vision of a hand writing on a wall?

_____

2 The infamous wife of King Ahab; whose name has become a byword for a scheming evil woman?

_____

3 Following David's killing of Goliath, the dead bodies of which people are said to have lain along the road from Gath to Ekron?

_____

4 In Genesis 32:15, how many bulls were given by Jacob to his Esau?

_____

5 Jesus said that he would send out his disciples as lambs among which kind of animals?

_____

6 What kind of birds did God send to alleviate the hunger of the Israelites in the desert?

_____

7 When Moses returned after receiving the Ten Commandments, he found the Israelites had made and were worshiping what false idol?

_____

8 Which mountain in Jordan is said to be the place from where Moses first saw the Promised Land?

_____

Shape-up

Every row and column in this grid originally contained one cross, one loaf, one fish, one star and two blank squares, although not necessarily in that order. Every symbol with a black arrow refers to the first of the four symbols encountered when traveling in the direction of the arrow. Every symbol with a white arrow refers to the second of the four symbols encountered in the direction of the arrow. Can you complete the original grid?

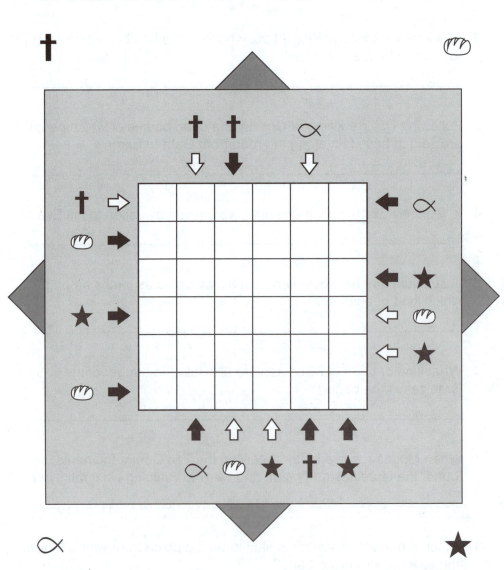

Paul's Pathfinder

The object of this puzzle is to trace a single path from the top left square to the bottom right square of the grid, traveling through all of the cells in either a horizontal, vertical or diagonal direction. Every cell must be entered once only and your path should take you through the letters in the sequence P-A-U-L-P-A-U-L, etc. Can you find the logical way through?

P	A	L	P	L	L	A	U
A	P	U	A	U	U	P	L
U	U	L	P	A	A	P	U
U	L	A	A	U	P	L	A
L	A	P	U	P	L	A	U
P	P	U	U	L	P	A	L
L	L	A	A	L	U	A	P
U	A	P	P	L	P	U	L

Simon's Squares

134

Fit the letters S, I, M, O and N into the grid in such a way that each horizontal row, each vertical column and each of the heavily outlined sections of five squares each contains a different letter. Some letters are already in place.

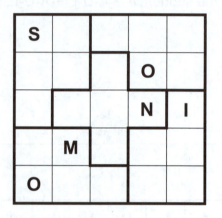

The Bottom Line

135

Can you fill each square in the bottom line with the correct symbol? Every square in the solution contains a symbol from each of the lines above, although two or more squares in the solution may contain the same symbol.

At the end of every row is a score, which shows:

a the number of symbols placed in the correct finishing position on the bottom line, as indicated by a tick; and

b the number of symbols which appear on the bottom line, but in a different position, as indicated by a cross.

SCORE

🍞	🏺	🗝	✝	✗ ✗
☆	🕯	✝	⊱	✗ ✗
✝	🍞	☆	🗝	✗ ✗
🕯	🕊	⊱	🏺	✗
🗝	✝	🍞	⊱	✓ ✓
				✓ ✓ ✓ ✓

124

Round Dozen

First solve the clues. All of the solutions end with the letter in the center of the circle, and in every word an additional letter is in place. When the puzzle is complete, you can then go on to discover the two names reading clockwise around the outermost ring of letters.

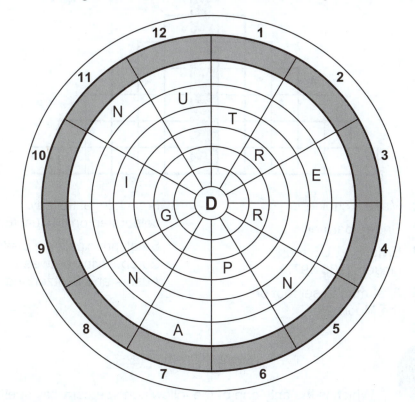

1 Caught and held
2 One of many minor planets orbiting between Mars and Jupiter
3 Frozen-in
4 Term used to describe North, Central and South America (3,5)
5 Expelled, sent away
6 Occulted, overshadowed

7 Recited a commentary accompanying a play
8 Quick, convenient comestibles of little nutritional value (4,4)
9 Shortened (version, eg of a book)
10 Unfavorably spoken about
11 Contaminated
12 Spayed

The names are:

_____ and _____

Pyracross

137

Solve the clues on each level of the pyramid and reveal the word in the central column of bricks.

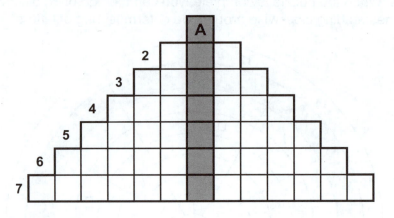

2 Make a choice

3 Bride's partner

4 Elvis ___, US rock singer (1935-1977)

5 First man to set foot on the Moon, Neil ___

6 French legal holiday celebrated on 14 July (8,3)

7 Small principality in central Europe, lying between Austria and Switzerland

Spelling Test

138

Which is the only one of the following to be correctly spelled?

a. DEUTORONOMY

b. DUTERONOMY

c. DEUTERONOMY

d. DUETERONOMY

Bookmark

Answer the clues by using the groups of letters in the lower box, crossing them out as you go. When finished, rearrange the remaining letters to make the name of a book of the Bible.

1 Violent release of energy caused by a chemical or nuclear reaction
2 US state in the Deep South on the gulf of Mexico
3 Circus swing performer (7,6)
4 Former UK prime minister, Winston ___
5 Members of a church, gathered together
6 Warm bedcover stuffed with feathers
7 Shortened form of a word or phrase
8 Vanishing from view
9 British author who created Sherlock Holmes (6,5,5)

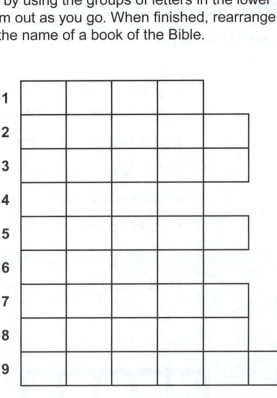

SS	URC	IST	PI	NAN	REG	LL	EI	PL
ON	ART	ZE	RE	OSI	AP	CO	CAH	HUR
RI	MI	WN	NG	VIA	HI	RDO	ON	ISS
ION	IP	DE	PE	DIS	MI	ART	TRA	PEA
CH	YLE	ABB	DO	EX	NG	CO	TI	AT

Book: _____

Character Assignation

Fill in the Across clues in this crossword in the normal way. Then read down the diagonal line of seven squares, to reveal the name of a character from the Bible.

1 Peter __ , French philosopher and theologian (1079-1142)

2 Relating to or characteristic of wolves

3 Son of Isaac and brother of Esau

4 Company emblem

5 Knight's title

6 Hawk-headed Egyptian sun-god

7 Chemical symbol for hydrogen

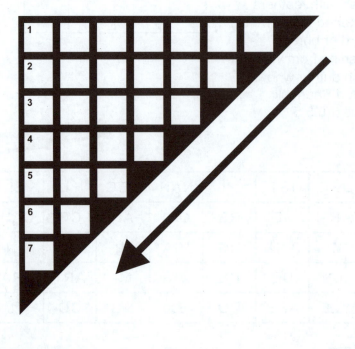

Character: ___ ___ ___ ___ ___ ___ ___

What's It Worth?

141

Each symbol stands for a different number. In order to reach the correct total at the end of each row and column, what is the value of the cross, dove, key and star?

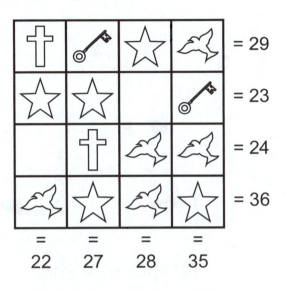

Pharaoh's Pyramid

142

Every brick in this pyramid contains a number which is the sum of the two numbers below it, so that F=A+B, etc. Just work out the missing numbers!

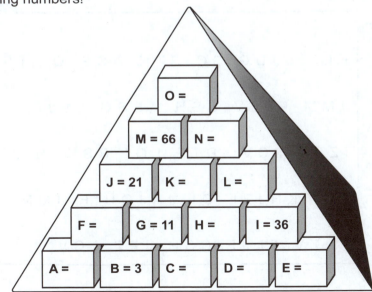

Jigsaw Puzzle

143

Which four pieces (two black and two white) fit together to make a copy of the cup shown here? Any piece may be rotated, but none may be flipped over.

A B C D

E F

G

H I J

Cryptography

144

Each letter of the alphabet in the scroll below has been replaced by another. Can you decipher the code to reveal the quotation, which is taken from Ezra 8:22?

FLZ LJUG SC STH ASG QI TRSU

JMM FLZV CSH ASSG FLJF

IZZP LQV; DTF LQI RSKZH JUG

LQI KHJFL QI JAJQUIF JMM

FLZV FLJF CSHIJPZ LQV.

The True Path

The chart gives directions to the church in the central square in the grid. Move the indicated number of spaces north, south, east and west (eg 4N means four squares north) stopping at each square once only to arrive there. At which square should you start?

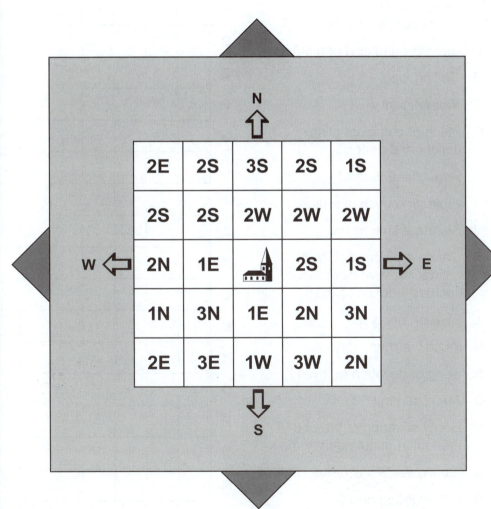

Acrostic

Solve the clues and enter the answers into the grid below. Then cross-reference the letters to their indicated positions in the grid on the opposite page to reveal a verse from the Bible.

A Impression that something might be the case

B Ninth planet from the sun

C Largest of the Dodecanese islands

D Underground part of a plant

E Golfing 'peg'

F Ripped, rent

G Place of complete bliss, delight and peace

H Republic of Ireland

I Projecting nose of a pig

J Secure a ship or boat

K Create a piece of cloth by interlacing strands of fabric, such as wool or cotton

L Division of a year

M Much warmer

N Song of devotion or loyalty

O Apex, summit

P Horny covering of the end of the foot in ungulate mammals

Q 'Sunflower State' of the USA

R Put baggage and provisions onto a ship

S Sufficient, more than enough

Acrostic

L5	Q5	M4	C2		A3	L2	O1		S5	N4	G2		O3	M2
N3	I5	H1	F3		S1	J3	K1	M5	H3		P3	G4	N5	D1
	L4	G1	E3		A4	B2	N1	S6 ,		D2	P4		E1
M1	S3		Q4	R3	L1	K5		R1	A2	J1	B1		M3	R2
	N6	K3	Q1	G5		I3	S4	C5		K4	E2	I1	C6	H4
S2		B3	I2	D4	P2		A1	F2	N2	B5	C1 ,		Q2
G6	R4		G3	F4	C3	B4	P1	K2	J4		I4	L3	F1	O2
	C4	H2	Q6	A5	D3	Q3	J2	M6	?					

Shape Spotter

Which is the only shape to appear twice in exactly the same shading (black, white or gray) in the box below? You'll need a keen eye for this one, as some shapes overlap others!

133

Riddle-Me-Ree

148

Find one letter per line, following the clues given in the verse below. For example, 'My first is in houses, but never in homes' gives the letter U as the first letter. When you have finished, the letters will spell a name.

My first's not in LIFE, though it is found in LIVING,

My second's in GETTING, and also in GIVING,

My third's found in ACTOR, though not seen in STAGE,

My fourth is in BLACK, but never in BEIGE,

My fifth's not in BEECH, though it is found in BIRCH,

My whole is a man often found in a church.

1st	2nd	3rd	4th	5th

Stop Gaps

149

Certain words from the text below have been removed and are listed to the right, in alphabetical order. Can you replace them in their correct positions?

Mark 7:32 And they bring unto him one that was _____, and had an _____ in his _____; and they beseech him to put his hand upon him.

Mark 7:33 And he took him aside from the multitude, and put his _____ into his ears, and he spit, and _____ his _____;

Mark 7:34 and looking up to _____, he _____, and saith unto him, Eph'phatha, that is, Be _____.

DEAF

FINGERS

HEAVEN

IMPEDIMENT

OPENED

SIGHED

SPEECH

TONGUE

TOUCHED

Scripture Knowledge

How's your knowledge of the scriptures? See if you can answer the questions below…

1 According to the Sermon on the Mount, what kind of fruit will be borne by a good tree?

_____

2 In Chapter 6 of the Book of Revelation, what are the names of the Four Horsemen of the Apocalypse?

_____

3 What are the colors of each of the four steeds ridden by the Four Horsemen?

_____

4 What is carried by the third Horseman, Famine?

_____

5 Which kind of fruit was taken by Eve from the forbidden tree in the Garden of Eden?

_____

6 According to Genesis 14, to which king did Abraham give a tenth-part of everything?

_____

7 To whom did King Balak of Moab offer a high reward if he could put a curse upon the Israelites?

_____

8 Who was the leader of the victorious Israelites at the Battle of Jericho?

_____

Jacob's Ladder

Change one letter at a time (but not the position of any letter) to make a new word – and move from the word at the top of each ladder to the word at the bottom, using the exact number of rungs provided.

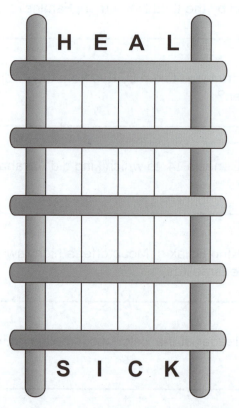

HEAL

SICK

Bitcoin

152

Bible Codeword

Every letter in this crossword has been replaced by a number, the number remaining the same for that letter wherever it occurs. Can you substitute numbers for letters and complete the crossword? The letters either side of the grid and the reference box showing which numbers have been decoded can also aid solving. One word has already been entered into the grid, to help you on your way. When finished, use the code to spell out a quotation from the Bible.

Reference Box

1	2	3	4	5 T	6	7	8	9	10	11 L	12	13 C
14	15	16	17	18 A	19	20	21	22	23	24	25	26

Quotation

18	7	6	22	15	11	25	18	20	11	9	18	20	23	4	18

15	6	1	18	8	9	24	18	13	26	1	18	23	26	7

137

S Bend

153

Place the letters of each word, one per cell, so that every word flows in a clockwise direction around a number. Where the hexagons of one word overlap with those of another, the letter in each cell is common to both.

When finished, rearrange the letters in the pale gray hexagons to form the name of a character from the Bible.

ADROIT

COWARD

CREASE

DOLLOP

DONATE

INSERT

NOBODY

OCELOT

SERENE

WHOLLY

WRAITH

N

3 2 1

4

T

5 6 7

8

I

11 10 9

B

The name is: _____

Phone-etics

Use the telephone dial in order to spell out the Bible quotation.

4 4193 26561732 8433, 6 50

5693, 86 1 2656160 64 467838 46

6417164'8 24174688. 840 243348

173 265350 9484 7698 64 439358,

840 6324 9484 241468 64 4652.

Wordwheel

155

How many words of three or more letters can you make from those in the wheel, without using plurals, abbreviations or proper nouns?

The central letter must appear once in every word and no letter in a section of the wheel may be used more than once.

There is at least one nine-letter word in the wheel, which is a proper noun: the name of a person in the Bible.

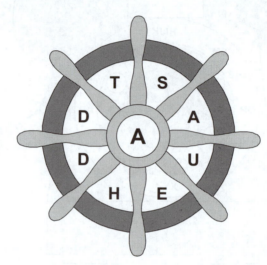

_____

_____

_____

_____

_____

_____

_____

_____

_____

The nine-letter word is: _____

Into the Ark

Can you discover the way through this maze, and thus help these animals to find their way into Noah's Ark at the center?

Books of the Bible

Can you find the listed books of the Bible, which are all hidden in the grid below?

Words may run forwards or backwards, either horizontally, diagonally or vertically, but always in a straight, uninterrupted line.

V	J	O	V	R	O	I	H	S	S	R	V	S
E	K	U	U	T	A	N	A	E	G	Z	J	D
L	Z	A	D	G	W	L	B	T	N	V	Q	G
Z	N	E	G	G	E	L	A	S	N	U	A	E
O	S	A	K	U	E	O	K	A	J	C	I	N
B	H	K	M	I	J	S	K	I	T	O	S	E
A	V	A	N	O	E	B	U	S	T	T	B	S
D	S	A	H	W	J	L	K	E	O	J	S	I
I	D	N	C	O	F	O	K	L	N	L	P	S
A	S	G	N	I	K	R	X	C	D	E	V	E
H	G	A	O	M	A	C	M	C	T	R	K	Z
Y	H	T	O	M	I	T	B	E	L	U	A	R
E	S	T	H	E	R	F	R	R	L	Z	N	A

ACTS

DANIEL

ECCLESIASTES

ESTHER

EZEKIEL

EZRA

GENESIS

HABAKKUK

HAGGAI

JOB

JOHN

JONAH

JUDGES

KINGS

LUKE

MARK

OBADIAH

PETER

SAMUEL

TIMOTHY

Keyword Crossword

Solve the crossword puzzle in the usual way, then rearrange the letters in the shaded squares to spell out a keyword, which is the name of place (it might be a country, region, river, garden, hill, mountain, town or city) that appears in the Bible.

Across

1 One of the Seven Deadly Sins (4)
3 Reply of denial (8)
9 Meet head-on (7)
10 Glue (5)
11 Made for or adjusted to a particular individual (12)
14 Deciduous tree (3)
16 Home planet (5)
17 Barrier which contains the flow of water (3)
18 Daughter of Nehru who served as prime minister of India (6,6)
21 Frequently (5)
22 Unexceptional (7)
23 Magician (8)
24 Succeeding (4)

Down

1 Put into code (8)
2 Exceptional or heroic courage when facing danger (5)
4 Female sheep (3)
5 Large oval stadium with tiers of seats (12)
6 As an alternative (7)
7 Biblical garden (4)
8 Failure to comply (12)
12 Largest artery of the body (5)
13 About to happen (8)
15 Watch (7)
19 Male duck (5)
20 Head honcho (4)
22 Took in solid food (3)

Bible Passage Storyword

Some of the words in the Bible passage below have been replaced with clue numbers. The missing words all fit into the grid opposite. For example, if the phrase is "Seek and ye 18A find", this indicates that the solution to 18 Across is 'SHALL', which can then be written into the grid.

Don't worry if you can't discover the precise word required at first glance – when more words are filled into the grid, the letters which intersect with others will help you discover further words.

This passage is taken from Judges, Chapter 16.

6: And Delilah said to Samson, 10D me, I pray thee, wherein thy great strength lieth, and wherewith thou mightest be bound to 14A thee.

7: And Samson said unto her, If they bind me with 40A green withs that were never dried, then shall I be weak, and be as another man.

8: Then the 46D of the Philistines 29D up to her seven 20D withs which had not been 32A, and she bound him with them.

9: Now there were men 2D in wait, abiding with her in the chamber. And she said unto him, The Philistines be upon thee, Samson. And he brake the 13D, as a thread of 23D is 49A when it 12A the 15D. So his strength was not 43D.

10: And 3A said unto Samson, 34A, thou hast mocked me, and told me 7A: now tell me, I pray thee, wherewith thou mightest be bound.

11: And he said unto her, If they 30A me 18D with new ropes that never were 47A, then shall I be weak, and be as 9D man.

12: Delilah 17A took new 33D, and 31D him therewith, and said 39D him, The Philistines be upon thee, Samson. And there were liers in 5D abiding in the chamber. And he brake them from off his arms like a 16D.

13: And Delilah said 39D Samson, 4D thou hast mocked me, and 45A me 7A: tell me wherewith thou mightest be bound. And he said unto her, If thou 8A the seven 44D of my head with the web.

14: And she fastened it with the 48D, and said unto him, The Philistines be upon thee, 26A. And he 22D out of his sleep, and went away with the pin of the beam, and with the 28A.

15: And she said unto him, How canst thou say, I 42D thee, when thine heart is not with me? Thou hast mocked me these 38A times, and hast 37A told me wherein thy 20A strength lieth.

16: And it came to 36A, when she 50A him 1A with her words, and 39A him, so that his 35A was 41D unto 21A;

17: That he told her all his heart, and said unto her. There hath not come a 19A upon mine 27D; for I have been a Nazarite unto God from my 24D womb: if I be 11D, then my 11A will go from me, and I shall become 25A, and be like any other 6A.

Bible Passage Storyword

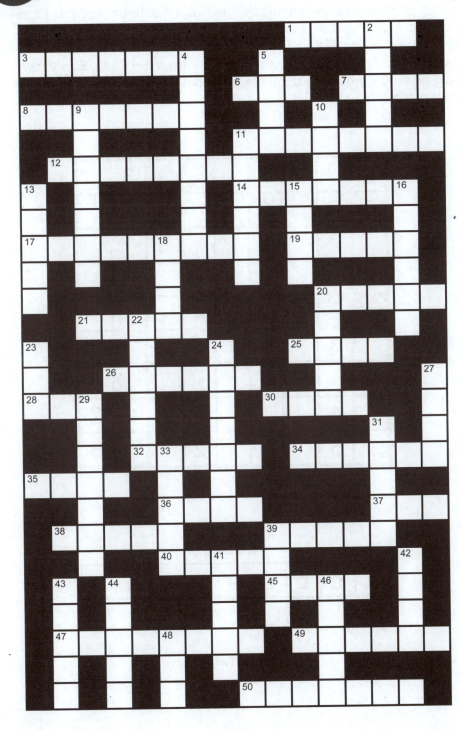

Bible Sudoku

Every row, every column and each of the nine smaller boxes of nine squares should be filled with a different number from 1 to 9 inclusive. Some numbers are already in place.

When the grid is completely filled, decode the numbers in the shaded squares to spell out the name of a character from the Bible. Every row should be read from left to right, starting from the top and working to the bottom of the grid.

2		1	7				3	
3	9		1				4	
						8		
5				2			6	
			3		4			
	3			1				8
		9						
	4				5		1	2
	5				2	7		6

Code

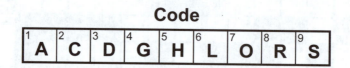

1	2	3	4	5	6	7	8	9
A	C	D	G	H	L	O	R	S

Name:

_____

Scripture Knowledge

How's your knowledge of the scriptures? See if you can answer the questions below…

1   What is referred to in James 3:8 as "a restless evil, full of deadly poison"?

   _____

2   What is the literal meaning of the name 'Israel'?

   _____

3   Which Old Testament prophet told King David to give his son, Solomon, the name of Jedediah?

   _____

4   According to Jesus' teaching what could move a mountain?

   _____

5   According to 2 Kings:19 the angel of the Lord killed 185,000 of which people?

   _____

6   Brothers Moses and Aaron turned their staffs into which creatures?

   _____

7   What is the usual name for the Sea of Lot, also known as the Sea of Salt and the Sea of Arabah?

   _____

8   What was the final plague inflicted on Pharaoh's Egypt, which convinced him to release the Israelites from slavery?

   _____

Shape-up

Every row and column in this grid originally contained one cross, one loaf, one fish, one star and two blank squares, although not necessarily in that order. Every symbol with a black arrow refers to the first of the four symbols encountered when traveling in the direction of the arrow. Every symbol with a white arrow refers to the second of the four symbols encountered in the direction of the arrow. Can you complete the original grid?

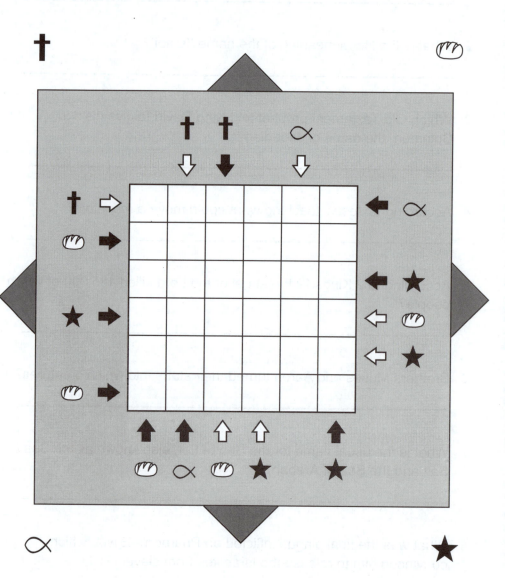

Paul's Pathfinder

The object of this puzzle is to trace a single path from the top left square to the bottom right square of the grid, traveling through all of the cells in either a horizontal, vertical or diagonal direction. Every cell must be entered once only and your path should take you through the letters in the sequence P-A-U-L-P-A-U-L, etc. Can you find the logical way through?

P	L	A	U	A	P	L	P
P	A	U	P	L	U	U	A
A	A	P	L	L	A	A	U
U	A	U	L	U	P	P	L
U	L	P	P	A	U	L	P
U	L	L	U	L	P	U	A
L	A	P	A	P	A	U	A
P	A	U	L	U	L	P	L

Simon's Squares

Fit the letters S, I, M, O and N into the grid in such a way that each horizontal row, each vertical column and each of the heavily outlined sections of five squares each contains a different letter. Some letters are already in place.

I			M	
		I		
	S			
N				O

The Bottom Line

Can you fill each square in the bottom line with the correct symbol? Every square in the solution contains a symbol from each of the lines above, although two or more squares in the solution may contain the same symbol.

At the end of every row is a score, which shows:

a the number of symbols placed in the correct finishing position on the bottom line, as indicated by a tick; and

b the number of symbols which appear on the bottom line, but in a different position, as indicated by a cross.

SCORE

candle	bread	chalice	†	✗ ✗
bread	☆	fish	†	✓ ✗
☆	chalice	key	fish	✓ ✗
dove	chalice	key	candle	✓ ✗
key	bread	☆	candle	✗ ✗
				✓ ✓ ✓ ✓

Round Dozen

First solve the clues. All of the solutions end with the letter in the center of the circle, and in every word an additional letter is in place. When the puzzle is complete, you can then go on to discover the two names reading clockwise around the outermost ring of letters.

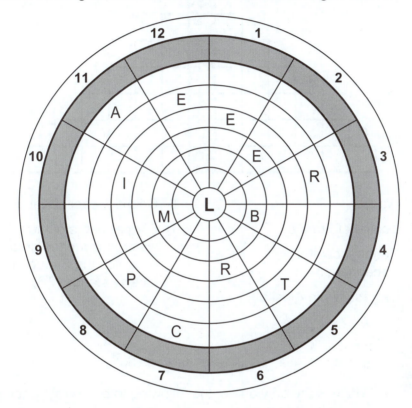

1 Swiss cheese with large holes

2 Bony, wasted

3 End-point

4 Carthaginian leader who crossed the Alps to defeat the Romans

5 Outside

6 An about-turn

7 Expressing contempt

8 Favorable reception

9 Tear-gland

10 Something that is left to choice, discretionary

11 The ___ Plan, otherwise known as the European Recovery Program

12 Full of incident

The names are:

_____ and _____

Pyracross

167

Solve the clues on each level of the pyramid and reveal the word in the central column of bricks.

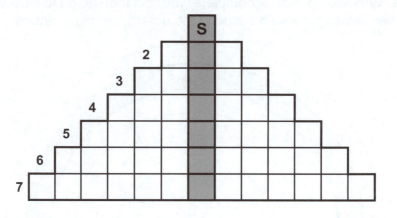

2 Wager

3 Capital of France

4 Country, capital Copenhagen

5 Largest city in Alaska

6 Country, capital Kabul

7 Former name of the water-surrounded area on which the Statue of Liberty stands (7,6)

Spelling Test

168

Which is the only one of the following to be correctly spelled?

a. **PHILIPPIANS**

b. **PHILIPEANS**

c. **PHILLIPPIANS**

d. **PHILIPIANS**

Bookmark

Answer the clues by using the groups of letters in the lower box, crossing them out as you go. When finished, rearrange the remaining letters to make the name of a book of the Bible.

1 Morning meal

2 Assortment

3 Color of the rainbow

4 Atmospheric disturbance often accompanied by lightning and rain

5 European sea

6 Gas which is abundant in the atmosphere

7 Violent, naturally occurring tremor

8 Country, capital Canberra

9 Massive herbivorous animal, with horns on the snout

10 Cautiousness

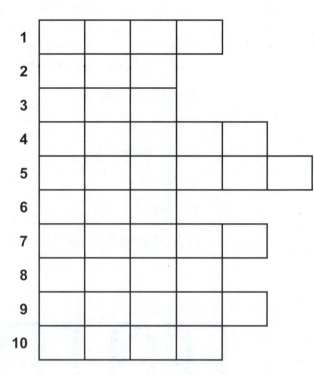

IA	RO	RRA	ER	MB	MIX	RH	EA	AU
AST	GO	NU	IN	DAT	RT	ME	ION	STO
UA	EA	UND	IN	AL	TRE	OS	NIT	HQ
DI	STR	GEN	DI	BR	TH	RM	AN	PI
TE	RE	ER	KE	TU	ERS	NE	KF	OC

Book: _____

Character Assignation

Fill in the Across clues in this crossword in the normal way.
Then read down the diagonal line of seven squares, to reveal
the name of a character from the Bible.

1 Hector _____, French composer
of the *Symphonie Fantastique*

2 Nun's headdress

3 Ascend

4 Christmastide

5 Assist

6 Myself

7 Compass point at 90 degrees

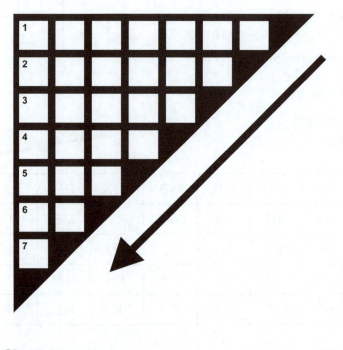

Character: ___ ___ ___ ___ ___ ___ ___

What's It Worth?

Each symbol stands for a different number. In order to reach the correct total at the end of each row and column, what is the value of the cross, dove, key and star?

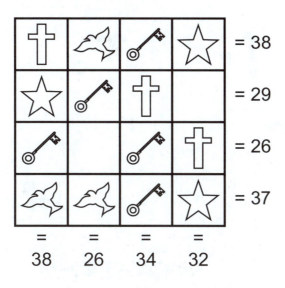

Pharaoh's Pyramid

Every brick in this pyramid contains a number which is the sum of the two numbers below it, so that F=A+B, etc. Just work out the missing numbers!

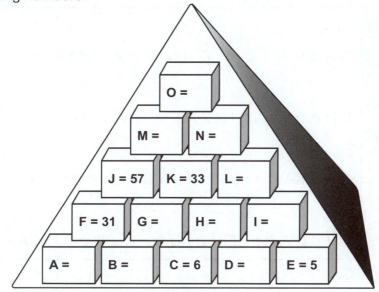

155

Jigsaw Puzzle

173

Which four pieces (two black and two white) fit together to make a copy of the cross shown here? Any piece may be rotated, but none may be flipped over.

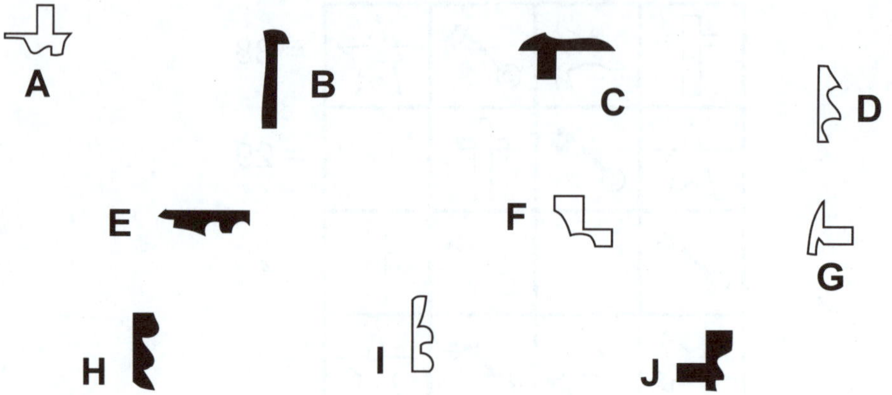

A

B

C

D

E

F

G

H

I

J

Cryptography

174

Each letter of the alphabet in the scroll below has been replaced by another. Can you decipher the code to reveal the quotation, which is taken from Proverbs 4:7?

GASKWJ AS DHN XZAPVAXBR

DHAPF; DHNZNEWZN FND

GASKWJ: BPK GADH BRR DHI

FNDDAPF FND OPKNZSDBPKAPF.

The True Path

The chart gives directions to the church in the central square in the grid. Move the indicated number of spaces north, south, east and west (eg 4N means four squares north) stopping at each square once only to arrive there. At which square should you start?

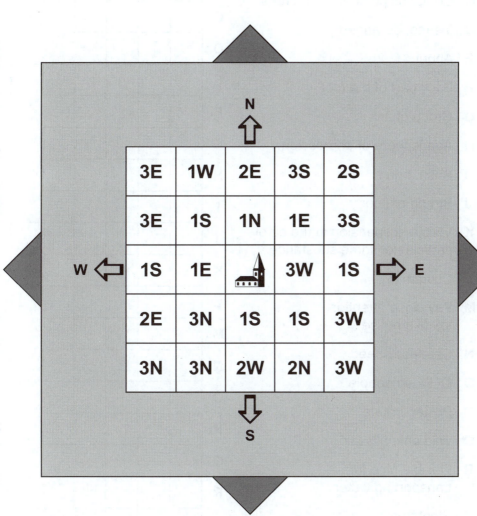

Acrostic

Solve the clues and enter the answers into the grid below.
Then cross-reference the letters to their indicated positions in
the grid on the opposite page to reveal a verse from the Bible.

A Stagger, walk unsteadily

B Very pleased

C Compass point at 90 degrees

D Insane, deranged

E About

F Back part of the foot

G Group of fish

H Atmosphere of depression

I Rush, hurry

J Strand of fiber

K Visible suspension in the air of
particles of some substance

L Custom

M Pay close attention
to, take notice

N Careless speed

O Of those people

P Pester, irritate

Q Wild animal's lair

R Flexible pipe for
transporting water

S Steal from

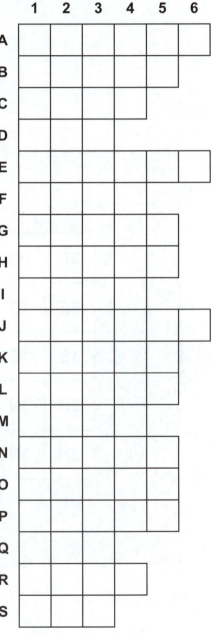

Acrostic

G4	P3	E6		A3	O2	J4		F4	H4	K5	Q1		R3	K2
L4	D3		E4	P2	C4	G3		H5	R2	G1	C1	N3	,	
C3	M3	O3	,		O4		B1	J5	K1	F3		D1	N2	I1
Q2		N4	J2	A5	F2		I2		H1	E3	J6		O1	K4
	B3	I4	D2	S1	E1	S2	L1	;		B2	E5	M4		C2
L2	A6	H3	Q3		A1	N1	P5		S3	O5	A2	J1	R1	M2
E2		I3	G2	P1	H2	G5		L3	N5		L5	M1	B5	
K3	J3	P4	B4	F1	R4	A4	.							

Shape Spotter

Which is the only shape to appear twice in exactly the same shading (black, white or gray) in the box below? You'll need a keen eye for this one, as some shapes overlap others!

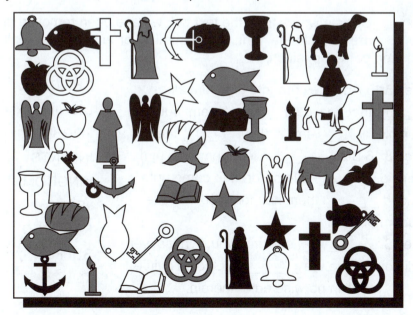

Riddle-Me-Ree

Find one letter per line, following the clues given in the verse below. For example, 'My first is in houses, but never in homes' gives the letter U as the first letter. When you have finished, the letters will spell a name.

My first's found in AUGUST, but never in JUNE,

My second's in RHYTHM, but never in TUNE,

My third is in SECOND, but never in TIME,

My fourth's found in MONEY and also in DIME,

My fifth is in SCREAMING, but never in SHOUTING,

My sixth's in DISCIPLE. Now, are you still doubting?

1st	2nd	3rd	4th	5th	6th

Stop Gaps

179

Certain words from the text below have been removed and are listed to the right, in alphabetical order. Can you replace them in their correct positions?

Luke 18:15 And they brought unto him also _____, that he would _____ them: but when his _____ saw it, they _____ them.
Luke 18:16 But _____ called them unto him, and said, _____ little children to come unto me, and _____ them not: for of such is the kingdom of God.
Luke 18:17 _____ I say unto you, Whosoever shall not receive the _____ of God as a little _____ shall in no wise enter therein.

CHILD

DISCIPLES

FORBID

INFANTS

KINGDOM

JESUS

REBUKED

SUFFER

TOUCH

VERILY

Scripture Knowledge

How's your knowledge of the scriptures? See if you can answer the questions below…

1 The reigns of how many judges are stated in the Book of Judges?

_____

2 After his arrest by King Herod, how was Peter able to escape from his imprisonment?

_____

3 During their wanderings in the desert, the Israelites stoned a man to death for collecting wood. Why?

_____

4 Which of Solomon's sons was the last king of a united Israel?

_____

5 Whose wife cautioned him to have nothing to do with Jesus?

_____

6 In Genesis 37, who bought Joseph from his brothers?

_____

7 Which three disciples did Jesus ask to keep watch with him in the Garden of Gethsemane?

_____

8 For how long had Lazarus been dead when Jesus restored him to life?

_____

Jacob's Ladder

Change one letter at a time (but not the position of any letter) to make a new word – and move from the word at the top of each ladder to the word at the bottom, using the exact number of rungs provided.

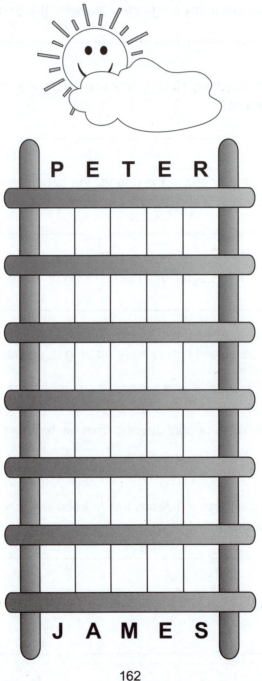

P E T E R

J A M E S

Bible Codeword

Every letter in this crossword has been replaced by a number, the number remaining the same for that letter wherever it occurs. Can you substitute numbers for letters and complete the crossword? The letters either side of the grid and the reference box showing which numbers have been decoded can also aid solving. One word has already been entered into the grid, to help you on your way. When finished, use the code to spell out a quotation from the Bible.

Left-side alphabet key: A B C D E F G H I J K L M
Right-side alphabet key: N O P Q R S T U V W X Y Z

7	2	6	21	24	■	7	18	1	8	12	5	1	8	25
19	■	11	■	3	■	11	■	21	■	18	■	■	■	18
21	11	19	24	9	15	6	2	4	■	9	26	15	6	2
1	■	15	■	4	■	21	■	11	■	6	■	16	■	20
25	5	9	15	15	11	■	23	19	2	25	21	1	6	9
2	■	■	■	1	■	17	■	8	■	10	■	8	■	■
15	19	8	1	12	■	2	1	14	24	■	24	3	1	4
9	■	11	■	24	■	15	■	1	■	22	■	18	■	2
14	11	11	21	■	24 (S)	15 (T)	19 (U)	8 (N)	■	2	5	9	2	14
■	■	14	■	24	■	18	■	25	■	19	■	■	■	18
7	11	18	18	11	16	9	14	■	1	8	14	1	25	11
18	■	9	■	7	■	24	■	9	■	14	■	12	■	12
1	8	24	9	15	■	5	2	8	14	1	16	11	6	3
8	■	■	■	9	■	1	■	13	■	12	■	8	■	9
25	9	11	25	6	2	4	5	10	■	9	2	24	9	14

Reference Box

1	2	3	4	5	6	7	8	9	10	11	12	13
							N					

14	15	16	17	18	19	20	21	22	23	24	25	26
	T				U					S		

Quotation

18	11	13	9	15	5	10	8	9	1	25	5
17	11	6	2	24	15	5	10	24	9	18	7

S Bend

183

Place the letters of each word, one per cell, so that every word flows in a clockwise direction around a number. Where the hexagons of one word overlap with those of another, the letter in each cell is common to both.

When finished, rearrange the letters in the pale gray hexagons to form the name of a character from the Bible.

ANTLER

BURIED

COUGAR

ISLAND

PASSES

QUORUM

SIGNAL

SPRITE

STAPLE

TEEING

TORPID

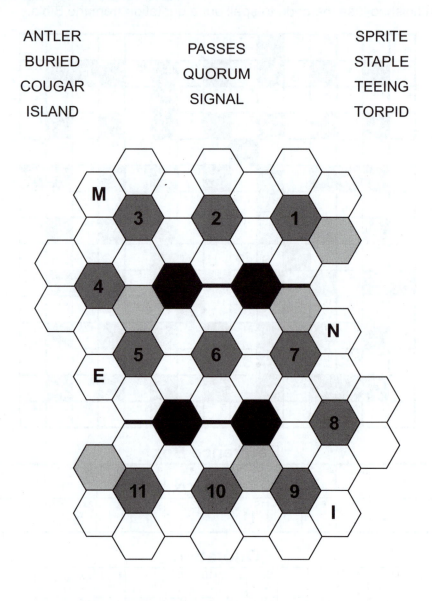

The name is: _____

Phone-etics

Use the telephone dial in order to spell out the Bible quotation.

4 27432 10 731866 63 5463

1335428466 9686 843 5672, 162

43 43172 53; 698 63 843 13550

63 4355 27432 4, 162 8469

43172388 50 96423.

Wordwheel

How many words of three or more letters can you make from those in the wheel, without using plurals, abbreviations or proper nouns?

The central letter must appear once in every word and no letter in a section of the wheel may be used more than once.

There is at least one nine-letter word in the wheel, which is a proper noun: the name of a book in the Bible.

_____

_____

_____

_____

_____

_____

_____

_____

The nine-letter word is: _____

Into the Ark

Can you discover the way through this maze, and thus help
these animals to find their way into Noah's Ark at the center?

Saints' Names

Can you find all of the 21 listed names of saints hidden in the grid below? Words may run forwards or backwards, either horizontally, diagonally or vertically, but always in a straight, uninterrupted line.

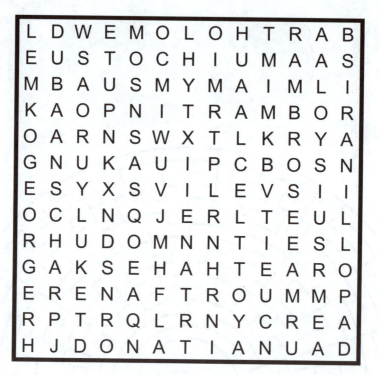

```
L D W E M O L O H T R A B
E U S T O C H I U M A A S
M B A U S M Y M A I M L I
K A O P N I T R A M B O R
O A R N S W X T L K R Y A
G N U K A U I P C B O S N
E S Y X S V I L E V S I I
O C L N Q J E R L T E U L
R H U D O M N N T I E S L
G A K S E H A H T E A R O
E R E N A F T R O U M M P
R P T R Q L R N Y C R E A
H J D O N A T I A N U A D
```

ALOYSIUS	CLEMENT	JOSEPH
AMBROSE	DEMETRIUS	LUKE
ANSCHAR	DONATIAN	MARK
ANTHONY	EUSTOCHIUM	MARTIN
APOLLINARIS	GEORGE	MARY
BARTHOLOMEW		PAUL
BERNHARD		PETER
BONA VENTURA		WILLIAM

Keyword Crossword

Solve the crossword puzzle in the usual way, then rearrange
the letters in the shaded squares to spell out a keyword,
which is the name of place (it might be a country, region, river, garden, hill,
mountain, town or city) that appears in the Bible.

Across

1 Two-wheeled horse-
   drawn battle vehicle (7)
5 Writing tables (5)
8 Rate or magnitude
   of change (9)
9 Long period of time (3)
10 Jewish spiritual leader (5)
12 Restricted (7)
13 Domestic thread-
   making machine (8,5)
15 Make more attractive (7)
17 Involving danger (5)
19 Stand for a golf ball (3)
20 Person who has
   religious faith (9)
22 Revolving blade (5)
23 Return to a former state (7)

Down

1 Conceal (5)
2 Ventilate (3)
3 Native of Rome, for
   example (7)
4 Experimenting until a
   solution is found (5,3,5)
5 Jeans material (5)
6 Emitting no odor (9)
7 Malicious gossip (7)
11 Most lustrous (9)
13 Protection (7)
14 African wild swine (7)
16 More recent (5)
18 Fine cords of twisted fibers (5)
21 Food in a pastry shell (3)

Bible Passage Storyword

Some of the words in the Bible passage below have been replaced with clue numbers. The missing words all fit into the grid opposite. For example, if the phrase is "Seek and ye 18A find", this indicates that the solution to 18 Across is 'SHALL', which can then be written into the grid.

Don't worry if you can't discover the precise word required at first glance – when more words are filled into the grid, the letters which intersect with others will help you discover further words.

This passage is taken from Psalms, Chapter 59.

1: Deliver me from mine 26D, O my God: defend me from them that 42A up 15A me.

2: Deliver me from the workers of 30A, and save me from 28D 32D.

3: For, lo, they lie in 37D for my 1A: the 24D are gathered against me; not for my 27A, nor for my sin, O LORD.

4: They run and prepare themselves 6D my fault: 31A to 40A me, and behold.

5: Thou therefore, O LORD God of 19D, the God of 23D, awake to 8A all the heathen: be not merciful to any wicked 9D. Selah.

6: They return at evening: they make a noise like a dog, and go 7D about the city.

7: 13A, they 28A out with their mouth: 36D are in their lips: for who, say they, doth 40D?

8: But thou, O 41D, shalt laugh at them; thou shalt have all the 29D in 20D.

9: 38A of his strength will I wait upon thee: for God is my defense.

10: The God of my mercy shall 5D me: God shall let me see my 34A upon mine enemies.

11: 16D them not, 22D my people forget: scatter them by thy 5A; and bring them down, O Lord our 18A.

12: For the 25D of their mouth and the words of their 14D let them even be taken in their 44A: and for cursing and 2D which they 36A.

13: Consume them in 45A, consume them, that they may not be: and let them 12A that God ruleth in Jacob unto the ends of the 39D. Selah.

14: And at evening let them return; and let them 35A a noise like a 17D, and go round 4D the city.

15: Let them wander up and down for 3A, and grudge if they be not 1D.

16: But I will 11A of thy power; yea, I will sing 21A of thy mercy in the morning: for thou hast been my 34D and 10A in the 33D of my trouble.

17: Unto thee, O my strength, will I sing: for 43A is my defense, and the God of my mercy.

Bible Passage Storyword

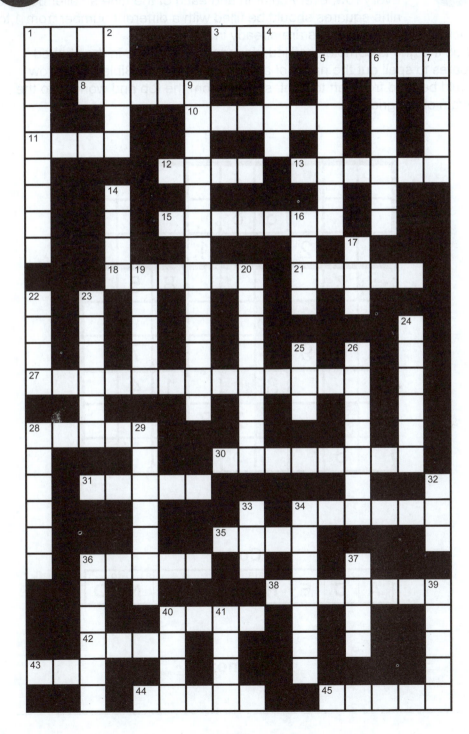

Bible Sudoku

190

Every row, every column and each of the nine smaller boxes of nine squares should be filled with a different number from 1 to 9 inclusive. Some numbers are already in place.

When the grid is completely filled, decode the numbers in the shaded squares to spell out the name of a character from the Bible. Every row should be read from left to right, starting from the top and working to the bottom of the grid.

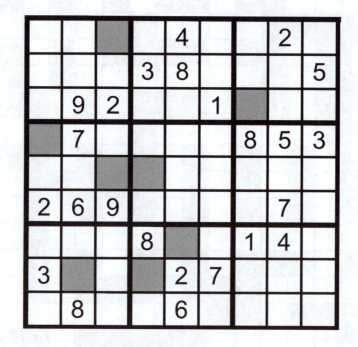

Code

1	2	3	4	5	6	7	8	9
A	D	E	H	I	J	M	N	O

Name:

172

Scripture Knowledge

How's your knowledge of the scriptures? See if you can answer the questions below…

1 Rahab and her family were the only people spared after the Israelites destroyed which city?

_____

2 From which place did Goliath come?

_____

3 For how many years did King David reign in Jerusalem?

_____

4 What did God command Moses to build to hold the tablets on which the Ten Commandments are inscribed?

_____

5 Why did King Saul attempt to have David killed on several occasions?

_____

6 Gomer was the wife of which Old Testament prophet?

_____

7 Gomer was a strange choice of wife for a religious man. Why?

_____

8 Who commanded the prophet's marriage to Gomer?

_____

Shape-up

Every row and column in this grid originally contained one cross, one loaf, one fish, one star and two blank squares, although not necessarily in that order. Every symbol with a black arrow refers to the first of the four symbols encountered when traveling in the direction of the arrow. Every symbol with a white arrow refers to the second of the four symbols encountered in the direction of the arrow. Can you complete the original grid?

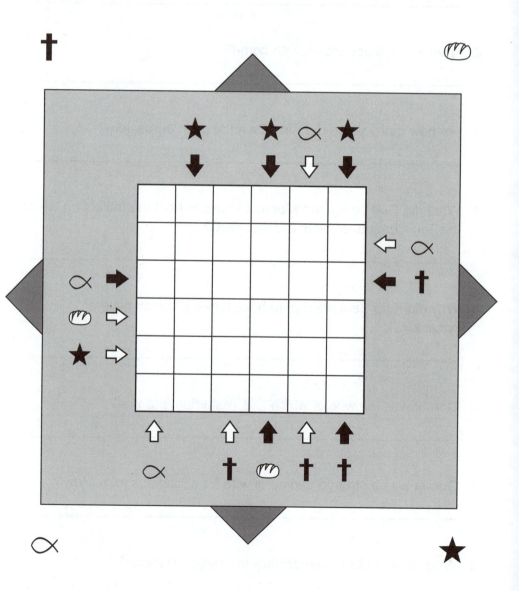

Paul's Pathfinder

The object of this puzzle is to trace a single path from the top left square to the bottom right square of the grid, traveling through all of the cells in either a horizontal, vertical or diagonal direction. Every cell must be entered once only and your path should take you through the letters in the sequence P-A-U-L-P-A-U-L, etc. Can you find the logical way through?

P	P	A	U	L	A	L	A
L	A	A	P	P	U	P	U
L	U	L	U	A	U	L	L
U	P	A	L	P	P	A	P
A	P	U	U	A	U	U	P
P	L	L	A	P	L	L	A
U	A	U	U	A	L	P	U
L	P	A	L	P	A	U	L

Simon's Squares

194

Fit the letters S, I, M, O and N into the grid in such a way that each horizontal row, each vertical column and each of the heavily outlined sections of five squares each contains a different letter. Some letters are already in place.

O				
I				
	S			O
		M		
				N

The Bottom Line

195

Can you fill each square in the bottom line with the correct symbol? Every square in the solution contains a symbol from each of the lines above, although two or more squares in the solution may contain the same symbol.

At the end of every row is a score, which shows:

a the number of symbols placed in the correct finishing position on the bottom line, as indicated by a tick; and

b the number of symbols which appear on the bottom line, but in a different position, as indicated by a cross.

SCORE

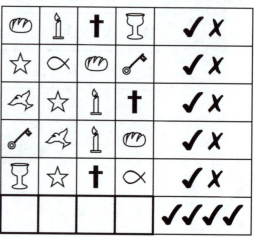

176

Round Dozen

First solve the clues. All of the solutions end with the letter in the center of the circle, and in every word an additional letter is in place. When the puzzle is complete, you can then go on to discover the two names reading clockwise around the outermost ring of letters.

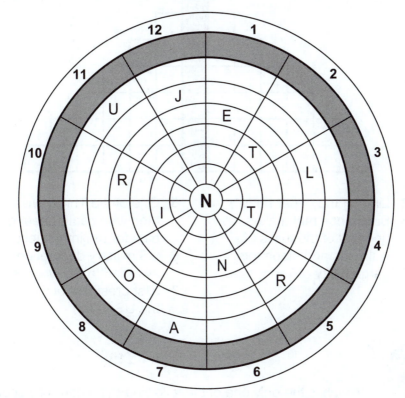

1 Ferdinand ____, explorer who led the first circumnavigation of the world
2 Aeronautics
3 Amulet, worn to ward off evil
4 Metal also known as wolfram
5 Scolding old woman
6 Canadian city, capital of Alberta province
7 Sentinel, lookout

8 Arachnid with long segmented stinger
9 Resident of Honolulu, for example
10 Hard physical or mental effort
11 Brief official report for immediate release
12 Russian-born US entertainer, original name Asa Yoelson (2,6)

The names are:

_____ and _____

Pyracross

197

Solve the clues on each level of the pyramid and reveal the word in the central column of bricks.

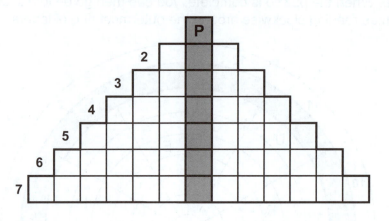

2 Limb of the upper body
3 Substance that makes up most of the tusks of walruses and elephants
4 Largest city of Tennessee

5 One of the Three Wise Men who came bearing gifts for the infant Jesus
6 US military decoration awarded to the wounded (6,5)
7 31st president of the USA (7,6)

Spelling Test

198

Which is the only one of the following to be correctly spelled?

a. EPIPANY

b. EPHIPHANY

c. EPHIPANY

d. EPIPHANY

Bookmark

Answer the clues by using the groups of letters in the lower box, crossing them out as you go. When finished, rearrange the remaining letters to make the name of a book of the Bible.

1 Below the Earth's surface

2 Sweets, candies

3 Proclaim

4 Representation carved in stone or wood

5 Sham, fake

6 Comprehending

7 Former US president, George ___

8 Sign of the zodiac

9 Going on for all time, enduring

10 Bringing up to date

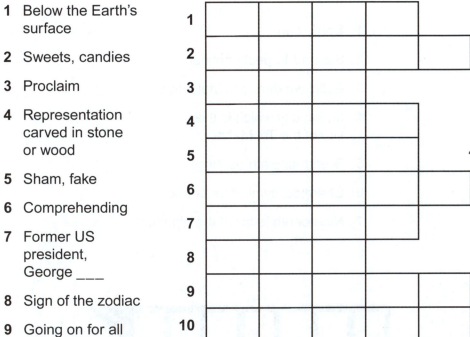

SHI	ING	DE	ULP	RL	ST	RIC	AS	GAL
RY	GRO	AN	DER	FEC	NG	COU	NE	EIT
NT	ZI	SC	DER	ATI	CAP	UN	RE	AND
ANS	NOU	ORN	ERF	CON	NCE	TI	WA	RNI
NG	UN	TIO	TON	MO	EVE	TU	NG	UND

Book: _____

Character Assignation

Fill in the Across clues in this crossword in the normal way.
Then read down the diagonal line of seven squares, to reveal
the name of a character from the Bible.

1 Spray can

2 Second-largest continent

3 Ballroom dance in triple time

4 Indian city which is the
  site of the Taj Mahal

5 Breathable atmosphere

6 Chemical symbol for copper

7 Nineteenth letter of the alphabet

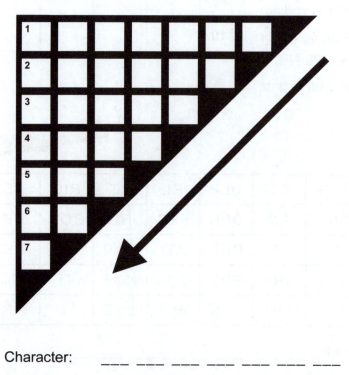

Character: ___ ___ ___ ___ ___ ___ ___

What's It Worth?

201 Each symbol stands for a different number. In order to reach the correct total at the end of each row and column, what is the value of the cross, dove, key and star?

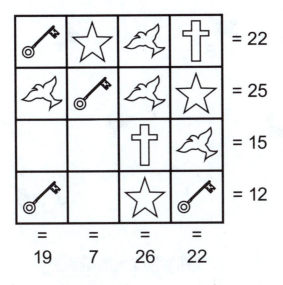

Pharaoh's Pyramid

202 Every brick in this pyramid contains a number which is the sum of the two numbers below it, so that F=A+B, etc. Just work out the missing numbers!

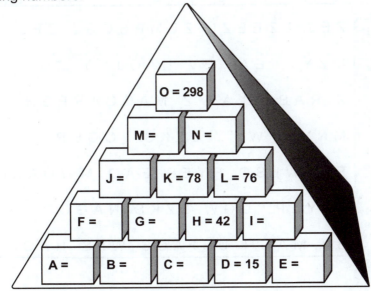

Jigsaw Puzzle

203

Which four pieces (two black and two white) fit together to make a copy of the star shown here? Any piece may be rotated, but none may be flipped over.

A

B

C

D

E

F

G

H

I

J

Cryptography

204

Each letter of the alphabet in the scroll below has been replaced by another. Can you decipher the code to reveal the quotation, which is taken from 1 Samuel 1:15?

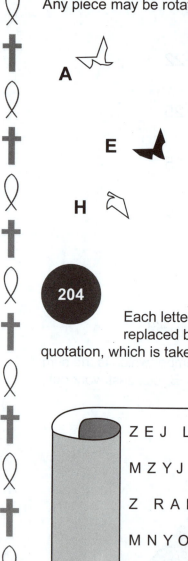

ZEJ LZEEZL ZEMRSOSJ ZEJ

MZYJ, EA, BV HAOJ, Y ZB

Z RABZE AF Z MAOOARFGH

MNYOYW: Y LZKS JOGEP

ESYWLSO RYES EAO MWOAEI

JOYEP, UGW LZKS NAGOSJ AGW

BV MAGH USFAOS WLS HAOJ.

The True Path

The chart gives directions to the church in the central square in the grid. Move the indicated number of spaces north, south, east and west (eg 4N means four squares north) stopping at each square once only to arrive there. At which square should you start?

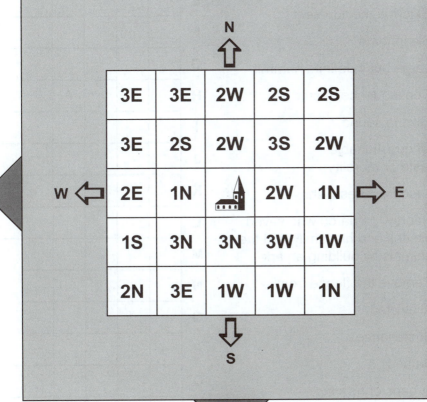

N

3E	3E	2W	2S	2S
3E	2S	2W	3S	2W
2E	1N		2W	1N
1S	3N	3N	3W	1W
2N	3E	1W	1W	1N

W ⇐ | | ⇒ E

S

Acrostic

Solve the clues and enter the answers into the grid below.
Then cross-reference the letters to their indicated positions in
the grid on the opposite page to reveal a verse from the Bible.

	1	2	3	4	5	6
A Narrowing of the body between the ribs and hips						
B Expel air through pursed lips						
C In this place						
D Light grayish-brown color						
E Express gratitude						
F External medicament						
G Blaspheme						
H Large but indefinite number						
I Consequence, result						
J Take in sound						
K Of questionable taste or morality						
L Lose freshness, shrivel						
M Hebrew patriarch who saved himself and his family and the animals by building an ark						
N Remove the fleece from						
O Alleviated						
P Sustenance						
Q Bathes						
R Organs of hearing						
S Lacking excess flesh						
T Verdant						

Acrostic

M1	P2	B4		H2	J3		Q4	C4		G2	R2	J1	E5
J5	O5		D1	K5		I6	E2	I1		K1	I4	Q2	
F5	P1		D4	A2	B2	L2	F1	O4	L5	,		S2	O1
	A4	N4	L1		R4	F4	H1	M2	S4		E3	T5	P4
	G4	E4	K4	L6	C2	A1		K2	D3	Q6		B1	N5
P3	F3	M4	D5	R3		I5	M3	G1	J4	S3	F6	T1	
O2		J6	G3	L3		J2	H3	S1	B3		A5	L4	N3
	O3	T3	K3	:		I3	F2	T2		E1	N2	R1	H4
	Q1	D2	C3	Q5		I2	A3	N1	C1	T4	G5	Q3	.

207

Shape Spotter

Which is the only shape to appear twice in exactly the same shading (black, white or gray) in the box below? You'll need a keen eye for this one, as some shapes overlap others!

Riddle-Me-Ree

208

Find one letter per line, following the clues given in the verse below. For example, 'My first is in houses, but never in homes' gives the letter U as the first letter. When you have finished, the letters will spell a name.

My first is in ORANGE, and also in GREEN,

My second's in EAGER, but never in KEEN,

My third's found in BAT, as well as in BALL,

My fourth's not in WALK, but is found in CRAWL,

My fifth is in DINNER, but not seen in SUPPER,

My sixth's found in LOWER, as well as in UPPER,

My Seventh's in GENTLE, but never in KIND,

My whole is the name of an angel, you'll find.

1st	2nd	3rd	4th	5th	6th	7th

Stop Gaps

209

Certain words from the text below have been removed and are listed to the right, in alphabetical order. Can you replace them in their correct positions?

Isaiah 2:17 And the _____ of man shall be _____ down, and the _____ of men shall be made low; and the LORD alone shall be _____ in that day.

Isaiah 2:18 And the _____ he shall utterly _____.

Isaiah 2:19 And they shall go into the _____ of the _____, and into the _____ of the earth, for fear of the Lord, and for the glory of his _____, when he ariseth to _____ terribly the earth.

ABOLISH

BOWED

CAVES

EXALTED

HAUGHTINESS

HOLES

IDOLS

LOFTINESS

MAJESTY

ROCKS

SHAKE

186

Scripture Knowledge

How's your knowledge of the scriptures? See if you can answer the questions below…

1 Which of King David's sons rebelled against his father and was eventually killed at the Battle of Ephraim Wood?

_____

2 Who was the military commander who slew David's rebellious son?

_____

3 What was the name of the inhabitants of the part of Israel known as Samaria?

_____

4 Which Assyrian king captured Samaria in 722 BC?

_____

5 To where did Joseph and Mary flee with the young Jesus?

_____

6 Approximately how old was Jesus when he was baptized?

_____

7 Who carried out Jesus' baptism?

_____

8 Who proffered the Three Temptations to Jesus?

_____

Jacob's Ladder

Change one letter at a time (but not the position of any letter) to make a new word – and move from the word at the top of each ladder to the word at the bottom, using the exact number of rungs provided.

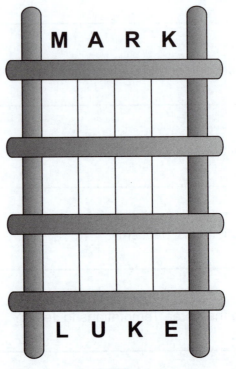

M A R K

L U K E

Bible Codeword

Every letter in this crossword has been replaced by a number, the number remaining the same for that letter wherever it occurs. Can you substitute numbers for letters and complete the crossword? The letters either side of the grid and the reference box showing which numbers have been decoded can also aid solving.
One word has already been entered into the grid, to help you on your way.
When finished, use the code to spell out a quotation from the Bible.

Left column labels: A B C D E F G H I J K L M

Right column labels: N O P Q R S T U V W X Y Z

3	17	15	4	26	19	3	3	9		18	17	26	7	19
16		4		17		17		17		3		17		5
13	19	17	23	2		26	17	3	6	17	25	23		2
26		6		21		26		23		11		22		3
17	2	21	7	19	2	25	11		15	2	3	20	1	19
		19		3			20		16					13
11	25	2	19		22	19	20	4	17	3	24	25	10	19
C	I	T	E											
21		2		3		17		19		19		23		7
3	21	25	23	19	15	2	20	23	19		17	11	21	9
9			21		15				14		16			
15	21	20	12	19	7		15	8	16	17	26	26	7	19
17		18		17		11		16		3		17		12
7		18	20	3	13	16	7	17		13	20	2	2	20
25		19		15		3		9		2		20		1
15	4	3	19	19		24	25	15	11	21	17	3	6	19

Reference Box

1	2 T	3	4	5	6	7	8	9	10	11 C	12	13
14	15	16	17	18	19 E	20	21	22	23	24	25 I	26

Quotation

| 13 | 17 | 23 | 24 | 20 | 2 | 21 | 23 | 20 | 2 | 7 | 25 | 12 |
| 19 | 26 | 9 | 26 | 3 | 19 | 17 | 24 | 20 | 23 | 7 | 9 | |

S Bend

Place the letters of each word, one per cell, so that every word flows in a clockwise direction around a number. Where the hexagons of one word overlap with those of another, the letter in each cell is common to both.

When finished, rearrange the letters in the pale gray hexagons to form the name of a character from the Bible.

BARREL

DEMURE

DISMAL

FORMAT

GYPSUM

LEADEN

PEDDLE

RESIDE

RHYTHM

SPOTTY

THRIFT

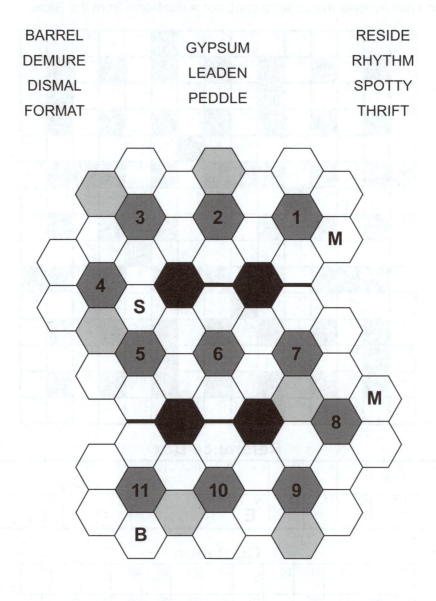

The name is: _____

Phone-etics

Use the telephone dial in order to spell out the Bible quotation.

162 03 84155 318 46 653680, 162

13 818483432, 162 671483 843 6153

63 843 5672 0697 362, 8418 4184

23158 9662769850 9484 069: 162 50

636653 84155 63937 13 1841532.

Wordwheel

How many words of three or more letters can you make from those in the wheel, without using plurals, abbreviations or proper nouns?

The central letter must appear once in every word and no letter in a section of the wheel may be used more than once.

There is at least one nine-letter word in the wheel, which is a proper noun: the name of a person in the Bible.

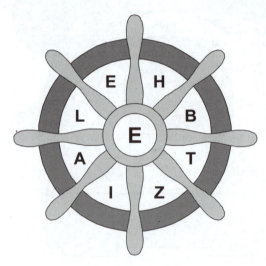

_____

_____

_____

_____

_____

_____

_____

_____

_____

_____

The nine-letter word is: _____

Into the Ark

Can you discover the way through this maze, and thus help these animals to find their way into Noah's Ark at the center?

Wedding Wordsearch

There are 21 words relating to the wedding ceremony hidden in the grid below. Can you find them all?
Words may run forwards or backwards, either horizontally, diagonally or vertically, but always in a straight, uninterrupted line.

```
M S O M V D R R K Z E Q C
O L A Z A U R P C P P E B
O L O Z O R S E H Y R C E
R E H N T R R O S E O P T
G B O U E E T I M S M R R
U H Q W S O U O A S I A O
E V O L G B N Q N G S Y T
N L E R E Y A I U V E E H
F B A R F D F N F O S R E
N P Y F I D P A D C B S D
H L D I W N Y H C R U H C
S N M Y H R G G B R I D E
A L T A R E T S I G E R O
```

ALTAR	FLOWERS	LOVE
BELLS	GROOM	MARRIAGE
BETROTHED	HONOUR	PHOTOGRAPH
BOUQUET	HUSBAND	PRAYERS
BRIDE	HYMNS	PROMISES
CEREMONY		REGISTER
CHURCH		RINGS
DRESS		WIFE

Keyword Crossword

Solve the crossword puzzle in the usual way, then rearrange the letters in the shaded squares to spell out a keyword, which is the name of place (it might be a country, region, river, garden, hill, mountain, town or city) that appears in the Bible.

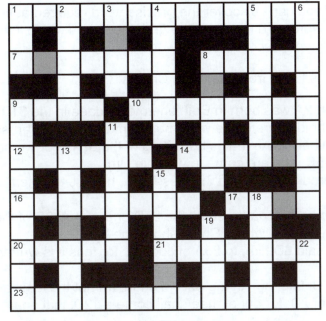

Across

1 Shame felt when a guilt is made public (13)
7 Rational motives (7)
8 Coconut meat (5)
9 Covering to disguise or conceal the face (4)
10 Formally arranged gatherings (8)
12 Leash (6)
14 Dinner jacket (6)
16 Text that is printed on paper (4,4)
17 Fury (4)
20 Run off to marry (5)
21 Old Testament prophet (7)
23 Temperateness (4-9)

Down

1 Organ of hearing (3)
2 Items strung to make a necklace (5)
3 Underground part of a plant (4)
4 Reply (6)
5 Cost (7)
6 Change the order or arrangement of (9)
8 Juicy fruit, such as lemon, orange, etc (6)
9 Above comparison (9)
11 Deliverance (6)
13 Violent disturbance (7)
15 Rates of travel (6)
18 Defense plea of being elsewhere (5)
19 Juicy, gritty-textured fruit (4)
22 Ignited (3)

Bible Passage Storyword

Some of the words in the Bible passage below have been replaced with clue numbers. The missing words all fit into the grid opposite. For example, if the phrase is "Seek and ye 18A find", this indicates that the solution to 18 Across is 'SHALL', which can then be written into the grid.

Don't worry if you can't discover the precise word required at first glance – when more words are filled into the grid, the letters which intersect with others will help you discover further words.

This passage is taken from Matthew, Chapter 2.

1: Now when 2A was born in Bethlehem of Judaea in the 31D of Herod the king, behold, there came wise men from the east to Jerusalem,

2: Saying, Where is he that is born King of the 37A? For we have 30A his star in the 35D, and are come to worship him.

3: When Herod the king had 7D these 36A, he was troubled, and all 20A with him.

4: And when he had gathered all the 27D priests and 8D of the people 11A, he 46A of them where Christ should be born.

5: And they said 6D him, In 29A of Judaea: for thus it is written by the prophet,

6: And thou Bethlehem, in the 42D of Juda, art not the least among the princes of 2D: for out of thee shall come a 12D, that shall 16D my people 9A.

7: Then Herod, when he had privily called the wise 25A, 44A of them diligently what 19D the star appeared.

8: And he sent them to Bethlehem, and said, Go and 1D 17D for the young child; and when ye have found him, bring me 43D again, that I may come and worship him 10A.

9: When they had heard the 34D, they departed; and, lo, the star, which they 1A in the east, went before them, 41D it came and stood over where the young 45A was.

10: When they saw the 28A, they rejoiced with 21D great joy.

11: And when they were come into the house, they saw the young child with Mary his 22D, and 5D down, and worshiped him: and when they had opened their 13D, they 26D unto him 18A; 38A, and 33A, and myrrh.

12: And being 23A of 15D in a dream that they should not return to Herod, they departed into their own country another way.

13: And when they were departed, behold, the 32D of the Lord 24D to Joseph in a 39D, saying, 4D, and take the young child and his mother, and flee into 40A, and be thou 36D until I 14A thee word: for 7A will 3D the young child to destroy him.

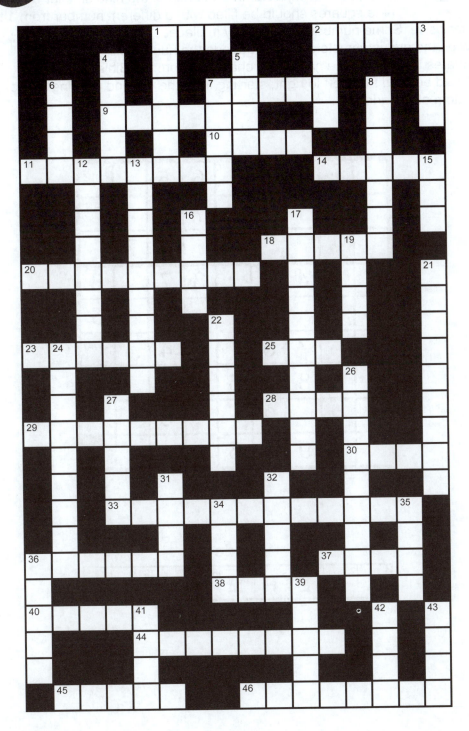

Bible Passage Storyword

Bible Sudoku

Every row, every column and each of the nine smaller boxes of nine squares should be filled with a different number from 1 to 9 inclusive. Some numbers are already in place.

When the grid is completely filled, decode the numbers in the shaded squares to spell out the name of a character from the Bible. Every row should be read from left to right, starting from the top and working to the bottom of the grid.

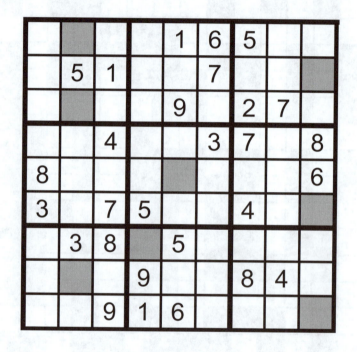

Code

1	2	3	4	5	6	7	8	9
A	B	E	H	M	N	O	R	T

Name:

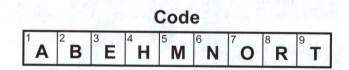

Scripture Knowledge

How's your knowledge of the scriptures? See if you can answer the questions below…

1 In which town did Jesus carry out an exorcism and heal Simon Peter's mother-in-law?

_____

2 What are the names of the eight blessings which Jesus gave at the Sermon on the Mount?

_____

3 What were the only provisions that Jesus' disciples had at the beginning of the Feeding of the Five Thousand?

_____

4 After the Five Thousand had eaten their fill, how many baskets of food were left?

_____

5 Who is said to have uttered the words "Get thee behind me, Satan!"?

_____

6 Which of the disciples were present at the transfiguration of Jesus?

_____

7 With which two important Old Testament figures did Jesus speak at his transfiguration?

_____

8 In return for thirty pieces of silver, which one of his twelve disciples betrayed Jesus?

_____

Shape-up

Every row and column in this grid originally contained one cross, one loaf, one fish, one star and two blank squares, although not necessarily in that order. Every symbol with a black arrow refers to the first of the four symbols encountered when traveling in the direction of the arrow. Every symbol with a white arrow refers to the second of the four symbols encountered in the direction of the arrow. Can you complete the original grid?

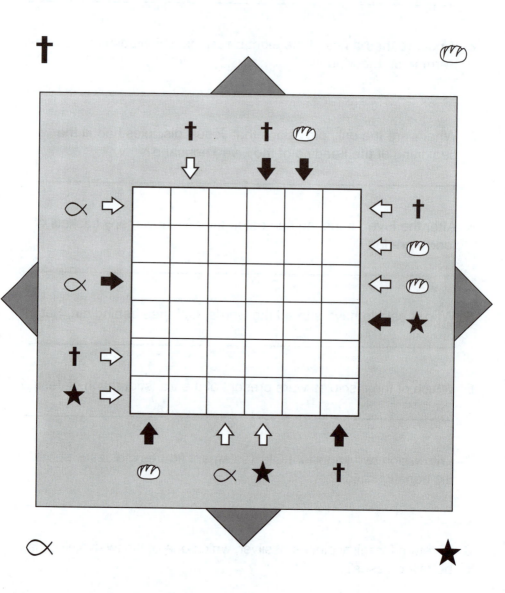

Paul's Pathfinder

The object of this puzzle is to trace a single path from the top left square to the bottom right square of the grid, traveling through all of the cells in either a horizontal, vertical or diagonal direction. Every cell must be entered once only and your path should take you through the letters in the sequence P-A-U-L-P-A-U-L, etc. Can you find the logical way through?

P	U	P	A	U	P	A	U
A	P	L	L	L	U	P	L
A	U	U	P	P	L	A	U
A	L	L	A	A	P	A	L
P	U	L	U	P	L	P	A
U	P	U	A	L	A	U	P
L	A	U	L	P	A	U	L
P	A	P	A	U	L	U	L

Simon's Squares

Fit the letters S, I, M, O and N into the grid in such a way that each horizontal row, each vertical column and each of the heavily outlined sections of five squares each contains a different letter. Some letters are already in place.

				I
	O			
N		S		
	N			
			M	

The Bottom Line

Can you fill each square in the bottom line with the correct symbol? Every square in the solution contains a symbol from each of the lines above, although two or more squares in the solution may contain the same symbol.

At the end of every row is a score, which shows:

a the number of symbols placed in the correct finishing position on the bottom line, as indicated by a tick; and

b the number of symbols which appear on the bottom line, but in a different position, as indicated by a cross.

SCORE

				SCORE
🕯	🍞	✝	🏆	✗ ✗
☆	🐟	🗝	🕯	✗
🍞	🕯	🗝	✝	✓ ✗
🍞	🏆	🕊	🗝	✗ ✗
✝	🕊	☆	🍞	✗ ✗
				✓✓✓✓

202

Round Dozen

First solve the clues. All of the solutions end with the letter in the center of the circle, and in every word an additional letter is in place. When the puzzle is complete, you can then go on to discover the two names reading clockwise around the outermost ring of letters.

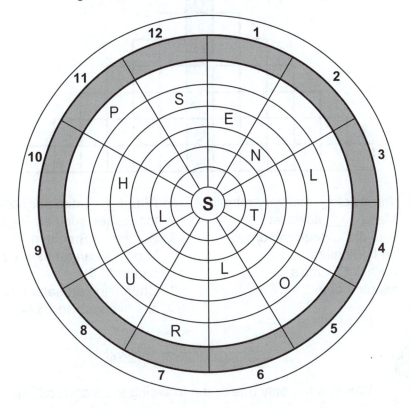

1 In a state of great hunger
2 Legendary mid-ocean island
3 Branch of mathematics
4 Ancient race of people who inhabited Anatolia and Syria around 2000BC
5 Exceedingly large
6 Dead

7 US river rising in the Rocky Mountains and flowing into the Mississippi
8 A mental or personality disturbance
9 Father of Icarus in Greek mythology
10 Remorseless
11 Book of the New Testament
12 Cowboy movies

The names are:

_____ and _____

227

Pyracross

Solve the clues on each level of the pyramid and reveal the word in the central column of bricks.

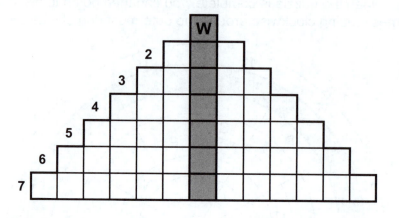

2 Immediately, this very minute
3 Marie ____, scientist who discovered radium and polonium
4 Barack Obama's middle name

5 Alfred ____, director noted for movies such as *Psycho*
6 Section of Brooklyn known as an amusement center (5,6)
7 Church in Jerusalem, on the site of Jesus' tomb (4,9)

228

Spelling Test

Which is the only one of the following to be correctly spelled?

a. HABBAKUK

b. HABAKUK

c. HABAKKUK

d. HABBAKKUK

Bookmark

Answer the clues by using the groups of letters in the lower box, crossing them out as you go. When finished, rearrange the remaining letters to make the name of a book of the Bible.

1 Exactly alike

2 Month of the year

3 Attracting debate

4 Safe haven for a ship

5 Acid found in milk

6 US national park

7 Division of the week

8 Relating to trade

9 Side opposite that of port on a ship

10 Preparation that reduces or prevents sweating

	IC	EN	NE	IR	IAL	YEL	RSP	
STA	WS	MB	CON	COM	TR	RB	CI	LA
LO	AL	HE	CT	ID	SA	DE	TO	CE
ANT	OVE	HA	TUR	ARD	AL	MER	RBO	IPE
RS	ER	TIC	OR		BRE	ANT	DAY	WS

Book: _____

Character Assignation

Fill in the Across clues in this crossword in the normal way. Then read down the diagonal line of seven squares, to reveal the name of a character from the Bible.

1 Mythical capital of King Arthur's kingdom

2 Alternative name for Mount McKinley

3 Sacred song

4 Mount ___, site of Moses' first view of the Promised Land

5 Explosive substance (inits)

6 Scale denoting acidity or alkalinity

7 Penultimate letter of the alphabet

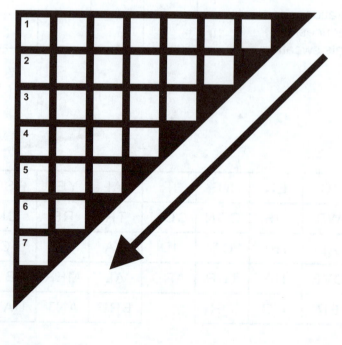

Character: ___ ___ ___ ___ ___ ___ ___

What's It Worth?

Each symbol stands for a different number. In order to reach the correct total at the end of each row and column, what is the value of the cross, dove, key and star?

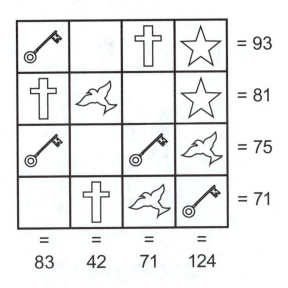

Pharaoh's Pyramid

Every brick in this pyramid contains a number which is the sum of the two numbers below it, so that F=A+B, etc. Just work out the missing numbers!

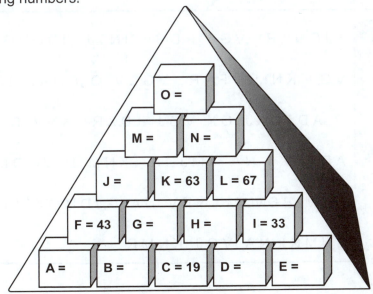

Jigsaw Puzzle

233

Which four pieces (two black and two white) fit together to make a copy of the angel shown here? Any piece may be rotated, but none may be flipped over.

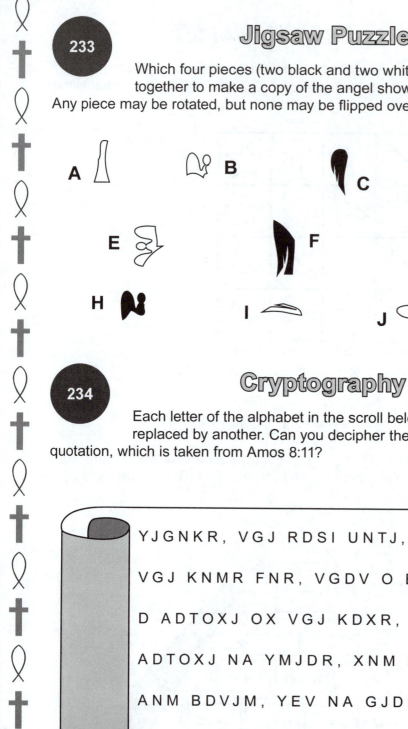

A

B

C

D

E

F

G

H

I

J

Cryptography

234

Each letter of the alphabet in the scroll below has been replaced by another. Can you decipher the code to reveal the quotation, which is taken from Amos 8:11?

YJGNKR, VGJ RDSI UNTJ, IDOVG

VGJ KNMR FNR, VGDV O BOKK IJXR

D ADTOXJ OX VGJ KDXR, XNV D

ADTOXJ NA YMJDR, XNM D VGOMIV

ANM BDVJM, YEV NA GJDMOXF VGJ

BNMRI NA VGJ KNMR.

The True Path

The chart gives directions to the church in the central square in the grid. Move the indicated number of spaces north, south, east and west (eg 4N means four squares north) stopping at each square once only to arrive there. At which square should you start?

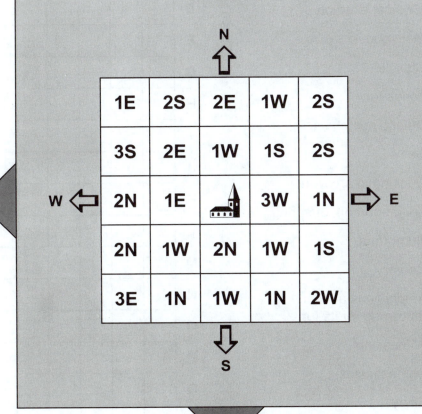

1E	2S	2E	1W	2S
3S	2E	1W	1S	2S
2N	1E		3W	1N
2N	1W	2N	1W	1S
3E	1N	1W	1N	2W

236

Acrostic

Solve the clues and enter the answers into the grid below. Then cross-reference the letters to their indicated positions in the grid on the opposite page to reveal a verse from the Bible.

A Umbra

B Chuckles with amusement

C Short swinging punch delivered from the side with the elbow bent

D Diversion requiring physical exertion

E Male goose

F Cubicle

G Longs for

H Defect, mistake

I Hazy

J Cooking in an oven

K Young person, offspring

L Humorous

M Country

N Amphibious animal renowned for its fur

O Witnessing

P Domesticates

Q Effigy

R Priest who is a member of a cathedral chapter

S Herb

	1	2	3	4	5	6
A						
B						
C						
D						
E						
F						
G						
H						
I						
J						
K						
L						
M						
N						
O						
P						
Q						
R						
S						

Acrostic

D5	K2	F2	B3	O6	C1		I2		G5	D2	N5	B2	J3
A6	J4	I4	G3		P1	A2	E5		M3	C2	R5	Q4	H3	O3
P5		M5	H1		I1	N2	M6		H2	S3	A4		D3	L1
	E2	R3	J6	G4	B1	B6	,	P2	E3	K5		F5	J2
N4	O2		L3	F3	H5		K1	B5	M2	D4	Q1	S4	I5	,
	K3		A3	S1		F1	Q5	R1	C3	Q2	P4		G1	I3
	O1	A5	L2	J5	E4	M4	O5	B4		J1	E6	N3	A1	D1
		R4	N6		Q3		F4	S2	L4	C4	H4	O4	M1	E1
,		G2	L5	P3	N1	R2	K4	.						

Shape Spotter

Which is the only shape to appear twice in exactly the same shading (black, white or gray) in the box below? You'll need a keen eye for this one, as some shapes overlap others!

211

Riddle-Me-Ree

238

Find one letter per line, following the clues given in the verse below. For example, 'My first is in houses, but never in homes' gives the letter U as the first letter. When you have finished, the letters will spell a name.

My first is in VISION, and also in SIGHT,

My second's in MIDDAY, but not in MIDNIGHT,

My third is in DIAMOND, as well as in MINE,

My fourth is in GRAPES, but it's not found in WINE,

My fifth is in HONEST, but not in SINCERE,

My sixth is in NOWHERE, but never in HERE.

My whole is a man who was robbed of his might,

By a woman with scissors who came in the night!

1st	2nd	3rd	4th	5th	6th

Stop Gaps

239

Certain words from the text below have been removed and are listed to the right, in alphabetical order. Can you replace them in their correct positions?

Ecclesiastes 3:1 To every _____ there is a _____, and a time to every _____ under the _____:

Ecclesiastes 3:2 a time to be _____, and a time to die; a time to _____, and a time to _____ up that which is planted;

Ecclesiastes 3:3 a time to _____, and a time to heal; a time to _____ down, and a time to _____ up.

BORN
BREAK
BUILD
HEAVEN
KILL
PLANT
PLUCK
PURPOSE
SEASON
THING

Scripture Knowledge

How's your knowledge of the scriptures? See if you can answer the questions below…

1 Which nation descended from Esau?

_____

2 Which Biblical man is said to have lived to the age of 969 years?

_____

3 Deborah is thought to be the longest-lived woman in the Bible. To what age did she live?

_____

4 Mentioned in the Bible as 'Alashiya', by what name is this island in the eastern Mediterranean Sea known today?

_____

5 To whom was King Ahab speaking when he said "Is that you, O troubler of Israel?"?

_____

6 Which Biblical figure has the reputation of 'slaying a thousand men with the jaw-bone of an ass'?

_____

7 According to Psalm 92, who 'spring up like grass'?

_____

8 What was the occupation of Zaccheus, the short man who was told to come down from a tree he had climbed in order to see Jesus?

_____

Jacob's Ladder

Change one letter at a time (but not the position of any letter) to make a new word – and move from the word at the top of each ladder to the word at the bottom, using the exact number of rungs provided.

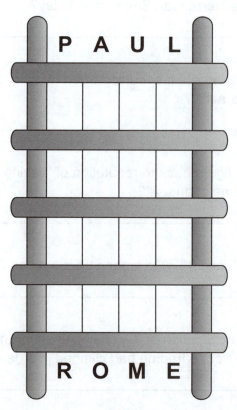

P A U L

R O M E

242

Bible Codeword

Every letter in this crossword has been replaced by a number, the number remaining the same for that letter wherever it occurs. Can you substitute numbers for letters and complete the crossword? The letters either side of the grid and the reference box showing which numbers have been decoded can also aid solving. One word has already been entered into the grid, to help you on your way. When finished, use the code to spell out a quotation from the Bible.

A B C D E F G H I J K L M

12	2	12	18	23	5	■	24	■	9	■	3	5	2	7
5	■	18	■	12	■	21	2	12	18	22	18	■	■	5
22	2	24	17	18	16	6	22	■	7	■	24 T	17 R	2 I	12 M
2	■	18	■	21	■	3	■	5	24	18	3	■	■	2
4	5	17	3	6	22	24	6	17	■	■	18	12	6	22
■	17	■	■	■	20	■	■	6	4	17	20	■	■	5
23	4	17	2	3	24	20	17	5	7	■	17	2	25	24
10	■	■	22	■	12	■	2	■	20	■	17	■	■	6
18	11	6	8	■	6	12	3	5	24	10	2	1	6	8
6	■	■	6	8	16	6	■	■	4	■	■	■	12	■
12	5	2	12	■	■	24	6	4	10	22	2	13	20	6
5	■	■	22	5	15	6	■	18	■	2	■	20	■	7
21	2	11	2	■	5	■	12	2	23	4	10	2	6	25
6	■	■	25	18	23	23	2	7	■	6	■	4	■	2
17	6	7	19	■	24	■	14	■	26	17	18	21	6	22

N O P Q R S T U V W X Y Z

Reference Box

1	2 I	3	4	5	6	7	8	9	10	11	12 M	13
14	15	16	17 R	18	19	20	21	22	23	24 T	25	26

Quotation

2	5	12	16	18	2	22	16	24	10	6	11	5	19
18	25	5	7	7	24	10	6	6	5	17	24	10	

S Bend

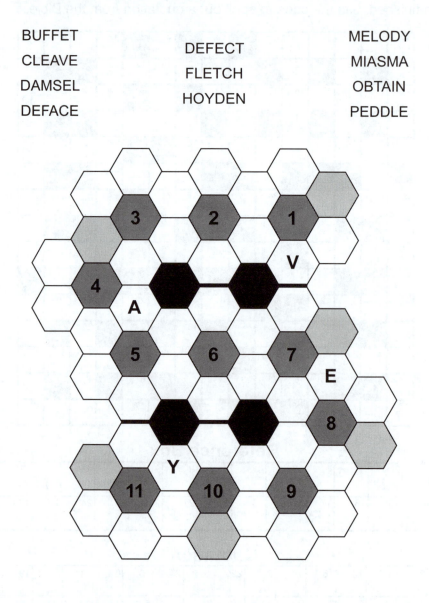

243

Place the letters of each word, one per cell, so that every word flows in a clockwise direction around a number. Where the hexagons of one word overlap with those of another, the letter in each cell is common to both.

When finished, rearrange the letters in the pale gray hexagons to form the name of a character from the Bible.

BUFFET

CLEAVE

DAMSEL

DEFACE

DEFECT

FLETCH

HOYDEN

MELODY

MIASMA

OBTAIN

PEDDLE

The name is: _____

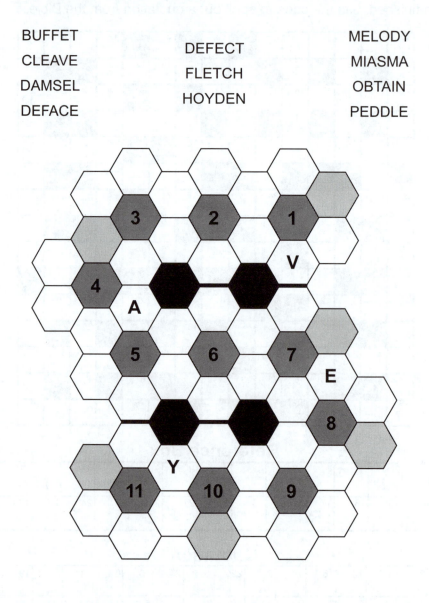

Phone-etics

Use the telephone dial in order to spell out the Bible quotation.

367 43 93 1354393 8418 43898

2432 162 7683 13146, 3936 86

8435 1586 94424 85336 46 43898

9455 362 17463 9484 445.

Wordwheel

How many words of three or more letters can you make from those in the wheel, without using plurals, abbreviations or proper nouns?

The central letter must appear once in every word and no letter in a section of the wheel may be used more than once.

There is at least one nine-letter word in the wheel, which is a proper noun: the name of a person in the Bible.

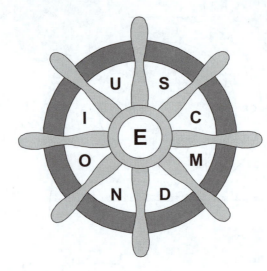

_____

_____

_____

_____

_____

_____

_____

_____

_____

_____

The nine-letter word is: _____

Into the Ark

Can you discover the way through this maze, and thus help these animals to find their way into Noah's Ark at the center?

Christening Conundrum

247

Mr & Mrs Wordsmith are having a hard time choosing a name for their baby daughter, who is due to be baptized next Wednesday morning. They have, however, narrowed the choice down to 21 possible names (some of them rather uncommon!). See if you can find them all hidden in the grid below.

Words may run forwards or backwards, either horizontally, diagonally or vertically, but always in a straight, uninterrupted line.

```
X X W H A G R E P Q Q X C
I E D N A L O Y X S M W M
E V E R A E S L A C Y X A
L O A L M S L Y Z U R N N
E I Z I E K A S S E T B D
M Z L N N D E E X O L E Y
I E Q Y I O A L I L E L L
L I E I R I S N L C L I K
Y L I I E Y E Q Z Y J N O
F L O C H T I J I E D D M
K I R O T P J F H A K A J
M M P E A N O H V E F O L
E E L U C Y B S Q G Y M G
```

ADELE	KELLY	MILLIE
ANTOINETTE	LEAH	MYRTLE
BELINDA	LILY	SONIA
CATHERINE	LUCY	SOPHIE
EMILY	MANDY	TESSA
HOPE		VERA
IRIS		YOLANDE
JOY		ZOE

248

Keyword Crossword

Solve the crossword puzzle in the usual way, then rearrange the letters in the shaded squares to spell out a keyword, which is the name of place (it might be a country, region, river, garden, hill, mountain, town or city) that appears in the Bible.

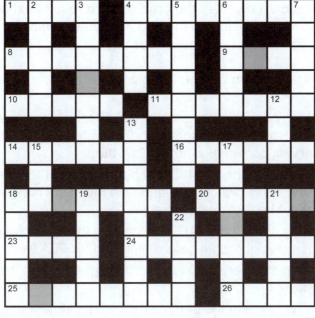

Across

1 Gumbo (4)
4 Computer package or program, for example (8)
8 Animal or plant that lives in or on a host (8)
9 Cogwheel (4)
10 Black and white, bamboo-eating mammal (5)
11 Culinary art (7)
14 Unbroken mustang (6)
16 Not far away (6)
18 Movement downward (7)
20 Freight (5)
23 Small rodents (4)
24 Popular frozen dessert (3,5)
25 Reduces in length (8)
26 Nearly all (4)

Down

2 Australian 'bear' (5)
3 Desert, leave (7)
4 Front part of the human leg below the knee (4)
5 Happening often (8)
6 Earnings (5)
7 Spooky (5)
12 Writing point of a pen (3)
13 Happen simultaneously (8)
15 Fish eggs (3)
17 Word of transposed letters (7)
18 Throws away as refuse (5)
19 Shout of approval (5)
21 Plant grown as a lawn (5)
22 Not as much (4)

Some of the words in the Bible passage below have been replaced with clue numbers. The missing words all fit into the grid opposite. For example, if the phrase is "Seek and ye 18A find", this indicates that the solution to 18 Across is 'SHALL', which can then be written into the grid.

Don't worry if you can't discover the precise word required at first glance – when more words are filled into the grid, the letters which intersect with others will help you discover further words.

This passage is taken from Daniel, Chapter 6.

16: Then the king commanded, and they 37A Daniel, and cast him into the den of lions. Now the king spake and said unto Daniel, Thy 25A whom thou servest continually, he will 21A thee.

17: And a 8A was brought and 40D upon the mouth of the den; and the king 36D it with his own signet, and with the 3D of his 42A; that the purpose might not be 29A 14D Daniel.

18: Then the king went to his 24D, and passed the 39D 2A: neither were instruments of musick brought before him: and his 23A went from him.

19: Then the king 16D very 34D in the morning, and went in haste 43A the den of lions.

20: And when he came to the den, he 18D with a lamentable 13A unto Daniel: and the king spake and said to Daniel, O Daniel, 30D of the 17A God, is thy God, whom thou servest 38A, able to deliver thee 11A the 28A?

21: Then said 27A unto the king, O king, live for ever.

22: My God hath sent his angel, and hath 1D the lions' mouths, that they have not 20A me: forasmuch as before him innocency was found in me; and also 6D thee, O king, have I done no hurt.

23: Then was the king exceeding 25D for him, and commanded that they should take Daniel up 10D of the den. So Daniel was 41A up out of the den, and no 15A of hurt was 19A upon him, because he 33A in his God.

24: And the king commanded, and they brought 9A men which had accused Daniel, and they 14A them into the 22A of lions, them, their children, and their 35A; and the lions had the mastery of them, and brake all their 26D in 5D or ever they came at the 32D of the den.

25: Then 7A Darius wrote unto all people, 4D, and 31D, that 22D in all the earth; Peace be 12D unto you.

Bible Passage Storyword

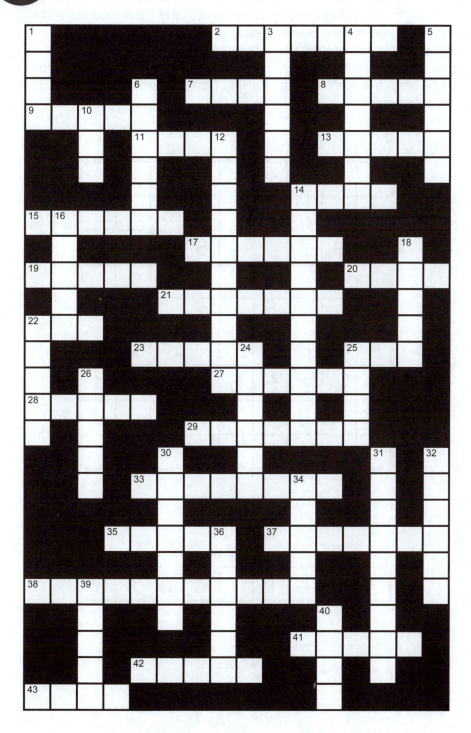

Bible Sudoku

Every row, every column and each of the nine smaller boxes of nine squares should be filled with a different number from 1 to 9 inclusive. Some numbers are already in place.

When the grid is completely filled, decode the numbers in the shaded squares to spell out the name of a character from the Bible. Every row should be read from left to right, starting from the top and working to the bottom of the grid.

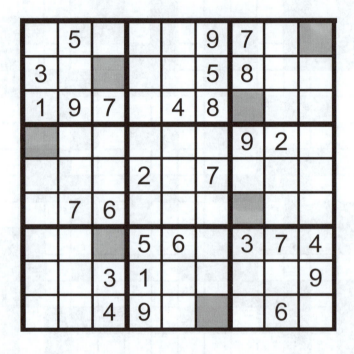

Code

1	2	3	4	5	6	7	8	9
A	B	G	H	I	O	N	S	Y

Name:

Scripture Knowledge

How's your knowledge of the scriptures? See if you can answer the questions below…

1 In the Old Testament Book of Judges, who is the only female Judge?

_____

2 On God's command, Gideon destroyed the altar to which pagan god?

_____

3 Which Old Testament prophet ascended into heaven in a chariot?

_____

4 Who warned of "False prophets who come as wolves in sheep's clothing"?

_____

5 Which of Jacob's sons did he consider to be "a ravenous wolf"?

_____

6 What does the Hebrew name-prefix 'Bar' translate as?

_____

7 "Choose for yourselves this day whom you will serve" was a choice put before the Israelites by which Old Testament figure?

_____

8 At the Last Supper, which of the disciples did Jesus foretell would deny him three times?

_____

Shape-up

252

Every row and column in this grid originally contained one cross, one loaf, one fish, one star and two blank squares, although not necessarily in that order. Every symbol with a black arrow refers to the first of the four symbols encountered when traveling in the direction of the arrow. Every symbol with a white arrow refers to the second of the four symbols encountered in the direction of the arrow. Can you complete the original grid?

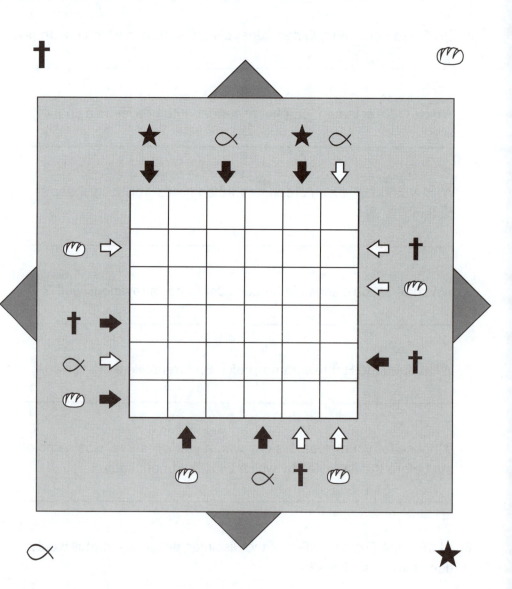

Paul's Pathfinder

The object of this puzzle is to trace a single path from the top left square to the bottom right square of the grid, traveling through all of the cells in either a horizontal, vertical or diagonal direction. Every cell must be entered once only and your path should take you through the letters in the sequence P-A-U-L-P-A-U-L, etc. Can you find the logical way through?

P	L	U	A	A	L	P	U
A	U	P	P	U	P	L	A
U	L	L	A	U	L	P	P
P	A	P	L	P	L	A	A
A	U	U	L	A	U	A	U
P	A	L	U	L	U	P	L
L	P	P	U	A	P	A	U
A	U	L	A	U	L	P	L

Simon's Squares

Fit the letters S, I, M, O and N into the grid in such a way that each horizontal row, each vertical column and each of the heavily outlined sections of five squares each contains a different letter. Some letters are already in place.

				S
				I
		M		
O				
			N	

255

The Bottom Line

Can you fill each square in the bottom line with the correct symbol? Every square in the solution contains a symbol from each of the lines above, although two or more squares in the solution may contain the same symbol.

At the end of every row is a score, which shows:

a the number of symbols placed in the correct finishing position on the bottom line, as indicated by a tick; and

b the number of symbols which appear on the bottom line, but in a different position, as indicated by a cross.

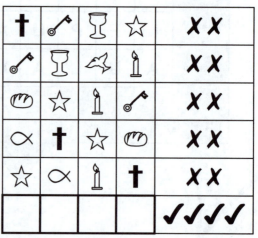

SCORE

228

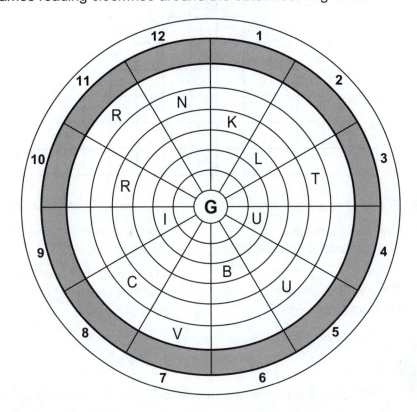

Round Dozen

256

First solve the clues. All of the solutions end with the letter in the center of the circle, and in every word an additional letter is in place. When the puzzle is complete, you can then go on to discover the two names reading clockwise around the outermost ring of letters.

1 Young domestic fowl

2 Underwater breathing apparatus

3 Riboflavin (7,1)

4 Medical respiration assisting machine (4,4)

5 Discouraging

6 Allen ___, US beat generation poet (1926-1997)

7 Too extended in duration

8 Finding

9 Getting in the way

10 Terminating prematurely

11 Tourist information film

12 Chinese island leased by Britain until 1997 (4,4)

The names are:

_____ and _____

Pyracross

Solve the clues on each level of the pyramid and reveal the word in the central column of bricks.

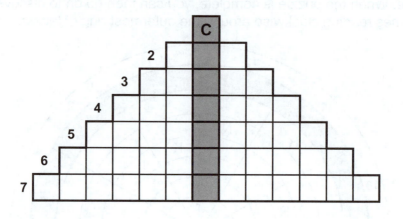

2 For what reason?

3 Ulysses Simpson ____, 18th president of the USA

4 Island country in the Persian Gulf off the coast of Saudi Arabia

5 Country, capital Lobamba

6 Body of water to the east of Italy (8,3)

7 US writer and poet noted for her sharp wit (7,6)

258

Spelling Test

Which is the only one of the following to be correctly spelled?

a. PHILLEMON

b. PHILEMON

c. PHYLEMON

d. PHILAMON

Bookmark

259

Answer the clues by using the groups of letters in the lower box, crossing them out as you go. When finished, rearrange the remaining letters to make the name of a book of the Bible.

1 Trade practiced by Joseph, father of Jesus

2 Massive, thick-skinned animal which lives in or near African rivers

3 Linking, joining together

4 Not living up to expectations

5 Marriage ceremony

6 Holy city

7 Mammal that carries its young in a pouch, for example a kangaroo or wallaby

8 Out of scale, comparatively

9 Mixture of gases surrounding a planet

10 Lucky

OS	SAL	SU	NA	DD	DIS	AP	JE	PPO
PO	TIO	NG	MES	CA	CON	AL	ATM	FO
PI	ING	TAM	UN	MAR	RU	PRO	ENT	TI
ATE	JA	DIS	ER	PHE	WE	HI	POI	TE
ING	EM	RE	POR	US	NT	NEC	RT	RP

Book: _____

Character Assignation

Fill in the Across clues in this crossword in the normal way.
Then read down the diagonal line of seven squares, to reveal
the name of a character from the Bible.

1 The 'Camellia State' of the USA

2 Winged child-angel

3 Greek epic poet credited with
writing the *Odyssey*

4 Ostrich-like South American bird

5 Initials denoting the speed of something

6 Informal term for a mother

7 Last letter of the first half
of the alphabet

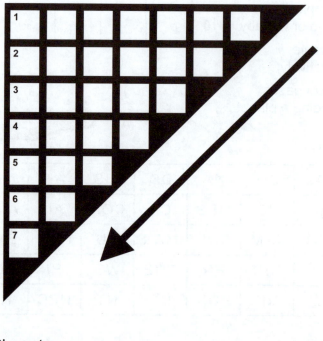

Character: ___ ___ ___ ___ ___ ___ ___

261 What's It Worth?

Each symbol stands for a different number. In order to reach the correct total at the end of each row and column, what is the value of the cross, dove, key and star?

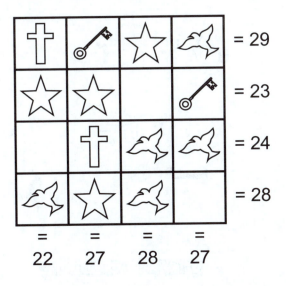

262 Pharaoh's Pyramid

Every brick in this pyramid contains a number which is the sum of the two numbers below it, so that F=A+B, etc. Just work out the missing numbers!

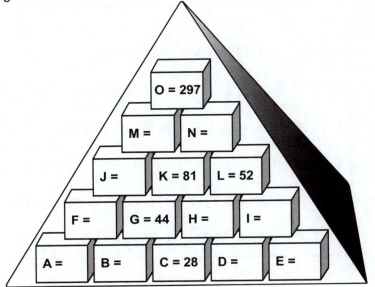

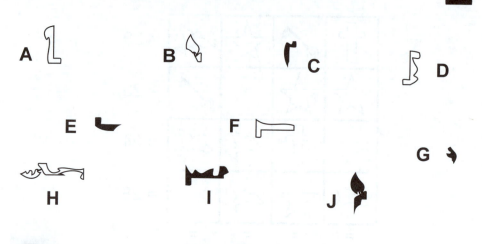

Jigsaw Puzzle

263

Which four pieces (two black and two white) fit together to make a copy of the candle shown here? Any piece may be rotated, but none may be flipped over.

A
B
C
D
E
F
G
H
I
J

Cryptography

264

Each letter of the alphabet in the scroll below has been replaced by another. Can you decipher the code to reveal the quotation, which is taken from Jonah 1:17?

UIH LEM AIXY EKY

RXMRKXMY K VXMKL GFQE

LI QHKAAIH BR DIUKE. KUY

DIUKE HKQ FU LEM WMAAC

IG LEM GFQE LEXMM YKCQ

KUY LEXMM UFVELQ.

The True Path

265

The chart gives directions to the church in the central square in the grid. Move the indicated number of spaces north, south, east and west (eg 4N means four squares north) stopping at each square once only to arrive there. At which square should you start?

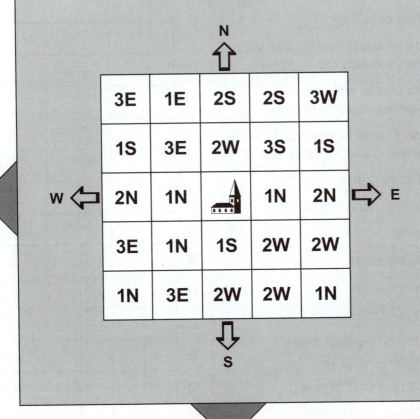

Acrostic

Solve the clues and enter the answers into the grid below.
Then cross-reference the letters to their indicated positions in
the grid on the opposite page to reveal a verse from the Bible.

	1	2	3	4	5	6

A Deposit of personal property as security for a debt

B Informal conversation

C Bike

D Summer month

E Long, narrow hill

F Item of cutlery

G Be similar in end sound, such as the words cat and mat

H Clock that wakes a sleeper at a preset time

I Mark used to indicate the word above it should be repeated

J Bride's partner

K Talk under one's breath

L Deed

M Gatehouse

N Wrongdoer

O Sign of the zodiac

P Alter or regulate so as to achieve accuracy

Q Carrying out (a task)

R Molars, for example

S Beating

T Expression of dislike

Acrostic

K3	S1	C5		A2	O3	H4	S3		T4	R5	L1	H2	M1	
D1	P4	Q1	A5	G5		B4	G2	N5		A1	R2	J4	F2	O1
R3	**:**		P3	D2	E3	Q5	A6		H5	O2	**,**	I5		
C4	Q2	J2	M3			H3	L2	C1	J3	E1	A4	I2	N4	S6
	P6	F4		J5 **,**	G3		G1	N2	E4	B2	R1	M5	L5	K2
N1	S5	K5	F1	T3 **,**			B3	D3	I1		H1	B1	C3	F3
N6	P2	E2	Q4	M4		I4	M2		G4	T2	L6	D4		S2
N3	L3	A3	J1	K6	Q3	R4	C2		I3	T1	P1	K4		L4
P5		S4	F5		K1	E5 **.**								

Shape Spotter

Which is the only shape to appear twice in exactly the same shading (black, white or gray) in the box below? You'll need a keen eye for this one, as some shapes overlap others!

Riddle-Me-Ree

Find one letter per line, following the clues given in the verse below. For example, 'My first is in houses, but never in homes' gives the letter U as the first letter. When you have finished, the letters will spell a name.

My first is in THIS, though it's never in THAT,

My second's in LEOPARD, and also in CAT,

My third is in OBOE, but not found in FLUTE,

My fourth's not in SHOE, but is seen in BOOT,

My fifth's found in HAPPINESS, never in SORROW,

My sixth is in YESTERDAY, also TOMORROW,

My seventh's not in TREASURE, although it's in CHEST,

My whole is a day used for prayer and rest.

1st	2nd	3rd	4th	5th	6th	7th

Stop Gaps

Certain words from the text below have been removed and are listed to the right, in alphabetical order. Can you replace them in their correct positions?

Zechariah 9:14 And the Lord shall be seen over them, and his _____ shall go forth as the _____: and the Lord God shall blow the _____, and shall go with _____ of the south.
Zechariah 9:15 The Lord of hosts shall defend them; and they shall _____, and subdue with _____ stones; and they shall _____, and make a _____ as through wine; and they shall be filled like _____, and as the corners of the _____.

ALTAR

ARROW

BOWLS

DEVOUR

DRINK

LIGHTNING

NOISE

SLING

TRUMPET

WHIRLWINDS

Scripture Knowledge

How's your knowledge of the scriptures? See if you can answer the questions below…

1 Why did Cain murder his brother, Abel?

_____

2 Who was the sister of Moses who was afflicted with leprosy?

_____

3 The Battle of Mount Gilboa saw the death of which Israelite king and several of his sons?

_____

4 In the Book of Joshua, what kind of weather phenomenon defeated the armies of the Amorite kings?

_____

5 In which book of the Bible does the account of Noah's Ark appear?

_____

6 In Genesis, who has a dream concerning fat cattle and thin cattle?

_____

7 How many virgins were there in Jesus' Parable of the Virgins?

_____

8 How many of them were 'foolish virgins'?

_____

Jacob's Ladder

Change one letter at a time (but not the position of any letter) to make a new word – and move from the word at the top of each ladder to the word at the bottom, using the exact number of rungs provided.

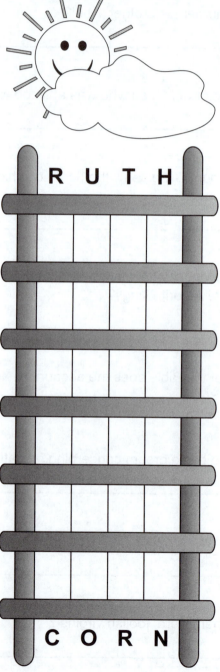

R U T H

C O R N

Bible Codeword

Every letter in this crossword has been replaced by a number, the number remaining the same for that letter wherever it occurs. Can you substitute numbers for letters and complete the crossword? The letters either side of the grid and the reference box showing which numbers have been decoded can also aid solving. One word has already been entered into the grid, to help you on your way. When finished, use the code to spell out a quotation from the Bible.

A															N
	1	10	4	15	20		16	9	13	10	2	23	16	6	4
B	10		20		10		2		6		10				20
C	17	23	13	12	12	14	10	6	12		15	18	25	8	16
D	5		23		20		15		18		6		3		23
E	16	14	5	11	22	17		6	25	3	10	12	25	4	16
F	14				25		11		15		15		18		
G	10	23	2	14	7		15	18	16	22		19	10	3	16
							C	R	E	W					
H	16		18		17		15		21		25		15		24
	21	14	16	24		12	13	18	13		15	18	16	2	4
I			4		22		18		14		15				18
J	22	10	8	25	18	1	18	7		15	13	15	26	11	11
	25		16		16		16		4		18		6		3
K	4	25	14	11	6		6	25	18	18	25	4	10	3	16
L	16				15		15		16		4		21		18
M	18	11	13	12	20	6	16	15	26		16	18	16	15,	4

Letters down right side: N O P Q R S T U V W X Y Z

Reference Box

1	2	3	4	5	6	7	8	9	10	11	12	13

14	15	16	17	18	19	20	21	22	23	24	25	26
	C	E		R				W				

Quotation

4	20	16	4	18	13	4	20	17	20	25	14
14	23	25	26	16	7	11	13	21	18	16	16

S Bend

Place the letters of each word, one per cell, so that every word flows in a clockwise direction around a number. Where the hexagons of one word overlap with those of another, the letter in each cell is common to both.

When finished, rearrange the letters in the pale gray hexagons to form the name of a character from the Bible.

AUTUMN

BEFALL

BEHAVE

CHERUB

GLASSY

HURRAH

INMATE

PLOVER

POSTAL

URGENT

VOTARY

The name is: _____

Phone-etics

Use the telephone dial in order to spell out the Bible quotation.

162 843 163358 94424 4368 668 84347

34788 388183, 198 5338 84347 696

4114818466, 43 4184 73837932 46

39375188463 241468 96237 21746388

9686 843 49235368 63 843 37318 210.

Wordwheel

How many words of three or more letters can you make from those in the wheel, without using plurals, abbreviations or proper nouns?

The central letter must appear once in every word and no letter in a section of the wheel may be used more than once.

There is at least one nine-letter word in the wheel, which is a proper noun: the name of a person in the Bible.

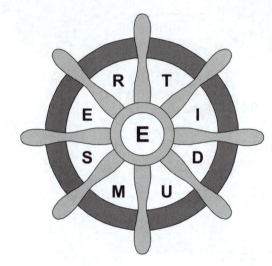

_____

_____

_____

_____

_____

_____

_____

_____

_____

_____

_____

_____

The nine-letter word is: _____

Into the Ark

Can you discover the way through this maze, and thus help these animals to find their way into Noah's Ark at the center?

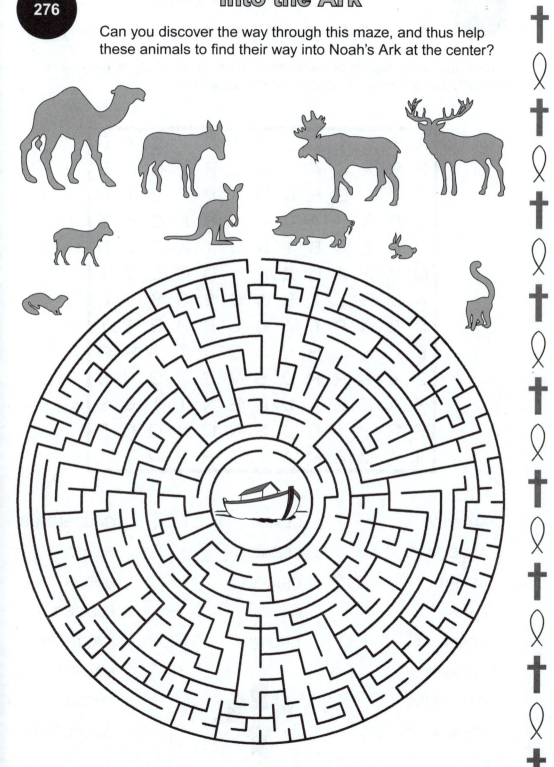

Saints' Names

277

Can you find all of the 21 listed names of saints hidden in the grid below?

Words may run forwards or backwards, either horizontally, diagonally or vertically, but always in a straight, uninterrupted line.

```
A I L I C E C A D Y B Z B
B R X C A T H E R I N E E
T Z W E R D N A P T V T N
H P A S A C L D N K O A E
O G Z W B I R U I K T L D
M V A A H B R I D G E T I
A M R L F B W C S G B V C
S B A P L W C L B P E T T
E C N U H U B E R T I R W
Z L S R R D S M J R G N B
T A E G A U D E N T I U S
F R L I C J S N Q L O C P
J A M S M A T T H E W T T
```

ANDREW	CLARA	GAUDENTIUS
ANSELM	CLEMENT	HILARY
ASAPH	CRISPIN	HUBERT
BARBE	DAVID	LUDGER
BENEDICT	GALLUS	MATTHEW
BRIDGET		MAURUS
CATHERINE		THOMAS
CECILIA		WALPURGIS

Keyword Crossword

Solve the crossword puzzle in the usual way, then rearrange the letters in the shaded squares to spell out a keyword, which is the name of place (it might be a country, region, river, garden, hill, mountain, town or city) that appears in the Bible.

Across
1 Make tidy (5,2)
5 Injured by a bee or wasp (5)
8 Tedium (7)
9 Month with 30 days (5)
10 Tennis stroke that puts the ball into play (5)
11 Christian recluse (7)
12 Period of 10 years (6)
14 Without obligation (6)
17 Cause to jump with fear (7)
19 Located (5)
22 Drama set to music (5)
23 Disease transmitted by the mosquito (7)
24 Honesty (5)
25 One division of a week (7)

Down
1 Blocks (5)
2 Mistake (5)
3 Person with bright auburn hair (7)
4 Treat with excessive indulgence (6)
5 No longer new, uninteresting (5)
6 Country, capital Kiev (7)
7 Series of rooms where works of art are exhibited (7)
12 Twist and press out of shape (7)
13 French castle (7)
15 Bring to an end, settle conclusively (7)
16 Armored hat (6)
18 Give instruction to (5)
20 Worn out (5)
21 Journal (5)

Bible Passage Storyword

Some of the words in the Bible passage below have been replaced with clue numbers. The missing words all fit into the grid opposite. For example, if the phrase is "Seek and ye 18A find", this indicates that the solution to 18 Across is 'SHALL', which can then be written into the grid.

Don't worry if you can't discover the precise word required at first glance – when more words are filled into the grid, the letters which intersect with others will help you discover further words.

This passage is taken from John, Chapter 6.

1: After these things Jesus went over the sea of 41A, which is the 39D of Tiberias.

2: And a great 40A followed him, because they saw his miracles which he did on them that were diseased.

3: And Jesus went up into a 7A, and there he sat with his disciples.

4: And the passover, a 36A of the 20A, was 43A.

5: When Jesus then lifted up his 8A, and saw a great company come unto him, he saith unto Philip, Whence shall we 15D bread, that these may 5D?

6: And this he said to 13D him: for he himself 17A what he would do.

7: 33A answered him, Two 11A pennyworth of 25D is not 24D for them, that every one of them may take a 10D.

8: One of his disciples, 4A, Simon Peter's brother, saith unto him,

9: There is a 29A here, which hath 28A barley loaves, and 16D 22D fishes: but what are they 35A so many?

10: And Jesus said, Make the men sit 19D. Now there was much 32D in the place. So the men 27A down, in 34A about five 2D.

11: And Jesus took the 44A; and when he had given 9D, he 14A to the disciples, and the 12D to them that were set down; and 23A of the fishes as much as they would.

12: When they were 18A, he said unto his disciples, 1A up the fragments that remain, that nothing be 42D.

13: Therefore they gathered them together, and filled 37D 38A with the fragments of the five barley loaves, which 3D over and 31D unto them that had eaten.

14: Then those 40D, when they had seen the 26A that Jesus did, said, This is of a 46A that prophet that should come into the 21D.

15: When Jesus therefore perceived that they would come and take him by 45A, to make him a 30D, he 6D again into a mountain himself 4D.

248

Bible Passage Storyword

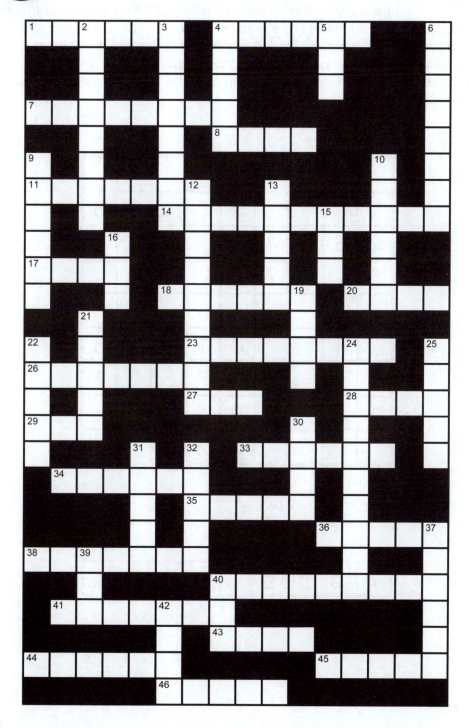

Bible Sudoku

Every row, every column and each of the nine smaller boxes of nine squares should be filled with a different number from 1 to 9 inclusive. Some numbers are already in place.

When the grid is completely filled, decode the numbers in the shaded squares to spell out the name of a character from the Bible. Every row should be read from left to right, starting from the top and working to the bottom of the grid.

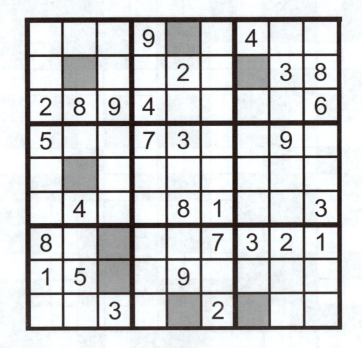

Code

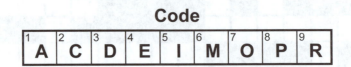

1	2	3	4	5	6	7	8	9
A	C	D	E	I	M	O	P	R

Name:

Scripture Knowledge

How's your knowledge of the scriptures? See if you can answer the questions below…

1 The marriage at Cana was the location for which of Jesus' miracles?

_____

2 How many Apostles were there?

_____

3 Which Old Testament prophet stated that "Gold and silver will not be able to deliver people from God's wrath."?

_____

4 According to The Book of Revelation 13:18, what is the "number of the Beast"?

_____

5 In the Book of Esther, who was the Persian minister who plotted to exterminate all Jews?

_____

6 On which Mediterranean island was St Paul shipwrecked in 60 AD?

_____

7 Which king's throne had six steps with two lions on each step?

_____

8 According to the Book of Job, a lion may perish for lack of what?

_____

Shape-up

282

Every row and column in this grid originally contained one cross, one loaf, one fish, one star and two blank squares, although not necessarily in that order. Every symbol with a black arrow refers to the first of the four symbols encountered when traveling in the direction of the arrow. Every symbol with a white arrow refers to the second of the four symbols encountered in the direction of the arrow. Can you complete the original grid?

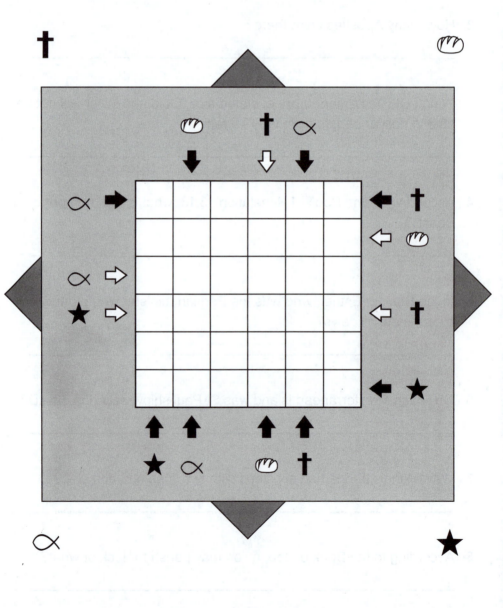

Paul's Pathfinder

The object of this puzzle is to trace a single path from the top left square to the bottom right square of the grid, traveling through all of the cells in either a horizontal, vertical or diagonal direction. Every cell must be entered once only and your path should take you through the letters in the sequence P-A-U-L-P-A-U-L, etc. Can you find the logical way through?

P	A	P	L	A	P	A	P
P	A	U	A	L	U	L	U
L	U	L	L	U	A	P	L
U	P	U	A	P	U	A	L
A	A	U	P	L	P	P	U
A	L	P	U	L	A	A	L
U	P	L	A	U	L	P	U
L	P	A	U	P	A	U	L

Simon's Squares

284

Fit the letters S, I, M, O and N into the grid in such a way that each horizontal row, each vertical column and each of the heavily outlined sections of five squares each contains a different letter. Some letters are already in place.

				I
	N			
M				S
			O	

The Bottom Line

285

Can you fill each square in the bottom line with the correct symbol? Every square in the solution contains a symbol from each of the lines above, although two or more squares in the solution may contain the same symbol.

At the end of every row is a score, which shows:

a the number of symbols placed in the correct finishing position on the bottom line, as indicated by a tick; and

b the number of symbols which appear on the bottom line, but in a different position, as indicated by a cross.

SCORE

🕯	🍞	†	🏆	X
∝	🏆	☆	🍞	X
🗝	∝	🏆	†	X
🍞	✝	🕊	∝	X
☆	☆	🗝	∝	X X
				✓✓✓✓

254

Round Dozen

First solve the clues. All of the solutions end with the letter in the center of the circle, and in every word an additional letter is in place. When the puzzle is complete, you can then go on to discover the two names reading clockwise around the outermost ring of letters.

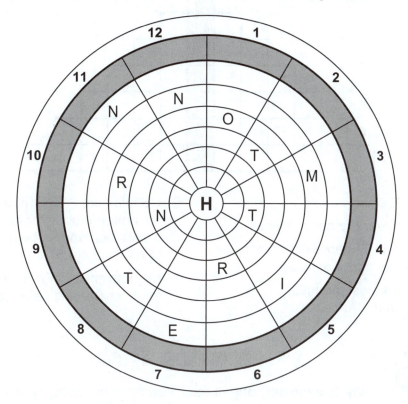

1 Biblical city destroyed by God

2 Contracted form for 'information technology'

3 Destroy, tear down

4 Uncanny, weird

5 Powerful businessman of post-cold war Russia

6 The home town of Joseph and Mary

7 Lamenting Israelite prophet

8 Exceed, surpass

9 Seaport in eastern Georgia and flat grassland of tropical regions

10 Impinge

11 Cambodian capital (4,4)

12 Jewish 'Festival of Lights' holiday

The names are:

_____ and _____

Pyracross

Solve the clues on each level of the pyramid and reveal the word in the central column of bricks.

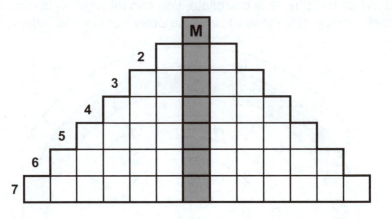

2 Set fire to

3 Elder brother of Moses

4 Old Testament patriarch, the father of Isaac

5 Highest mountain in the Andes

6 US folk hero (1734-1820) a pioneer famous for his exploration and settlement of Kentucky (6,5)

7 Major avenue in Paris, famous for its shops and cafes (6,7)

Spelling Test

288

Which is the only one of the following to be correctly spelled?

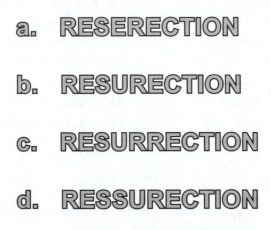

a. RESERECTION

b. RESURECTION

c. RESURRECTION

d. RESSURECTION

Bookmark

289

Answer the clues by using the groups of letters in the lower box, crossing them out as you go. When finished, rearrange the remaining letters to make the name of a book of the Bible.

1. Huge, ferocious fire
2. Starting, commencing
3. Subject to alteration
4. Piece of frozen rain
5. Word made from the letters of another word
6. Town, the birthplace of Jesus
7. Number represented by the Roman XVII
8. Ownership
9. Put out, as with a flame on a candle
10. Continent of the world

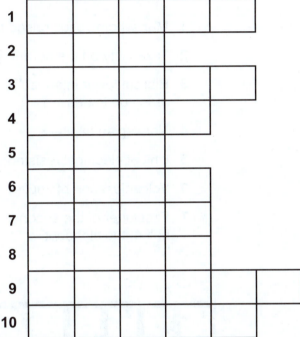

ION	TI	RC	VE	AB	WF	TI	UI	AGR
ING	THL	ION	FL	NG	AN	PO	KE	AM
ED	LA	GE	OS	AM	INN	AN	BE	EEN
TA	CON	SE	SNO	CH	EX	EM	AT	BEG
SH	AGR	AN	ESS	EH	CA	LE	NT	SS

Book: _____

Character Assignation

Fill in the Across clues in this crossword in the normal way. Then read down the diagonal line of seven squares, to reveal the name of a character from the Bible.

1 Man whom Jesus raised from the dead

2 Texan city on the border with Mexico (2,4)

3 Biblical tower intended to reach up to heaven

4 Norwegian capital

5 Unit of electrical resistance

6 Volcanic moon of Jupiter

7 First letter of the second half of the alphabet

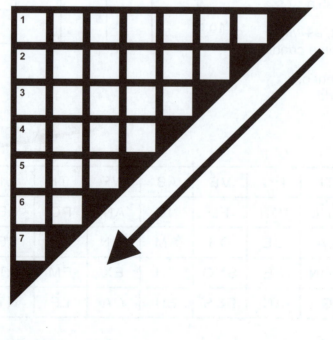

Character: ___ ___ ___ ___ ___ ___ ___

What's It Worth?

Each symbol stands for a different number. In order to reach the correct total at the end of each row and column, what is the value of the cross, dove, key and star?

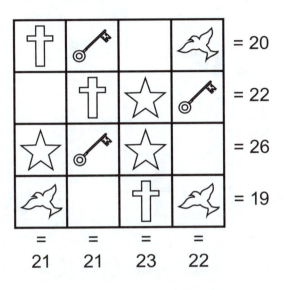

Pharaoh's Pyramid

Every brick in this pyramid contains a number which is the sum of the two numbers below it, so that F=A+B, etc. Just work out the missing numbers!

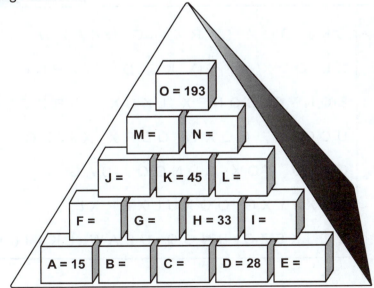

Jigsaw Puzzle

293

Which four pieces (two black and two white) fit together to make a copy of the preacher shown here? Any piece may be rotated, but none may be flipped over.

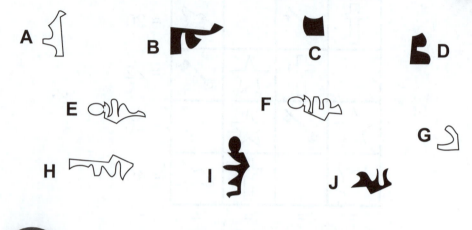

A   B   C   D

E   F   G

H   I   J

Cryptography

294

Each letter of the alphabet in the scroll below has been replaced by another. Can you decipher the code to reveal the quotation, which is taken from 1 Timothy 6:10?

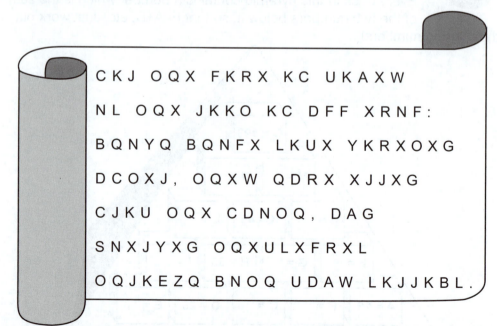

CKJ OQX FKRX KC UKAXW

NL OQX JKKO KC DFF XRNF:

BQNYQ BQNFX LKUX YKRXOXG

DCOXJ, OQXW QDRX XJJXG

CJKU OQX CDNOQ, DAG

SNXJYXG OQXULXFRXL

OQJKEZQ BNOQ UDAW LKJJKBL.

The True Path

The chart gives directions to the church in the central square in the grid. Move the indicated number of spaces north, south, east and west (eg 4N means four squares north) stopping at each square once only to arrive there. At which square should you start?

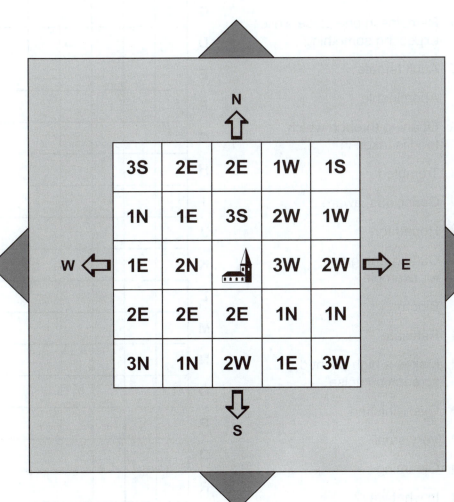

296

Acrostic

Solve the clues and enter the answers into the grid below. Then cross-reference the letters to their indicated positions in the grid on the opposite page to reveal a verse from the Bible.

A Infinitesimal

B Deluges

C Kitchen appliance

D Remains in one place while expecting something

E Adult female

F Abominable

G Opening through which food is taken in

H Trembled

I Conscious, aware

J Hoped for

K Cutting (the grass, for example)

L Bloom

M Retaliate

N Makes a high-pitched, screeching noise

O Over, finished

P Very small

Q Gleaming

R In what way?

S Rises to one's feet

	1	2	3	4	5	6
A						
B						
C						
D						
E						
F						
G						
H						
I						
J						
K						
L						
M						
N						
O						
P						
Q						
R						
S						

Acrostic

296

D1	J4	L3		N3	S6		M1		J1	F3	N6	C5		K1
I1	N4		S3	Q4	P3		O4	A3	F2	G3	M3	B5		E1
J2	A5	H2		C4	S4	B4	I2	L2	P5	O1	K6	N5		I3
G1	C2	E5	M5		Q5	O2	F5	?		B2	I5	G4		Q2
D3	P1		D5	N2	R2	L4		F1	A4	P6		C3	B1	
E4		P4	G2	B3	J6		C1	K2	O3	M2	A6	L6	H1	D2
S2	K4	F4	M4		R1	A2	J3		K3	H3	C6	H5	Q1	
N1	Q3	D4	G5		E3	M6	J5	I4	K5	L5	F6	S1		E2
L1		R3	P2	B6	S5	H4	A1	.						

Shape Spotter

297

Which is the only shape to appear twice in exactly the same shading (black, white or gray) in the box below? You'll need a keen eye for this one, as some shapes overlap others!

Riddle-Me-Ree

298

Find one letter per line, following the clues given in the verse below. For example, 'My first is in houses, but never in homes' gives the letter U as the first letter. When you have finished, the letters will spell a word.

My first is in CAROL, but never in SONG,

My second's in TALL, but never in LONG,

My third is in ASTER, as well as in ROSE,

My fourth's not in RHYME, though it is found in PROSE,

My fifth is in THOUSAND, and also in TWO,

My sixth's not in DOVE, but it is found in COO,

My seventh's in CHICKEN, never in PERCH,

My whole's often worn by a man of the church.

1st	2nd	3rd	4th	5th	6th	7th

Stop Gaps

299

Certain words from the text below have been removed and are listed to the right, in alphabetical order. Can you replace them in their correct positions?

Exodus 17:5 And the Lord said unto _____, Go on before the _____, and take with thee of the _____ of Israel; and thy rod, wherewith thou smotest the _____, take in thine _____, and go.

Exodus 17:6 Behold, I will stand before thee there upon the _____ in Horeb; and thou shalt smite the rock, and there shall come _____ out of it, that the people may _____. And Moses did so in the _____ of the elders of Israel.

DRINK

ELDERS

HAND

MOSES

PEOPLE

RIVER

ROCK

SIGHT

WATER

Scripture Knowledge

How's your knowledge of the scriptures? See if you can answer the questions below…

1 Where did Cain go after he left Eden?

_____

2 What were the three gifts that were given to Jesus by the Magi?

_____

Holy
Bible

3 What was the name of Moses' mother?

_____

4 In the Creation, what did God create on the sixth day?

_____

5 In Mark 4:39, what miracle did Jesus perform?

_____

6 What is the name given to the practice in a Law by Moses whereby a tenth part of a person's crops or income should be given over for religious purposes?

_____

7 In the Bible, who are the only three people not begotten of human fathers?

_____

8 In the Song of Songs, which king is described as "coming up from the desert like a column of smoke"?

_____

Jacob's Ladder

Change one letter at a time (but not the position of any letter) to make a new word – and move from the word at the top of each ladder to the word at the bottom, using the exact number of rungs provided.

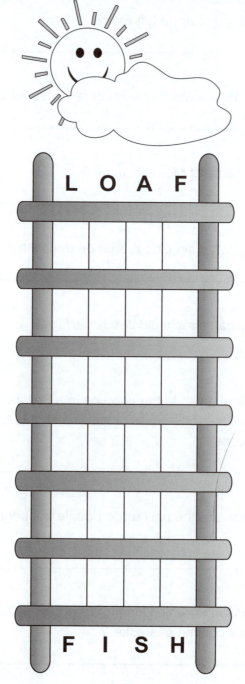

L O A F

F I S H

Bible Codeword

Every letter in this crossword has been replaced by a number, the number remaining the same for that letter wherever it occurs. Can you substitute numbers for letters and complete the crossword? The letters either side of the grid and the reference box showing which numbers have been decoded can also aid solving.
One word has already been entered into the grid, to help you on your way.
When finished, use the code to spell out a quotation from the Bible.

Left side letters (rows A–M): A B C D E F G H I J K L M
Right side letters (rows A–M): N O P Q R S T U V W X Y Z

Grid:

A	7	■	26	■	4	■	9	11	21	12	23	20	3	2	12
B	19	21	15	26	23	10	■	■	19	■	9	■	23	■	8
C	17	■	12	■	26	■	18	12	2	2	11	5	17	16	9
D	4	■	16	■	10	■	■	16	■	8	■	6	■	■	3
E	14	24	3	15	2	12	10	6	12	■	9	12	26	21	16
F	16	■	1	■	12	■	23	■	■	1	■	1			
G	26	22	12	10	■	19	24	12	22	4	17	8	17	24	6
G	24	■	■	16	■	■	24	■	■	4	■	■	■	26	
H	10	12	1	3	8	17	13	26	8	12	■	4(C)	2(L)	3(O)	8(T)
I	■	19	■	19	■	■	10	■	■	26	■	3	■	9	
J	3	3	25	12	10	■	4	12	2	12	20	23	26	8	12
J	4	■	25	■	12	■	2	■	■	23	■	10	■	23	
K	4	3	2	3	24	24	26	10	12	■	3	■	17	■	17
L	19	■	12	■	8	■	24	■	4	26	24	24	3	24	
M	23	12	10	12	16	17	6	24	16	■	10	■	6	■	6

Reference Box

1	2	3	4	5	6	7	8	9	10	11	12	13
	L	O	C				T					
14	15	16	17	18	19	20	21	22	23	24	25	26

Quotation

9	3	15	2	3	24	6	9	26	2	8	11	12	20	12	8
15	12	12	24	8	15	3	3	21	17	24	17	3	24	16	

S Bend

Place the letters of each word, one per cell, so that every word flows in a clockwise direction around a number. Where the hexagons of one word overlap with those of another, the letter in each cell is common to both.

When finished, rearrange the letters in the pale gray hexagons to form the name of a character from the Bible.

DILUTE

EVENTS

FILTER

FRIGID

KIDNEY

MARGIN

RATHER

SORREL

STAMEN

TURBID

TUSSLE

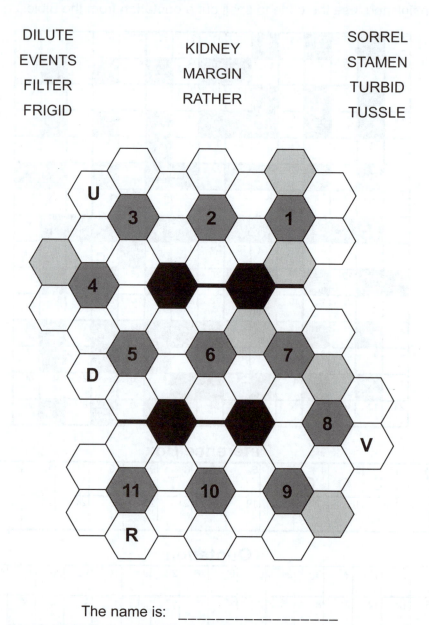

The name is: _____

Phone-etics

Use the telephone dial in order to spell out the Bible quotation.

162 43 431532 5160 8418 9373

8424 63 249378 24831838, 162

2188 698 5160 239458; 162

89333732 668 843 239458 86

86314, 1321983 8430 4639 445.

Wordwheel

How many words of three or more letters can you make from those in the wheel, without using plurals, abbreviations or proper nouns?

The central letter must appear once in every word and no letter in a section of the wheel may be used more than once.

There is at least one nine-letter word in the wheel, which is a proper noun: the name of a person in the Bible.

_____

_____

_____

_____

_____

_____

_____

_____

_____

_____

_____

_____

The nine-letter word is: _____

Into the Ark

Can you discover the way through this maze, and thus help these animals to find their way into Noah's Ark at the center?

Books of the Bible

Can you find the listed books of the Bible, which are all hidden in the grid below?

Words may run forwards or backwards, either horizontally, diagonally or vertically, but always in a straight, uninterrupted line.

```
A  I  N  S  B  W  E  H  T  T  A  M  D
F  H  E  C  Z  E  P  H  A  N  I  A  H
I  C  H  R  O  N  I  C  L  E  S  F  B
Y  A  E  H  A  L  C  S  G  N  I  K  N
G  L  M  A  R  V  O  S  Z  Q  M  O  E
E  A  I  N  Z  T  R  S  C  I  I  M  X
N  M  A  O  E  E  T  S  S  T  J  W  O
E  X  H  J  B  W  O  Y  A  I  I  T  D
S  K  L  M  J  M  J  L  T  B  A  U  U
I  Y  U  D  A  L  E  W  B  Y  J  N  S
S  N  T  L  M  V  H  E  B  R  E  W  S
D  E  U  T  E  R  O  N  O  M  Y  R  F
H  T  U  R  S  B  R  E  V  O  R  P  L
```

AMOS	JAMES	MALACHI
CHRONICLES	JONAH	MATTHEW
COLOSSIANS	KINGS	NEHEMIAH
DEUTERONOMY	LUKE	NUMBERS
EXODUS		PROVERBS
EZRA		REVELATION
GENESIS		RUTH
HEBREWS		ZEPHANIAH

Keyword Crossword

Solve the crossword puzzle in the usual way, then rearrange the letters in the shaded squares to spell out a keyword, which is the name of place (it might be a country, region, river, garden, hill, mountain, town or city) that appears in the Bible.

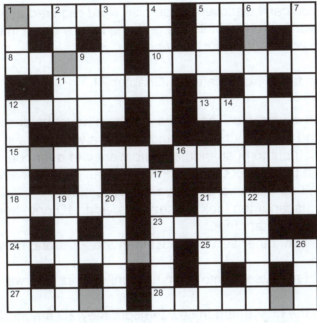

Across

1 Building for housing poultry (3-4)
5 Japanese rice dish (5)
8 Russian pancake (5)
10 Continuing forever or indefinitely (7)
11 Jet-black (5)
12 Synthetic silk-like fabric (5)
13 Mood disorder (5)
15 Seafarer (6)
16 Borne on the water (6)
18 Drinking vessel (5)
21 Contrite (5)
23 Identifying appellation (5)
24 Look over carefully (7)
25 Remark made spontaneously (2,3)
27 Formal visitor (5)
28 Act of God (7)

Down

1 Central part of a car wheel (3)
2 Clamorous (5)
3 Pungent vegetable (5)
4 Message communicated to God (6)
5 Water vapor (5)
6 Luster (5)
7 Without delay or hesitation (9)
9 Thin strips of pasta (7)
12 Voluntarily leaving a job or post (9)
14 In total (3,4)
17 Lowest part of anything (6)
19 Church passage (5)
20 Perspiration (5)
21 Step (5)
22 Remnant of the past (5)
26 Honey-producing insect (3)

Bible Passage Storyword

Some of the words in the Bible passage below have been replaced with clue numbers. The missing words all fit into the grid opposite. For example, if the phrase is "Seek and ye 18A find", this indicates that the solution to 18 Across is 'SHALL', which can then be written into the grid.

Don't worry if you can't discover the precise word required at first glance – when more words are filled into the grid, the letters which intersect with others will help you discover further words.

This passage is taken from Matthew, Chapter 21.

33: Hear another parable: There was a certain householder, which 24D a vineyard, and 44A it round 37D, and digged a winepress in it, and built a 23D, and let it out to husbandmen, and went into a far country:

34: And when the 42A of the fruit drew near, he sent his servants to the husbandmen, that they might receive the fruits of it.

35: And the husbandmen took his servants, and 11D one, and 32D another, 16A stoned another.

36: Again, he sent other servants 38D than the 22A: and they did unto them likewise.

37: But 39D of all he sent unto them his son, saying, 20A will reverence my 17A.

38: But when the husbandmen saw the son, they 2D among 26A, This is the 27D; come, let us kill him, and let us 13A on his 5D.

39: And they caught him, and cast him out of the vineyard, and 25D him.

40: When the lord therefore of the vineyard cometh, what will he do unto those 15D?

41: They say unto him, He will 40A 30D those wicked men, and will let out his vineyard unto other husbandmen, which shall 34A him the fruits in their seasons.

42: 8A saith unto them, Did ye 35D 4A in the 9D, The stone which the builders 4D, the same is become the 3D of the 1D: this is the Lord's 33A, and it is marvelous in our 10A?

43: Therefore say I unto you, The kingdom of God shall be 21A from you, and 7D to a 28A 6A forth the fruits thereof.

44: And whosoever shall fall on this 43A shall be 12D: but on whomsoever it shall 36A, it will grind him to 41A.

45: And when the 19A priests and 18D had 29A his parables, they 31D that he spake of them.

46: But when they 2A to lay hands on him, they feared the multitude, because they took him for a 14A.

Bible Passage Storyword

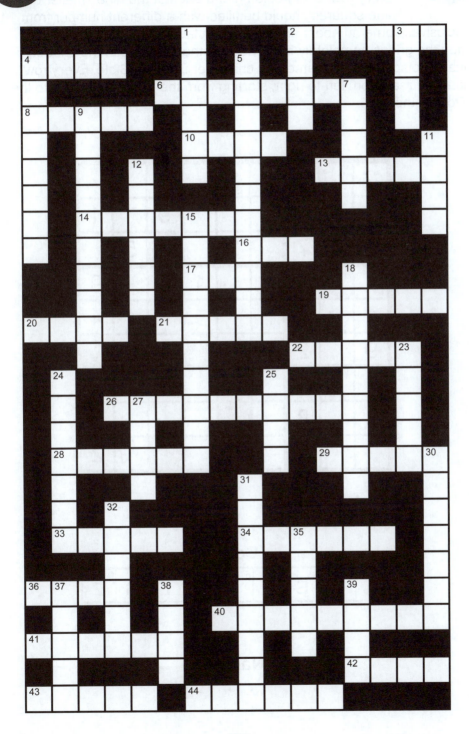

Bible Sudoku

Every row, every column and each of the nine smaller boxes of nine squares should be filled with a different number from 1 to 9 inclusive. Some numbers are already in place.

When the grid is completely filled, decode the numbers in the shaded squares to spell out the name of a character from the Bible. Every row should be read from left to right, starting from the top and working to the bottom of the grid.

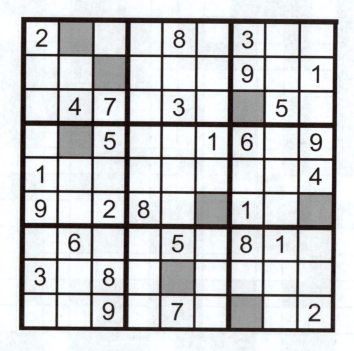

Code

1	2	3	4	5	6	7	8	9
A	D	E	H	I	K	L	S	Z

Name:

Scripture Knowledge

How's your knowledge of the scriptures? See if you can answer the questions below…

1 Which is the very first murder recorded in the Bible?

_____

2 "The Spirit lifted me up between Earth and Heaven and in visions of God took me to ____" – which city?

_____

3 What was the name of King Saul's lame grandson?

_____

4 An angel visited Mary during the sixth month of which other woman's pregnancy?

_____

5 To the Pharisees and Law-teachers, who said "A wicked and adulterous generation seeks a miraculous sign"?

_____

6 'The ____ of money is the root of all evil'. What is the word missing from this famous saying?

_____

7 God showed the Valley of the Bones to which prophet?

_____

8 At the Synagogue of which city did Jesus drive out an evil spirit from a man?

_____

Shape-up

312

Every row and column in this grid originally contained one cross, one loaf, one fish, one star and two blank squares, although not necessarily in that order. Every symbol with a black arrow refers to the first of the four symbols encountered when traveling in the direction of the arrow. Every symbol with a white arrow refers to the second of the four symbols encountered in the direction of the arrow. Can you complete the original grid?

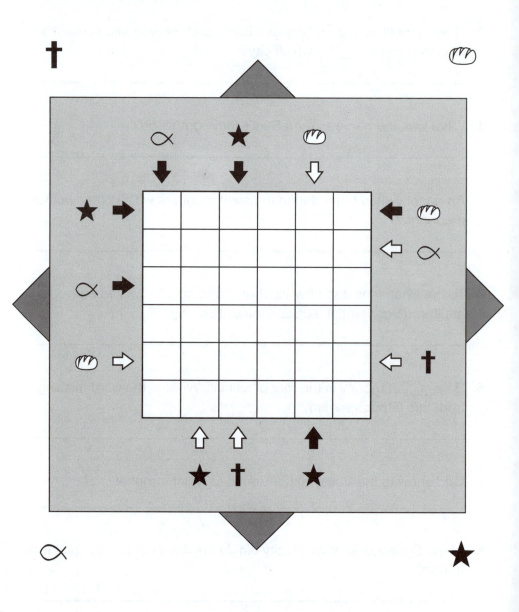

Paul's Pathfinder

The object of this puzzle is to trace a single path from the top left square to the bottom right square of the grid, traveling through all of the cells in either a horizontal, vertical or diagonal direction. Every cell must be entered once only and your path should take you through the letters in the sequence P-A-U-L-P-A-U-L, etc. Can you find the logical way through?

P	A	L	U	A	P	L	U
U	P	A	L	P	A	U	A
L	P	U	U	L	A	L	P
A	A	P	L	U	P	P	L
L	U	L	U	P	A	U	A
U	P	A	P	U	U	P	A
L	A	P	L	A	L	U	L
P	A	U	L	P	A	U	L

Simon's Squares

Fit the letters S, I, M, O and N into the grid in such a way that each horizontal row, each vertical column and each of the heavily outlined sections of five squares each contains a different letter. Some letters are already in place.

		N		
M				
		I		
	S			
				O

The Bottom Line

Can you fill each square in the bottom line with the correct symbol? Every square in the solution contains a symbol from each of the lines above, although two or more squares in the solution may contain the same symbol.

SCORE

At the end of every row is a score, which shows:

a the number of symbols placed in the correct finishing position on the bottom line, as indicated by a tick; and

b the number of symbols which appear on the bottom line, but in a different position, as indicated by a cross.

1	2	3	4	Score
key	star	fish	dove	✗ ✗
bread	chalice	candle	star	✗ ✗
cross	dove	chalice	key	✗ ✗
star	fish	bread	candle	✗ ✗
key	candle	dove	cross	✗ ✗
				✓✓✓✓

280

Round Dozen

First solve the clues. All of the solutions end with the letter in the center of the circle, and in every word an additional letter is in place. When the puzzle is complete, you can then go on to discover the two names reading clockwise around the outermost ring of letters.

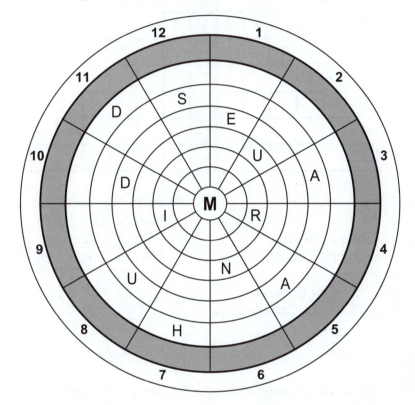

1 Product of a body's mass and its velocity

2 Selflessness

3 Confirm again

4 Mythical lover of Iseult (Isolde)

5 Available height clearance

6 Radioactive element

7 Type of angel whose gift is knowledge

8 Common light metal

9 Devil-worship

10 Clock's oscillating apparatus

11 Postscript in a book

12 Public bathroom facility

The names are:

_____ and _____

Pyracross

317

Solve the clues on each level of the pyramid and reveal the word in the central column of bricks.

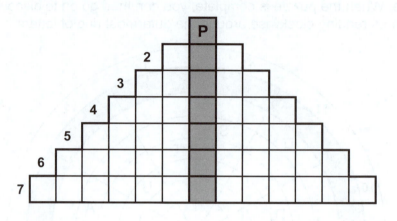

2 Feline creature
3 Christ
4 US confectioner and philanthropist, Milton Snavely ____
5 Body of water between Greenland and Canada (6,3)

6 Body of water to the north-east of Alaska (8,3)
7 'I am ____, the beginning and the end, the first and the last', Revelation 22:13 (5,3,5)

Spelling Test

318

Which is the only one of the following to be correctly spelled?

a. ISREALITE

b. ISRAELLITE

c. ISRELLITE

d. ISRAELITE

Bookmark

319

Answer the clues by using the groups of letters in the lower box, crossing them out as you go. When finished, rearrange the remaining letters to make the name of a book of the Bible.

1 Former US president, Theodore ___

2 Often

3 Cut out of a will

4 Without stopping, unbroken

5 Not suitable or fitting

6 Instrument used by doctors for listening to a heart beating

7 Thoughtful, especially for the feelings of others

8 Male chicken, rooster

9 Bright red

10 Brought together, assembled

1				
2				
3				
4				
5				
6				
7				
8				
9				
10				

TED	TED	PP	LY	MAL	NSI	DI	TE	UO
KER	EQ	LEC	US	RL	RI	OS	VE	ATE
ROP	DER	HI	CO	RO	NT	COC	FR	NHE
OSE	ETH	SCA	UE	INA	ST	AC	RIA	CO
ET	SI	CO	COL	PE	NT	EL	IN	LT

Book: _____

Character Assignation

Fill in the Across clues in this crossword in the normal way. Then read down the diagonal line of seven squares, to reveal the name of a character from the Bible.

1 Alan ___, first American in space

2 Person descended from French ancestors in southern United States

3 Honey badger

4 Japanese sacred volcanic peak

5 Snake-like sea or freshwater fish

6 California's largest city (inits)

7 William (Billy the Kid) Bonney's middle initial

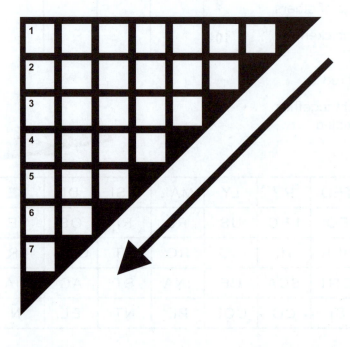

Character: ___ ___ ___ ___ ___ ___ ___

What's It Worth?

321

Each symbol stands for a different number. In order to reach the correct total at the end of each row and column, what is the value of the cross, dove, key and star?

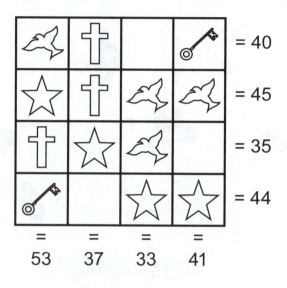

Pharaoh's Pyramid

322

Every brick in this pyramid contains a number which is the sum of the two numbers below it, so that F=A+B, etc. Just work out the missing numbers!

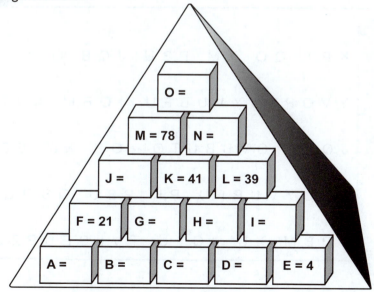

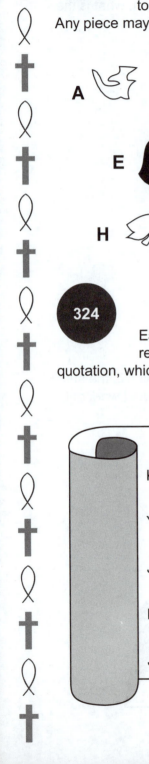

Jigsaw Puzzle

323

Which four pieces (two black and two white) fit together to make a copy of the apple shown here? Any piece may be rotated, but none may be flipped over.

A

B

C

D

E

F

G

H

I

J

Cryptography

324

Each letter of the alphabet in the scroll below has been replaced by another. Can you decipher the code to reveal the quotation, which is taken from Romans 5:19?

KPT QO XM PBU JQB'O

YVOPXUYVUBFU JQBM AUTU

JQYU OVBBUTO, OP XM ESU

PXUYVUBFU PK PBU OSQGG

JQBM XU JQYU TVLSEUPZO.

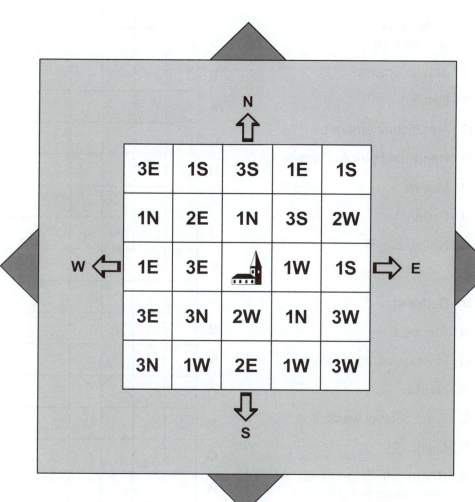

The True Path

325

The chart gives directions to the church in the central square in the grid. Move the indicated number of spaces north, south, east and west (eg 4N means four squares north) stopping at each square once only to arrive there. At which square should you start?

		N		
3E	1S	3S	1E	1S
1N	2E	1N	3S	2W
1E	3E	🏠	1W	1S
3E	3N	2W	1N	3W
3N	1W	2E	1W	3W

W ⬅ ➡ E

S

326

Acrostic

Solve the clues and enter the answers into the grid below. Then cross-reference the letters to their indicated positions in the grid on the opposite page to reveal a verse from the Bible.

A Close

B Fireplace

C Clean with soap and water

D Letter such as a, e or i, for example

E At high volume

F Battle

G A sufficient amount

H Hand-held piece of armor

I Motive

J Experiment

K Not so bright

L Love intensely

M Battered

N Stopped

O Division of the weekend

P Midday

Q Tract of level wasteland

R Giant

S Chemically-tipped strip of wood used to light a fire

	1	2	3	4	5	6
A						
B						
C						
D						
E						
F						
G						
H						
I						
J						
K						
L						
M						
N						
O						
P						
Q						
R						
S						

Acrostic

I3	M6	E4	▓	A5	G6	D4	▓	S2	P1	G5	M2	J5	▓	S4
C2	K3	L5	▓	K2	R5	▓	O2	I6	F5	E2	▓	B1	G1	K6
,	▓	J4	P4	N6	▓	C3	Q3	A2	H6	,	▓	S5	O5	H3
N3	, ▓	▓	S3	F4	P3	G4	▓	B5	H2	M3	J1	▓	R4	B4
R3	▓	Q5	F2	A3	C4	D5	O6	▓	F1	N2	D1	I5	I1	B2
O4	, ▓	▓	M4	N1	H4	▓	E1	P2	L4	K1	▓	R2	H1	▓
D3	J3	Q4	A4	▓	N4	B6	K5	I2	: ▓	▓	M1	H5	Q2	O1
I4	N5	L2	▓	B3	J2	R1	▓	A1	Q1	G3	E3	▓	L1	S1
D2	O3	F3	▓	C1	L3	K4	M5	G2	. ▓	▓	▓	▓	▓	▓

Shape Spotter

Which is the only shape to appear twice in exactly the same shading (black, white or gray) in the box below? You'll need a keen eye for this one, as some shapes overlap others!

Riddle-Me-Ree

328

Find one letter per line, following the clues given in the verse below. For example, 'My first is in houses, but never in homes' gives the letter U as the first letter. When you have finished, the letters will spell a name.

My first is in ANIMAL, but not in BEAST,

My second's in PARTY, as well as in FEAST,

My third's found in PENCIL, but never in WRITE,

My fourth is in SHINING, and also in BRIGHT,

My fifth's seen in FORTUNE, but never in LUCK,

My sixth is in CAR, as well as in TRUCK,

My whole is a place where Jesus first lay,

Think of a stable, with cattle … and hay.

1st	2nd	3rd	4th	5th	6th

Stop Gaps

329

Certain words from the text below have been removed and are listed to the right, in alphabetical order. Can you replace them in their correct positions?

Galatians 6:8 For he that soweth to his _____ shall of the flesh reap _____; but he that soweth to the _____ shall of the Spirit reap life _____.

Galatians 6:9 And let us not be _____ in well doing: for in due _____ we shall reap, if we _____ not.

Galatians 6:10 As we have therefore _____, let us do good unto all men, especially unto them who are of the _____ of faith.

CORRUPTION

EVERLASTING

FAINT

FLESH

HOUSEHOLD

OPPORTUNITY

SEASON

SPIRIT

WEARY

Scripture Knowledge

How's your knowledge of the scriptures? See if you can answer the questions below…

1 During the Israelites' Exodus from Egypt, what phenomenon guided them by day?

_____

2 In Numbers 28, how many burnt offerings of lambs were to be made each day?

_____

3 At the command of God, which kind of birds fed Elijah as he hid in the wilderness?

_____

4 What is the 'second death', stated in Revelation 20?

_____

5 Which of Jesus' parables concerns a swineherd who throws himself on his father's mercy?

_____

6 Which king conquered Jerusalem in 587 BC?

_____

7 For what reason did Joseph and Mary travel to Bethlehem, the place of Jesus' birth?

_____

8 Where was the 'Land of Milk and Honey'?

_____

Jacob's Ladder

Change one letter at a time (but not the position of any letter) to make a new word – and move from the word at the top of each ladder to the word at the bottom, using the exact number of rungs provided.

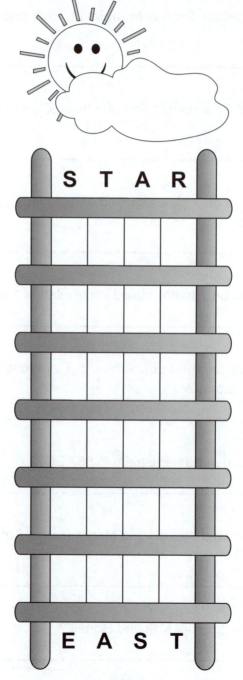

S T A R

E A S T

Bible Codeword

Every letter in this crossword has been replaced by a number, the number remaining the same for that letter wherever it occurs. Can you substitute numbers for letters and complete the crossword? The letters either side of the grid and the reference box showing which numbers have been decoded can also aid solving. One word has already been entered into the grid, to help you on your way. When finished, use the code to spell out a quotation from the Bible.

A / **N**
B / **O**
C / **P**
D / **Q**
E / **R**
F / **S**
G / **T**
H / **U**
I / **V**
J / **W**
K / **X**
L / **Y**
M / **Z**

A	5	17	16	3	7	5		8	9	12	5	1	2	5	1
B	17		5		3			8		17		5			5
C	19	8	26	25	13	23	23		17		5	3	12	5	7
D	5		26		1		13	26	6	22	1		19		13
E	1	8	3	1	12		12		3		25	1	5	5	12
F	25			13		6	16	3	1	25			1		16
G	7	3	24	23	22	7		7		16 (H)	5 (E)	15 (M)	12 (S)		
H	21			7		3	10	8	26	21		8			11
I			9	5	3	15		16		15	3	26	25	7	5
J	8		22			19	16	3	12	5		25			25
K	19	13	4	4	3		5		5		12	16	3	23	25
L	3		4		12	16	3	15	5		3		16		13
M	20	22	13	1	14		1		15	3	7	7	5	25	12
	22		26		5		25			12		3			8
	5	18	10	5	24	3	21	12		15	3	13	18	5	26

Reference Box

1	2	3	4	5 E	6	7	8	9	10	11	12 S	13
14	15 M	16 H	17	18	19	20	21	22	23	24	25	26

Quotation

24	5	5	19	26	8	25	12	16	5	13	12	26	8	25
18	5	3	18	9	22	25	12	7	5	5	19	5	25	16

S Bend

Place the letters of each word, one per cell, so that every word flows in a clockwise direction around a number. Where the hexagons of one word overlap with those of another, the letter in each cell is common to both.

When finished, rearrange the letters in the pale gray hexagons to form the name of a character from the Bible.

ALLURE
BUSTLE
KAISER
KNIGHT

OPPOSE
RATHER
REWARD

SCULPT
TAKING
THROES
WEIGHT

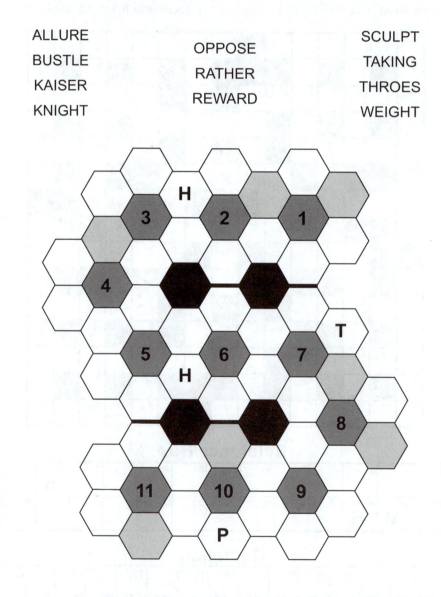

The name is: _____

Phone-etics

Use the telephone dial in order to spell out the Bible quotation.

4 215532 367 50 569378, 198 8430

23234932 53: 50 6743888 162 5463

352378 3193 96 843 34688 46 843

2480, 94453 8430 869348 84347

5318 86 7354393 84347 86958.

Wordwheel

How many words of three or more letters can you make from those in the wheel, without using plurals, abbreviations or proper nouns?

The central letter must appear once in every word and no letter in a section of the wheel may be used more than once.

There is at least one nine-letter word in the wheel, which is a proper noun: the name of a person in the Bible.

_____

_____

_____

_____

_____

_____

_____

_____

_____

_____

_____

The nine-letter word is: _____

Into the Ark

Can you discover the way through this maze, and thus help these animals to find their way into Noah's Ark at the center?

Christening Conundrum

Mr & Mrs Wordsmith are having a hard time choosing a name for their baby son, who is due to be baptized next Wednesday morning. They have, however, narrowed the choice down to 21 possible names (some of them rather uncommon!). See if you can find them all hidden in the grid below.

Words may run forwards or backwards, either horizontally, diagonally or vertically, but always in a straight, uninterrupted line.

```
M J W P R B X S E C D K O
C Z V W E O C E D U L R I
A N Y Q Y R V L B Q A D L
L P O J X R E I A J N Y X
E C N E R E T G R U O S M
B C U B L O O W R U D D A
W D R U A M Y A S I Y E R
X L G K A R G S B X N D M
H O A R O R M V T E D E A
F N K R L E R O Y O L E D
D R T Y R O N E R V N F U
N A X E L E A F I H M U K
R K G X E X X N R A G D E
```

ABEL	GILES	MELVIN
AMYAS	IVOR	NOEL
ARNOLD	LEROY	PEREGRINE
AXEL	MARK	REX
CALEB	MARMADUKE	RORY
CLAUDE		ROYSTON
DONALD		TERENCE
EDGAR		TYRONE

Keyword Crossword

Solve the crossword puzzle in the usual way, then rearrange the letters in the shaded squares to spell out a keyword, which is the name of place (it might be a country, region, river, garden, hill, mountain, town or city) that appears in the Bible.

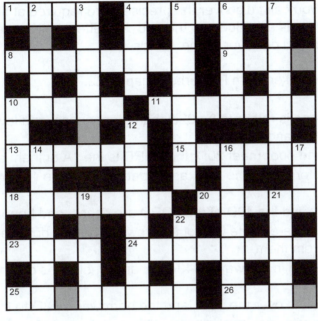

Across

1 Professional charges (4)
4 Going from one side to the other (8)
8 Undiplomatic (8)
9 Robe (4)
10 Watery fluid of the blood (5)
11 Large feline of tropical America (7)
13 Break free (6)
15 Women (6)
18 Forceful and extreme (7)
20 Contented (5)
23 Sticky paste (4)
24 Fluent, smooth-spoken (8)
25 Kept apart (8)
26 Throb dully (4)

Down

2 Rub out (5)
3 Variety of mandarin orange (7)
4 Organized group of workmen (4)
5 Barrier (8)
6 Instance of visual perception (5)
7 Not in any place (7)
10 Her (3)
12 Expressing remorse for misdeeds (8)
14 More than is needed (7)
16 Bram Stoker's vampire (7)
17 Put into words (3)
19 Carapace (5)
21 Squeeze with the fingers (5)
22 Highway (4)

Bible Passage Storyword

Some of the words in the Bible passage below have been replaced with clue numbers. The missing words all fit into the grid opposite. For example, if the phrase is "Seek and ye 18A find", this indicates that the solution to 18 Across is 'SHALL', which can then be written into the grid.

Don't worry if you can't discover the precise word required at first glance – when more words are filled into the grid, the letters which intersect with others will help you discover further words.

This passage is taken from Proverbs, Chapter 22.

1: A good name is rather to be 32D than great riches, and loving favor rather than 40A and 12A.

2: The rich and poor meet 20D: the LORD is the 1A of them all.

3: A 5A man foreseeth the 10A, and hideth 4D: but the 11A pass on, and are punished.

4: By humility and the 19D of the LORD are riches, and honor, and life.

5: 25D and 15D are in the way of the froward: he that doth keep his 30A shall be far from them.

6: 42A up a child in the way he 43A go: and when he is old, he will not 27D from it.

7: The 41D ruleth over the poor, and the borrower is 18D to the 21A.

8: He that soweth iniquity shall reap 37D: and the rod of his anger shall fail.

9: He that hath a bountiful eye shall be 23D; for he giveth of his 8A to the 34A.

10: Cast out the 16A, and 17D shall go out; yea, strife and 38A shall 33A.

11: He that loveth 5D of heart, for the 14D of his 9A the 2D shall be his 36D.

12: The eyes of the 13D preserve 3D; and he overthroweth the 6D of the transgressor.

13: The slothful man saith, There is a 26A without, I shall be 7D in the streets.

14: The mouth of 24A women is a deep pit: he that is abhorred of the LORD shall 35D therein.

15: 28A is 39D in the heart of a child; but the rod of 22A shall drive it far from him.

16: He that oppresseth the poor to 31A his riches, and he that giveth to the rich, shall 29D come to 6A.

Bible Passage Storyword

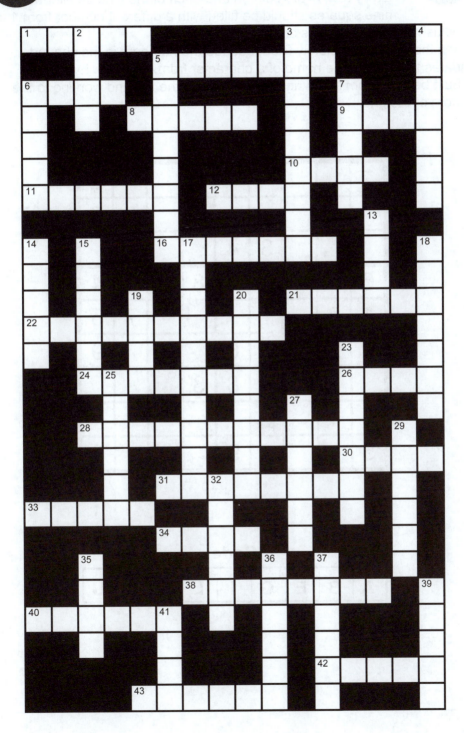

Bible Sudoku

340

Every row, every column and each of the nine smaller boxes of nine squares should be filled with a different number from 1 to 9 inclusive. Some numbers are already in place.

When the grid is completely filled, decode the numbers in the shaded squares to spell out the name of a character from the Bible. Every row should be read from left to right, starting from the top and working to the bottom of the grid.

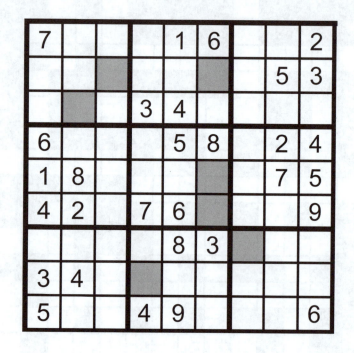

Code

1	2	3	4	5	6	7	8	9
A	B	E	G	I	L	R	S	U

Name:

Scripture Knowledge

How's your knowledge of the scriptures? See if you can answer the questions below...

1 Which Israelite leader burned the northern city of Hazor?

_____

2 Jehoiakim is famed as the king who burned the manuscript of a prophesy of which prophet?

_____

3 According to Jesus, what is "as treasure found in a field"?

_____

4 Which King of Judah required the Ammonites to give him silver, wheat and barley for three years, after he had defeated them in battle?

_____

5 Which prophet bought his wife for fifteen shekels and a sheaf of barley?

_____

6 Who betrayed Samson for a cask of silver coins?

_____

7 To Paul he was the 'Man of Lawlessness', in Revelation he is 'The Beast', who is 'he'?

_____

8 What did Jacob see rising from Earth to Heaven in his dream at Bethel?

_____

Shape-up

342

Every row and column in this grid originally contained one cross, one loaf, one fish, one star and two blank squares, although not necessarily in that order. Every symbol with a black arrow refers to the first of the four symbols encountered when traveling in the direction of the arrow. Every symbol with a white arrow refers to the second of the four symbols encountered in the direction of the arrow. Can you complete the original grid?

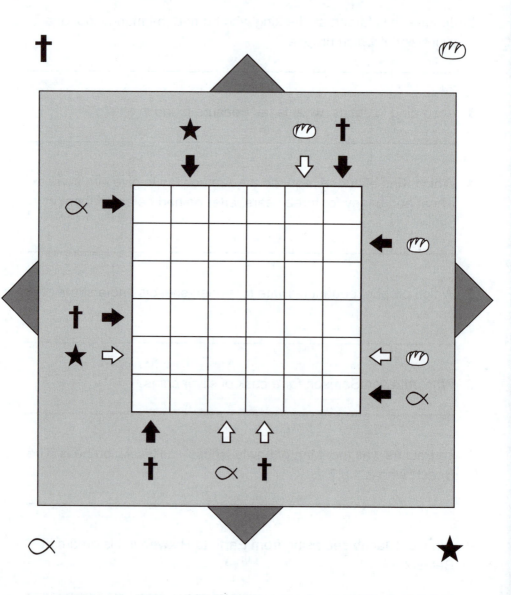

Paul's Pathfinder

The object of this puzzle is to trace a single path from the top left square to the bottom right square of the grid, traveling through all of the cells in either a horizontal, vertical or diagonal direction. Every cell must be entered once only and your path should take you through the letters in the sequence P-A-U-L-P-A-U-L, etc. Can you find the logical way through?

P	L	U	U	L	P	U	L
A	P	A	A	U	A	P	A
P	U	P	L	U	L	A	P
L	A	U	P	A	P	L	U
L	L	U	L	P	U	A	L
P	U	P	A	L	A	P	A
U	A	A	P	L	U	U	U
L	P	A	U	A	P	L	L

Simon's Squares

344

Fit the letters S, I, M, O and N into the grid in such a way that each horizontal row, each vertical column and each of the heavily outlined sections of five squares each contains a different letter. Some letters are already in place.

I				
		S		
			O	
	M			N

The Bottom Line

345

Can you fill each square in the bottom line with the correct symbol? Every square in the solution contains a symbol from each of the lines above, although two or more squares in the solution may contain the same symbol.

At the end of every row is a score, which shows:

a the number of symbols placed in the correct finishing position on the bottom line, as indicated by a tick; and

b the number of symbols which appear on the bottom line, but in a different position, as indicated by a cross.

SCORE

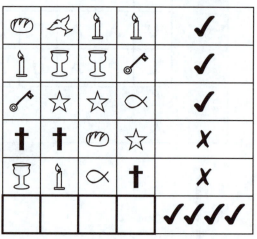

306

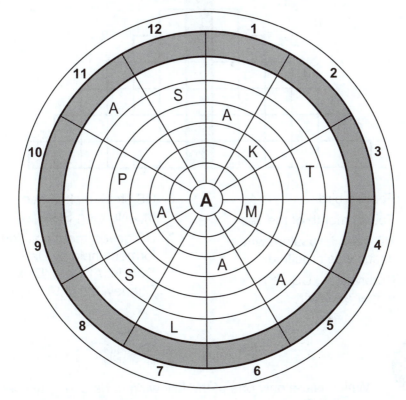

Round Dozen

First solve the clues. All of the solutions end with the letter in the center of the circle, and in every word an additional letter is in place. When the puzzle is complete, you can then go on to discover the two names reading clockwise around the outermost ring of letters.

1 Famous Moorish palace near Granada in Spain
2 Sea bordered by Turkey, Russia, Ukraine, etc (5,3)
3 South American ranch
4 Cancer of the blood
5 The official emblem of Nazi Germany
6 Native American chief, subject of a poem by Longfellow
7 Hair-loss condition
8 Reading disability
9 Edible yellow turnip
10 Sung without accompaniment (1,7)
11 Roman emperor famous for his cruelty and madness.
12 Violent mental agitation

The names are:

_____ and _____

Pyracross

347

Solve the clues on each level of the pyramid and reveal the word in the central column of bricks.

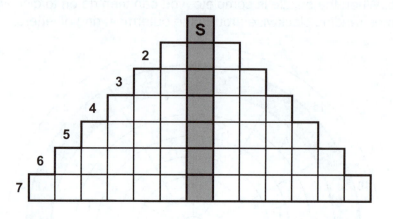

2 Female bird

3 Fourth month of the year

4 Hill near Jerusalem where Jesus was crucified

5 Barbra ___, US singer and actress

6 US state, nicknamed the 'Nutmeg State'

7 US government position formerly held by Dan Quayle, Al Gore, Dick Cheney, etc (4,9)

Spelling Test

348

Which is the only one of the following to be correctly spelled?

a. ECCUMENICAL

b. ECUMENICLE

c. ECUMENICAL

d. ECUMENNICAL

Bookmark

Answer the clues by using the groups of letters in the lower box, crossing them out as you go. When finished, rearrange the remaining letters to make the name of a book of the Bible.

1 Construction of large ocean-going vessels

2 Country, capital Lisbon

3 Science dealing with the study of stars, planets, etc

4 Watching closely

5 Person who travels into space

6 Wariness

7 What is left over

8 Structure built by bees

9 Distance around the perimeter of a circle

10 Each person, without exception

1					
2					
3					
4					
5					
6					
7					
8					
9					
10					

NEY	RY	OB	IND	TRO	RT	MFE	TR	NG
NCE	IP	JU	TRO	EP	VI	RE	NO	NG
MA	CO	UT	PO	CU	HO	UG	LDI	NA
DY	MY	AT	AS	SH	SER	ION	BO	MB
ID	BUI	RE	ER	AS	DE	EVE	AL	CIR

Book: _____

Character Assignation

Fill in the Across clues in this crossword in the normal way. Then read down the diagonal line of seven squares, to reveal the name of a character from the Bible.

1 Biblical person asked by God to sacrifice his son, Isaac

2 Imaginary perfect land

3 Robert Lee ____, New England poet (1874-1963)

4 27th president of the USA

5 Residue after a fire

6 Archaic form of 'you'

7 Compass point at 270 degrees

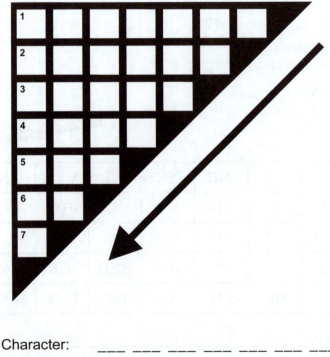

Character: ___ ___ ___ ___ ___ ___ ___

What's It Worth?

351

Each symbol stands for a different number. In order to reach the correct total at the end of each row and column, what is the value of the cross, dove, key and star?

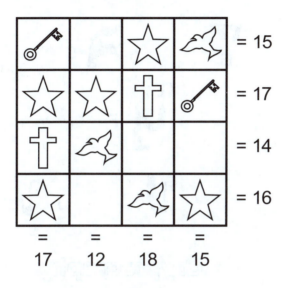

Pharaoh's Pyramid

352

Every brick in this pyramid contains a number which is the sum of the two numbers below it, so that F=A+B, etc. Just work out the missing numbers!

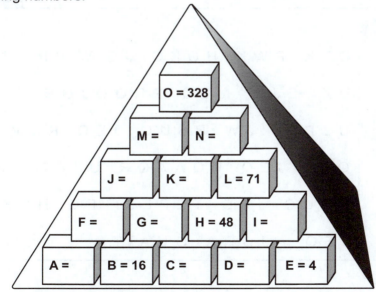

Jigsaw Puzzle

353

Which four pieces (two black and two white) fit together to make a copy of the shepherd here? Any piece may be rotated, but none may be flipped over.

A

B

C

D

E

F

G

H

I

J

Cryptography

354

Each letter of the alphabet in the scroll below has been replaced by another. Can you decipher the code to reveal the quotation, which is taken from Genesis 1:16?

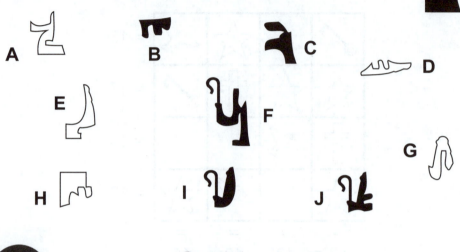

```
OTK  PWK  HOKQ  JGW  PRQOJ

UZPEJA;  JEQ  PRQOJQR

UZPEJ  JW  RSUQ  JEQ  KOM,

OTK  JEQ  UQAAQR  UZPEJ  JW

RSUQ  JEQ  TZPEJ:  EQ  HOKQ

JEQ  AJORA  OUAW.
```

The True Path

The chart gives directions to the church in the central square in the grid. Move the indicated number of spaces north, south, east and west (eg 4N means four squares north) stopping at each square once only to arrive there. At which square should you start?

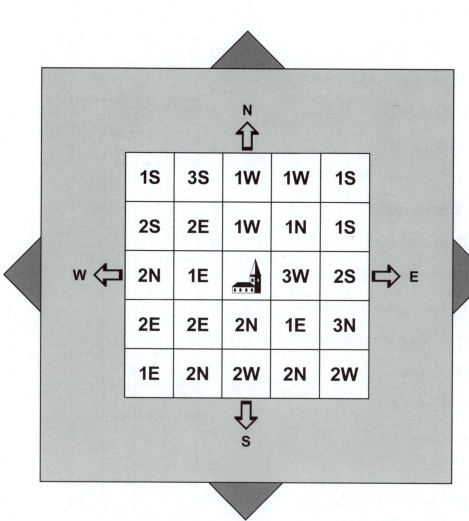

356

Acrostic

Solve the clues and enter the answers into the grid below. Then cross-reference the letters to their indicated positions in the grid on the opposite page to reveal a verse from the Bible.

A Controlled a vehicle

B Hypothesis

C Intonate

D Possessing

E External medicament

F Coupled

G Army rank

H Frequently visited place

I Boulevard

J Foot digit

K Intense burst of radiant energy

L Disappearing gradually

M Made neat and orderly

N Agitated

O Frail

P Glisten

Q Abode

R Part of the leg between the hip and the knee

	1	2	3	4	5	6
A						
B						
C						
D						
E						
F						
G						
H						
I						
J						
K						
L						
M						
N						
O						
P						
Q						
R						

Acrostic

C3	E6	M6			B1	R5	I6		E1	A3	G5	F6		K4	D2
P3	O4		H3	F4	O1	Q2		G3	J2	N1	C2	I5	H2		,
	P1	M5	N5	,		L4		N2	I1	D3	Q4		D6	M4	
A4	O5	L5		E4	O3	J1	B4		M1	R2	F3	N6	A5		
D1	N3	I4	M3		F1	P5	A2	M2	C1	Q1	F2	,		G2	
P4	L3		H5	K5	O2		N4	D4	H4	L6		E3	H1	I3	
O6	B3	E5	K1	,		L2	C4	A1		C5	B2	J3		G1	
R3	R4	P2	R1	B6		Q3	F5	D5		E2	L1		I2	K3	
K2	G4	B5	.												

Shape Spotter

Which is the only shape to appear twice in exactly the same shading (black, white or gray) in the box below? You'll need a keen eye for this one, as some shapes overlap others!

Riddle-Me-Ree

358

Find one letter per line, following the clues given in the verse below. For example, 'My first is in houses, but never in homes' gives the letter U as the first letter. When you have finished, the letters will spell a name.

My first is in MAJOR, but not found in MAIN,

My second's in THUNDER, but never in RAIN,

My third is in SPRING, and in SUMMER, too,

My fourth's found in VIOLET, but not in BLUE,

My fifth is in CHEESE, as well as in CREAM,

My sixth is in NIGHTMARE, but never in DREAM,

My seventh's in FOOTBALL, but never in GAME,

My whole once had walls – then Joshua came!

1st	2nd	3rd	4th	5th	6th	7th

Stop Gaps

359

Certain words from the text below have been removed and are listed to the right, in alphabetical order. Can you replace them in their correct positions?

1 John 4:8 He that loveth not, knoweth not God; for God is _____.

1 John 4:9 In this was _____ the love of God _____ us, because that God sent his only _____ Son into the _____, that we might live through him.

1 John 4:10 _____ is love, not that we loved God, but that he loved us, and sent his Son to be the _____ for our _____.

1 John 4:11 Beloved, if God so loved us, we _____ also to love one _____.

ANOTHER

BEGOTTEN

HEREIN

LOVE

MANIFESTED

OUGHT

PROPRIATION

SINS

TOWARD

WORLD

Scripture Knowledge

How's your knowledge of the scriptures? See if you can answer the questions below…

1 How is Jerub-Baal better known?

_____

2 Which place name in the Bible means 'house of bread'?

_____

3 Which son of Jacob had a 'coat of many colors'?

_____

4 After the Crucifixion, who gave his own tomb for the burial of Jesus?

_____

5 What is the translated meaning of Via Dolorosa, the route in Jerusalem which Jesus was forced to walk on the way to his crucifixion?

_____

6 Who was the twin brother of Jacob?

_____

7 On the way to his wedding, who saw bees in the carcass of a lion?

_____

8 Purim is the Jewish feast day that celebrates the prevention of a massacre of the Jews whilst in captivity in which land?

_____

Holy Bible

Jacob's Ladder

Change one letter at a time (but not the position of any letter) to make a new word – and move from the word at the top of each ladder to the word at the bottom, using the exact number of rungs provided.

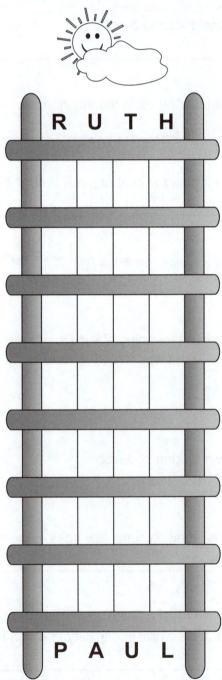

Bible Codeword

Every letter in this crossword has been replaced by a number, the number remaining the same for that letter wherever it occurs. Can you substitute numbers for letters and complete the crossword? The letters either side of the grid and the reference box showing which numbers have been decoded can also aid solving. One word has already been entered into the grid, to help you on your way. When finished, use the code to spell out a quotation from the Bible.

Left side labels: A B C D E F G H I J K L M
Right side labels: N O P Q R S T U V W X Y Z

11	7	26	9	16	17		19	24	23	23	22	19	26	7
3		12		24		21		11		26		5		24
24	5	11	22	12		26	20	4	8	12	19	26	12	9
7		26		19	24	10		26		24		23		8
7	24	19		23		8	11	3	24	7	24	17	22	5
22		8		25			7		5		20		2	
4	24	5	24	7	15	18	8		5	24	26	11	26	12
	18		26		24		8		22		12		19	
14	25	24	11	24	5		1	22	13	17	22	13	8	19
	5		7		19		8		13		24		5	
12	8	3	8	11	11	24	5	15(Y)		8		5	15	8
24		7		26		9		24(A)	13	7		23		11
11	3	24	5	8	3	5	22	13(W)		23	7	24	15	11
24		11		6		8		12(N)		17		5		8
7	26	11	17	8	12	8	5		11	16	5	8	13	19

Reference Box

| 1 | 2 | 3 | 4 | 5 | 6 | 7 | 8 | 9 | 10 | 11 | 12 N | 13 W |
| 14 | 15 Y | 16 | 17 | 18 | 19 | 20 | 21 | 22 | 23 | 24 A | 25 | 26 |

Quotation

| 24 | 20 | 8 | 12 | 19 | 15 | 22 | 25 | 5 | 13 | 24 | 15 | 11 |
| 24 | 12 | 19 | 15 | 22 | 25 | 5 | 19 | 22 | 26 | 12 | 9 | 11 |

319

S Bend

Place the letters of each word, one per cell, so that every word flows in a clockwise direction around a number. Where the hexagons of one word overlap with those of another, the letter in each cell is common to both.

When finished, rearrange the letters in the pale gray hexagons to form the name of a character from the Bible.

CIPHER

CITRIC

CLOSED

ENTITY

LOAVES

MARLIN

MORTAR

PARIAH

RAMROD

REVOLT

SOLEMN

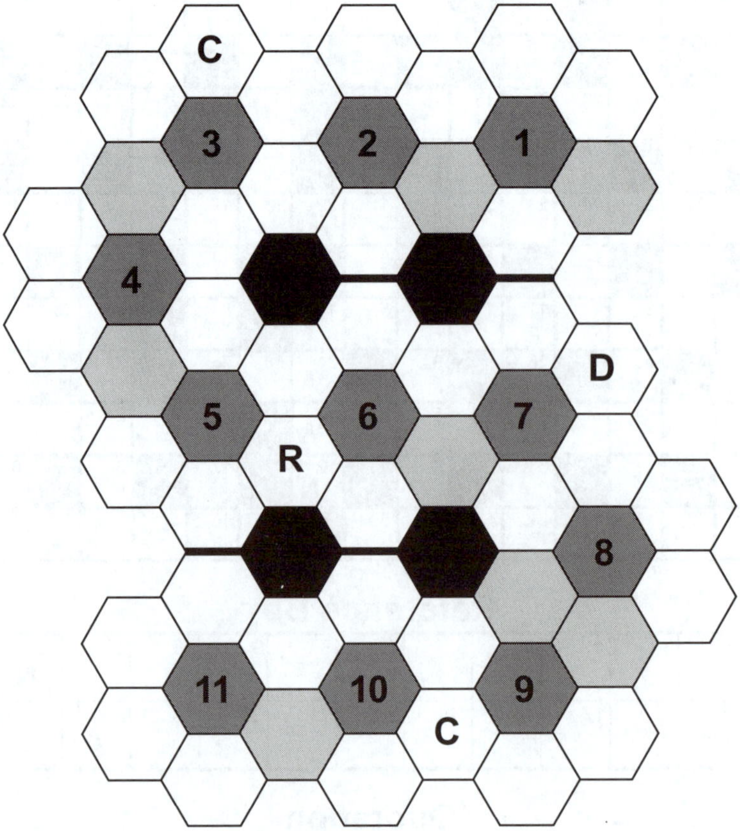

The name is: _____

Phone-etics

Use the telephone dial in order to spell out the Bible quotation.

4 3   4   4 1 9 3   8 6 5 2   0 6 9   3 1 7 8 4 5 0

8 4 4 6 3 8 ,   1 6 2   0 3   1 3 5 4 3 9 3   6 6 8 ,

4 6 9   8 4 1 5 5   0 3   1 3 5 4 3 9 3 ,   4 3   4

8 3 5 5   0 6 9   6 3   4 3 1 9 3 6 5 0   8 4 4 6 3 8 ?

Wordwheel

How many words of three or more letters can you make from those in the wheel, without using plurals, abbreviations or proper nouns?

The central letter must appear once in every word and no letter in a section of the wheel may be used more than once.

There is at least one nine-letter word in the wheel, which is a proper noun: the name of a person in the Bible.

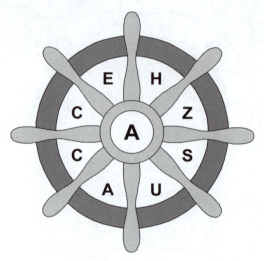

_____

_____

_____

_____

_____

_____

_____

_____

_____

_____

The nine-letter word is: _____

Into the Ark

366

Can you discover the way through this maze, and thus help these animals to find their way into Noah's Ark at the center?

Christmas Conundrum

367

There are 21 words relating to Christmas hidden in the grid below. Can you find them all?

Words may run forwards or backwards, either horizontally, diagonally or vertically, but always in a straight, uninterrupted line.

H	P	E	S	O	J	C	H	K	R	S	V	T
A	E	E	N	B	C	R	A	E	E	F	G	B
J	B	S	I	H	R	I	N	C	G	I	Y	G
G	E	R	N	Y	G	B	G	U	N	W	E	A
D	T	S	M	E	D	O	E	O	A	J	K	B
H	H	H	U	M	C	T	L	R	M	C	N	R
S	L	E	X	S	K	N	S	D	A	C	O	I
T	E	P	R	S	G	N	I	D	I	T	D	E
A	H	H	G	O	Q	M	F	K	M	J	S	L
B	E	E	C	I	D	W	A	Y	N	C	B	P
L	M	R	O	K	F	K	A	R	R	A	X	M
E	A	D	V	E	N	T	G	V	Y	U	R	V
W	I	S	N	E	M	E	S	I	W	U	T	F

ADVENT	GIFTS	MANGER
ANGELS	GOLD	MARY
BETHLEHEM	HEROD	MYRRH
BIRTH	JESUS	SHEPHERDS
CRIB	JOSEPH	STABLE
DONKEY		STAR
FRANKINCENSE		TIDINGS
GABRIEL		WISE MEN

Keyword Crossword

Solve the crossword puzzle in the usual way, then rearrange the letters in the shaded squares to spell out a keyword, which is the name of place (it might be a country, region, river, garden, hill, mountain, town or city) that appears in the Bible.

Across

3 Poverty-stricken (9)
8 Submerged ridge of rock or coral (4)
9 Gland located behind the stomach (8)
10 Capital of Lebanon (6)
13 Burn with steam (5)
14 Theft by threat of violence (7)
15 Device for creating a current of air (3)
16 Large mass of frozen water (7)
17 Constructed (5)
21 Out of sight (6)
22 Fabric (8)
23 Disease of the skin (4)
24 Convalesced (9)

Down

1 Long flexible snout (9)
2 Devoted to a cause or purpose (9)
4 Containing nothing (5)
5 Stress (7)
6 Hoop that covers a wheel (4)
7 Item used to carry many cups at once (4)
11 Dwelling place (9)
12 Onlooker (9)
14 Piece of scrap material (3)
15 Delicate, frail (7)
18 Protrude outwards (5)
19 Container for a bird (4)
20 Courageous man (4)

Bible Passage Storyword

Some of the words in the Bible passage below have been replaced with clue numbers. The missing words all fit into the grid opposite. For example, if the phrase is "Seek and ye 18A find", this indicates that the solution to 18 Across is 'SHALL', which can then be written into the grid.

Don't worry if you can't discover the precise word required at first glance – when more words are filled into the grid, the letters which intersect with others will help you discover further words.

This passage is taken from Deuteronomy, Chapter 9.

9: When I was gone up into the mount to receive the tables of stone, even the tables of the covenant which the LORD made with you, then I 43D in the mount 6D days and forty nights; I neither did eat 40D nor drink 4A.

10: And the LORD delivered unto me two tables of 46A written with the finger of God; and on them was 19D according to all the words which the LORD spake with you in the mount, out of the 45A of the fire, in the day of the 18D.

11: And it came to pass at the 10A of forty 27A and forty nights, that the LORD gave me the two tables of stone, even the tables of the 30D.

12: And the LORD said unto me, 28D, get thee down quickly from hence; for thy 37A which thou hast 21D forth out of 42D have 13D themselves; they are quickly turned aside out of the way which I commanded them; they have made them a 3D 32D.

13: 25A the LORD spake unto me, saying, I have 29D this people, and, behold, it is a stiffnecked people.

14: Let me alone, that I may 34D them, and 21A out their name from under 26A: and I will make of thee a nation mightier and greater than they.

15: So I turned and came 44A from the mount, and the mount burned with 1A: and the two 39A of the covenant were in my two 7D.

16: And I looked, and, behold, ye had sinned against the LORD your 33A, and had made you a molten 8A: ye had 11A aside 12A out of the way which the LORD had commanded you.

17: And I took the two tables, and 20A them out of my 9A hands, and brake them before your eyes.

18: And I 6A down before the LORD, as at the 1D, forty days and forty nights: I did neither eat bread nor 31A water, 16D of all your sins which ye sinned, in doing 4D in the sight of the LORD, to 17A him to 41A.

19: For I was 24D of the anger and hot 23A, wherewith the LORD was wroth against you to destroy you. But the 14A hearkened unto me at that time also.

20: And the LORD was very angry with Aaron to have destroyed him: and I prayed for 22D also the same 2A.

21: And I took your 35A, the calf which ye had made, and burnt it with fire, and stamped it, and 38D it very 36A, even until it was as small as dust: and I cast the 15D thereof into the 5D that descended out of the mount.

Bible Passage Storyword

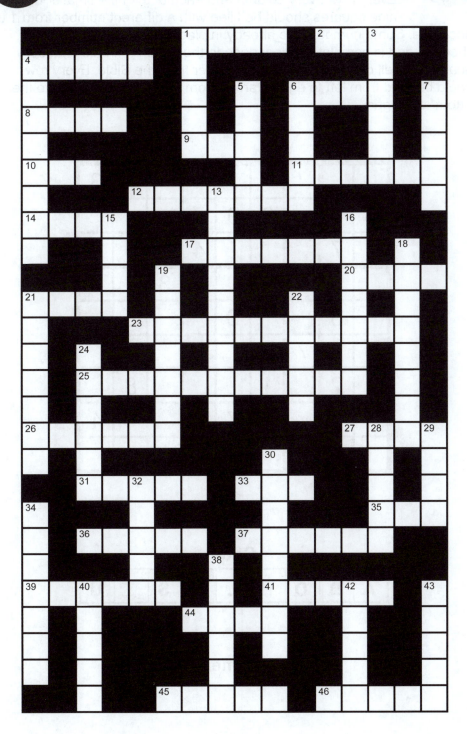

Bible Sudoku

370

Every row, every column and each of the nine smaller boxes of nine squares should be filled with a different number from 1 to 9 inclusive. Some numbers are already in place.

When the grid is completely filled, decode the numbers in the shaded squares to spell out the name of a character from the Bible. Every row should be read from left to right, starting from the top and working to the bottom of the grid.

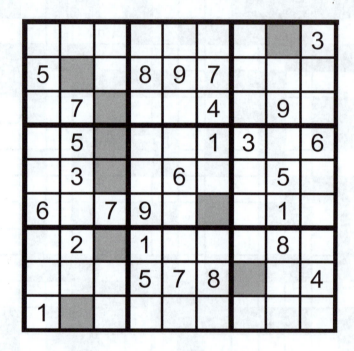

Code

1	2	3	4	5	6	7	8	9
A	B	D	H	L	N	S	T	U

Name:

Scripture Knowledge

How's your knowledge of the scriptures? See if you can answer the questions below…

1 According to Paul's letter to the Galatians, 'a man reaps ___'?

_____

2 In Genesis, an angel with a flaming sword guards the way to which tree?

_____

3 In Luke 1:13, an angel appears before Zacharias and tells him that his son is to be named what?

_____

4 What is the eighth of the Ten Commandments?

_____

5 In the Old Testament, to whom did God say, "Whoever sheds the blood of man, shall his blood also be shed."?

_____

6 Which disciple asked of Jesus, "Lord, how many times shall I forgive my brother when he sins against me?"?

_____

7 What is the sixth of the Ten Commandments?

_____

8 In which book of the Old Testament is the quotation; "From dust you are and to dust you will return."?

_____

Shape-up

372

Every row and column in this grid originally contained one cross, one loaf, one fish, one star and two blank squares, although not necessarily in that order. Every symbol with a black arrow refers to the first of the four symbols encountered when traveling in the direction of the arrow. Every symbol with a white arrow refers to the second of the four symbols encountered in the direction of the arrow. Can you complete the original grid?

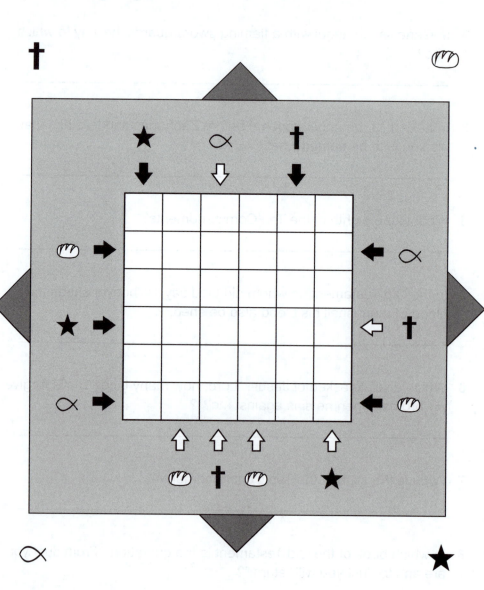

Paul's Pathfinder

The object of this puzzle is to trace a single path from the top left square to the bottom right square of the grid, traveling through all of the cells in either a horizontal, vertical or diagonal direction. Every cell must be entered once only and your path should take you through the letters in the sequence P-A-U-L-P-A-U-L, etc. Can you find the logical way through?

P	A	U	A	A	P	L	U
P	U	L	P	U	P	A	U
L	A	P	L	L	P	A	L
U	L	U	A	U	A	L	P
A	P	P	U	L	U	P	A
L	U	A	L	P	U	L	U
U	L	A	A	P	A	L	U
A	P	P	L	U	P	A	L

Simon's Squares

374

Fit the letters S, I, M, O and N into the grid in such a way that each horizontal row, each vertical column and each of the heavily outlined sections of five squares each contains a different letter. Some letters are already in place.

The Bottom Line

375

Can you fill each square in the bottom line with the correct symbol? Every square in the solution contains a symbol from each of the lines above, although two or more squares in the solution may contain the same symbol.

At the end of every row is a score, which shows:

a the number of symbols placed in the correct finishing position on the bottom line, as indicated by a tick; and

b the number of symbols which appear on the bottom line, but in a different position, as indicated by a cross.

SCORE

Round Dozen

First solve the clues. All of the solutions end with the letter in the center of the circle, and in every word an additional letter is in place. When the puzzle is complete, you can then go on to discover the two names reading clockwise around the outermost ring of letters.

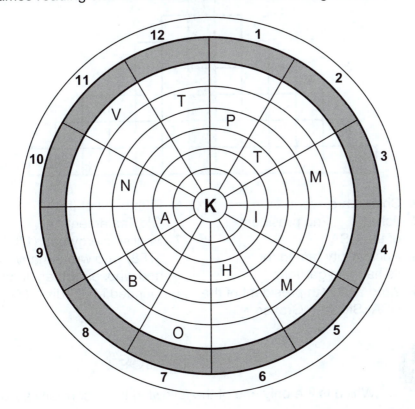

1 Part of a ship's superstructure (4,4)

2 Gossip (4,4)

3 Five-line humorous verse

4 Star-shaped character

5 Native American weapon

6 Kitchen beater

7 Collected volume of sung texts

8 Hebrew prophet, author of an Old Testament book of the same name

9 African nocturnal burrowing mammal

10 In Norse mythology, event describing the end of the world

11 Fail to notice

12 Compact portable computer

The names are:

_____ and _____

Pyracross

Solve the clues on each level of the pyramid and reveal the word in the central column of bricks.

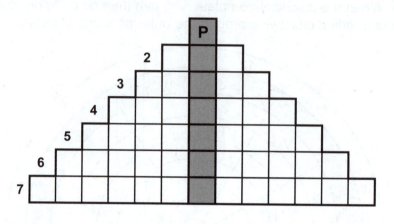

2 Shed tears, weep
3 John ____, 2nd president of the USA
4 Ancient city famed for its hanging gardens
5 22nd and 24th president of the USA, Stephen Grover ___

6 Fifth book of the Old Testament
7 English clergyman (1707-1788) who wrote many hymns and whose brother, John, founded Methodism (7,6)

Spelling Test

Which is the only one of the following to be correctly spelled?

a. **NAZARENE**

b. **NAZERENE**

c. **NAZARINE**

d. **NAZERINE**

Bookmark

Answer the clues by using the groups of letters in the lower box, crossing them out as you go. When finished, rearrange the remaining letters to make the name of a book of the Bible.

1 Ocean to the east of America

2 Home of the US film industry

3 German dish of pickled red cabbage

4 Apostle, follower of Jesus

5 Country, capital Caracas

6 Instrument for measuring temperature

7 Person who acts for or speaks in place of another

8 Art of taking pictures with a camera

9 Naval vessel from which planes can be launched (8,7)

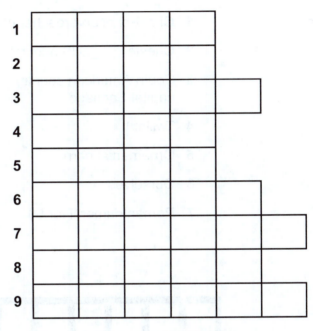

YW	ELA	TI	ER	UE	NT	ARR	ER	UT
RA	NE	LE	SEA	OG	AI	SC	HO	ESE
RK	VE	LL	IER	NTA	VE	PH	RA	OOD
RC	LA	MET	SA	IC	OT	TH	AT	RE
IP	TC	ZU	PHY	MO	HO	DI	PR	RAF

Book: _____

Character Assignation

380

Fill in the Across clues in this crossword in the normal way. Then read down the diagonal line of seven squares, to reveal the name of a character from the Bible.

1 Christ-chosen preacher of the Gospel

2 Chester ____, US admiral (1885-1966)

3 South American country, capital Santiago

4 Twilight

5 Ornamental carp

6 Ourselves

7 Roman numeral for 50

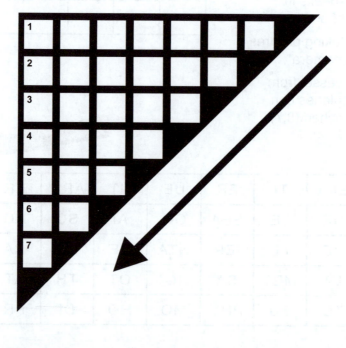

Character: ___ ___ ___ ___ ___ ___ ___

What's It Worth?

Each symbol stands for a different number. In order to reach the correct total at the end of each row and column, what is the value of the cross, dove, key and star?

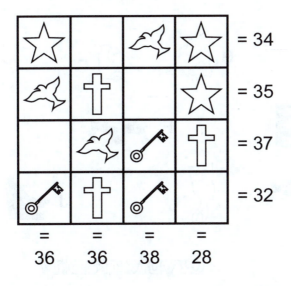

Pharaoh's Pyramid

Every brick in this pyramid contains a number which is the sum of the two numbers below it, so that F=A+B, etc. Just work out the missing numbers!

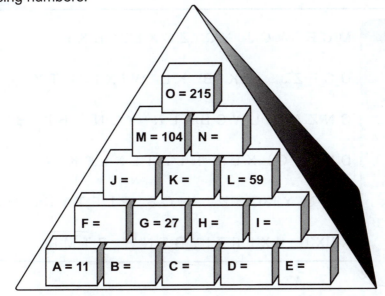

Jigsaw Puzzle

383

Which four pieces (two black and two white) fit together to make a copy of the book shown here? Any piece may be rotated, but none may be flipped over.

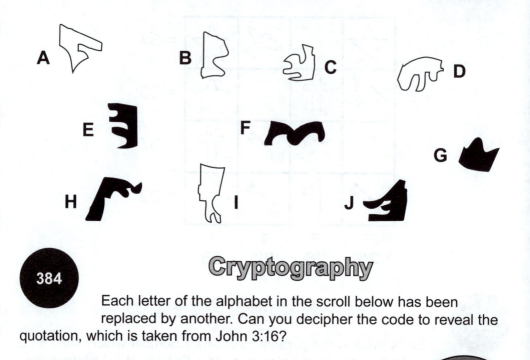

A   B   C   D

E   F   G

H   I   J

Cryptography

384

Each letter of the alphabet in the scroll below has been replaced by another. Can you decipher the code to reveal the quotation, which is taken from John 3:16?

MCF WCJ YC ZCXLJ BKL

DCFZJ, BKIB KL WIXL KTY

CNZA HLWCBBLN YCN, BKIB

DKCYCLXLF HLZTLXLBK TN

KTQ YKCSZJ NCB PLFTYK, HSB

KIXL LXLFZIYBTNW ZTML.

The True Path

The chart gives directions to the church in the central square in the grid. Move the indicated number of spaces north, south, east and west (eg 4N means four squares north) stopping at each square once only to arrive there. At which square should you start?

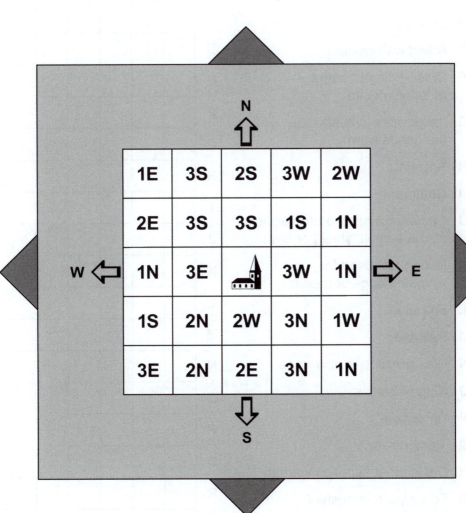

Acrostic

Solve the clues and enter the answers into the grid below. Then cross-reference the letters to their indicated positions in the grid on the opposite page to reveal a verse from the Bible.

A Bureau, place of work

B Having the leading position

C Clear

D Desired

E Affect with wonder

F Close-fitting trousers of heavy denim

G Items worn to keep the hands warm

H Applying

I Commend

J Circular rounded protuberance (as on a vault, shield or belt)

K Mixing tool used for whipping eggs or cream

L Fall silent

M Reliable

N Was present, is now gone

O King of beasts

P Egotistical

Q Track down

R Device that supplies warmth

S Force used in pushing

T Revised

	1	2	3	4	5	6
A						
B						
C						
D						
E						
F						
G						
H						
I						
J						
K						
L						
M						
N						
O						
P						
Q						
R						
S						
T						

Acrostic

Q4	R1	A6	P4		I1	G5	S6	F2	J1		S5	D3	O2	B5
,		K4	T3	C2	G4	B3	D2		E1	M3	T6		H5	A1
O1	T2		L4	F3	D4	T5		P3		O4	M2	Q3	E5	**;**
	N1	Q2	S1		H2	L2	A5	K2		B1	G6		I4	
Q1	E3	P1	T1		G1	K3	J3	N3		J2		M6	S2	R2
I6	**:**		A4	C5		J5	M1	R5		N4	C3	E2	D5	
G3	A3		F1	J4	L3	H1	M5		D1	L1	R6	C4	F5	R4
	O3	A2		H4	R3	E4	P2	I2	N2	T4	B2		S3	H3
I5	M4		S4	C1		I3	F4	D6		K1	B4	G2	K5	**.**

Shape Spotter

Which is the only shape to appear twice in exactly the same shading (black, white or gray) in the box below? You'll need a keen eye for this one, as some shapes overlap others!

Riddle-Me-Ree

388

Find one letter per line, following the clues given in the verse below. For example, 'My first is in houses, but never in homes' gives the letter U as the first letter. When you have finished, the letters will spell a name.

My first is in MESSAGE, but never in LETTER,

My second's in WORSE, and it's also in BETTER,

My third's seen in SERMON, but never in PREACH,

My fourth's not in TUTOR, but is found in TEACH,

My fifth is in SLENDER, and also in SLIGHT,

My sixth's found in EVENING, also in NIGHT,

My seventh's in MUSTANG, as well as in HORSE,

My whole is a book of the Bible, of course!

1st	2nd	3rd	4th	5th	6th	7th

Stop Gaps

389

Certain words from the text below have been removed and are listed to the right, in alphabetical order. Can you replace them in their correct positions?

Mark 14:23 And he took the _____, and when he had given _____, he gave it to them: and they all _____ of it.

Mark 14:24 And he said unto them, This is my _____ of the new _____, which is shed for _____.

Mark 14:25 Verily I say unto you, I will drink no more of the _____ of the _____, until that day that I drink it _____ in the _____ of God.

BLOODY

CUP

DRANK

FRUIT

KINGDOM

MANY

NEW

TESTAMENT

THANKS

VINE

Scripture Knowledge

How's your knowledge of the scriptures? See if you can answer the questions below…

1 What is the seventh of the Ten Commandments?

_____

2 Who "became leprous, like the snow" because she had spoken against Moses?

_____

3 According to Zechariah's prediction, which mountain will split apart?

_____

4 On his sea-voyage to Rome, a wind blew Paul's boat from Regium to which city?

_____

5 Who said that the end of the age would see the wicked cast into a fiery furnace where there would be "weeping and gnashing of teeth"?

_____

6 Which Old Testament prophet predicted that the Lord's coming "would be a unique day, without day or night"?

_____

7 As a dowry, which town was given to Solomon's wife by her father?

_____

8 What is the tenth of the Ten Commandments?

_____

Jacob's Ladder

Change one letter at a time (but not the position of any letter) to make a new word – and move from the word at the top of each ladder to the word at the bottom, using the exact number of rungs provided.

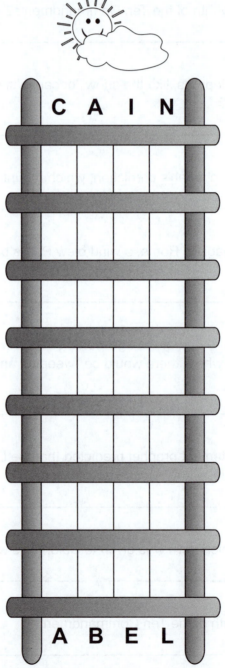

C A I N

A B E L

Phone-etics

Use the telephone dial in order to spell out the Bible quotation.

1 5 3 8 8 3 2   1 7 3   8 4 3 0   8 4 1 8   2 6   4 4 8

2 6 5 5 1 6 2 5 3 6 8 8 ,   8 4 1 8   8 4 3 0   5 1 0

4 1 9 3   7 4 3 4 8   8 6   8 4 3   8 7 3 3   6 3

5 4 3 3 ,   1 6 2   5 1 0   3 6 8 3 7   4 6   8 4 7 6 9 3 4

8 4 3   3 1 8 3 8   4 6 8 6   8 4 3   2 4 8 0 .

Solutions

1

JUDE, rude, ruse, rush, RUTH
(Other solutions may also exist)

3

The character is: SAMUEL

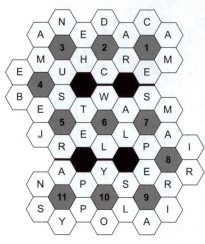

5

The Bible book is: ZECHARIAH

6

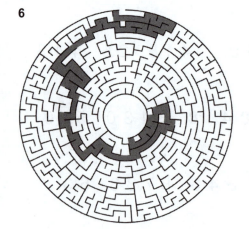

2

Let not the sun go down upon your wrath.
Ephesians 4:26

4

Judge not, and ye shall not be judged: condemn not, and ye shall not be condemned: forgive, and ye shall be forgiven.
Luke 6:37

7

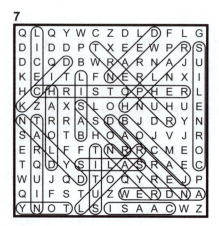

8

Across: 1 Comedy, 4 Utmost, 9 Agitate, 10 Piano, 11 There, 12 Yiddish, 13 Substantial, 18 Abscess, 20 Rogue, 22 Turns, 23 Avarice, 24 Clever, 25 Coffee.
Down: 1 Chaste, 2 Maize, 3 Drawers, 5 Tepid, 6 Ocarina, 7 Trophy, 8 New Year's Day, 14 Upsurge, 15 Tornado, 16 Tactic, 17 Recede, 19 Ensue, 21 Grief.
Answer: NAZARETH

Solutions

9

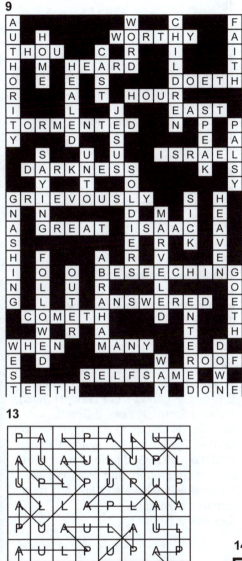

10

1	5	4	6	9	3	2	7	8
9	7	8	1	2	5	3	4	6
6	2	3	7	8	4	1	5	9
8	3	7	4	1	9	6	2	5
2	1	6	5	3	7	9	8	4
5	4	9	2	6	8	7	1	3
7	8	1	9	5	6	4	3	2
3	6	2	8	4	1	5	9	7
4	9	5	3	7	2	8	6	1

Name: DELILAH

11

1 Claudia Procula, 2 Thou shalt not bear false witness against thy neighbor, 3 John the Baptist, 4 Zebedee, 5 In, 6 Joshua, 7 27, 8 Jacob.

12

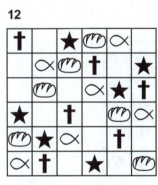

13

14

M	S	I	O	N
S	I	O	N	M
O	M	N	S	I
I	N	S	M	O
N	O	M	I	S

15

16

1 Pacifist, 2 Occupant, 3 Trappist, 4 Ignorant, 5 Pamphlet, 6 Hedonist, 7 Adjacent, 8 Regiment, 9 Schubert, 10 Heaviest, 11 Elephant, 12 Monument.
The names are: POTIPHAR and SHEM

Solutions

17

2 Pig, 3 Miser, 4 Amusing, 5 Tradition, 6 Annie Oakley, 7 Argumentative.
The central column reads: MISSION

20

1 Albania, 2 Cobweb, 3 Lotus, 4 Toga, 5 All, 6 Go, 7 M.
The character is: ABSALOM

21

Cross=13, dove=10, key=17, star=12.

23

25

2E	1W	4S	1S	3W
1S	2S	2E	3W	2S
4E	2S	■	1W	3W
2E	2E	2N	1N	3N
1N	3N	1E	4N	4W

27

28
MOSES

30

1 River Jordan, 2 Jerusalem, 3 Honey and locusts, 4 Damascus, 5 The Ten Commandments, 6 To take his wife, 7 He was stoned to death, 8 The time of Jesus' second coming.

18

The correct spelling is a.

19

1 Disgraceful, 2 Lithuania, 3 Population, 4 Information, 5 Disadvantaged, 6 Switzerland, 7 Wisconsin, 8 Embassy, 9 Quarter, 10 Encyclopedia.
The remaining letters form: LEVITICUS

22

A=5, B=12, C=7, D=9, E=3, F=17, G=19, H=16, I=12, J=36, K=35, L=28, M=71, N=63, O=134.

24

Therefore all things whatsoever ye would that men should do to you, do ye even so to them: for this is the law and the prophets.

26

A Heat, B Camel, C Invade, D Hated, E Bread, F London, G Found, H Blood, I Golf, J Storm, K Fish, L Death, M Editor, N Lather, O Hound, P Honing, Q Brief, R Giants, S Summer, T Fatten.
And the LORD God formed man of the dust of the ground, and breathed into his nostrils the breath of life; and man became a living soul.
Genesis 2:7

29

Revelation 1:1 The Revelation of Jesus Christ, which God gave unto him, to shew unto his servants things which must shortly come to pass; and he sent and signified it by his angel unto his servant John:
Revelation 1:2 Who bare record of the word of God, and of the testimony of Jesus Christ, and of all things that he saw.

Solutions

31
HOLY, hold, hood, hook, BOOK
(Other solutions may also exist)

33
The character is: EUTYCHUS

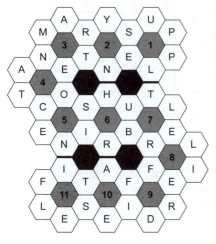

35
The nine-letter name is: PRISCILLA

36

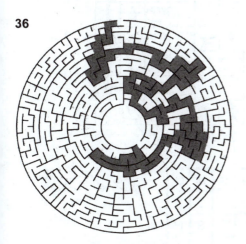

32

Unto the pure all things are pure.
Titus 1:15

34
And the earth was without form, and void; and darkness was upon the face of the deep. And the Spirit of God moved upon the face of the waters.
Genesis 1:2

37

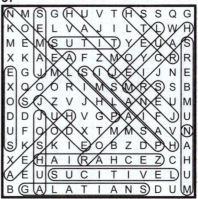

38
Across: 1 Knot, 4 Exciting, 8 Vertical, 9 Lose, 10 Beard, 11 Passion, 14 Spider, 16 Steady, 19 Mailbag, 21 Beast, 24 Dead, 25 Impaired, 26 Movement, 27 Gate.
Down: 2 Niece, 3 Tutored, 4 Each, 5 Collapse, 6 Tales, 7 Green, 10 Bus, 12 Odd, 13 Organize, 15 Pea, 17 Evening, 18 Yet, 19 Modem, 20 Ledge, 22 Scent, 23 Spot.
Answer: GALILEE

Solutions

39

40

3	4	9	2	5	6	1	8	7
2	1	7	3	8	9	5	4	6
6	5	8	4	7	1	3	2	9
8	9	2	6	1	5	4	7	3
4	7	5	9	2	3	8	6	1
1	3	6	8	4	7	9	5	2
7	6	1	5	3	4	2	9	8
5	2	3	7	9	8	6	1	4
9	8	4	1	6	2	7	3	5

Name: GAMALIEL

41

1 Gate, 2 Zipporah, 3 Pentateuch,
4 A drought, 5 Peter, 6 Fish, 7 Adultery,
8 INRI.

42

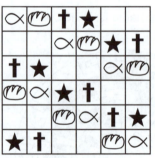

43

R	U	A	P	U	A	U	A
K	A	U	L	P	L	P	P
A	P	L	L	P	L	U	A
U	A	A	L	R	U	R	U
U	L	P	L	P	U	A	A
A	L	U	A	L	L	P	A
U	P	A	L	P	L	U	U
L	P	P	A	U	A	R	L

44

I	N	S	M	O
N	M	I	O	S
M	I	O	S	N
S	O	M	N	I
O	S	N	I	M

45

46

1 Jeopardy, 2 Emissary, 3 Treasury, 4 Humanity, 5 Rosemary, 6 Ordinary, 7 February,
8 Eternity, 9 Symphony, 10 Threnody, 11 Unsteady, 12 Sacristy.
The names are: JETHRO and FESTUS

Solutions

47

2 Car, 3 Japan, 4 Matthew, 5 Continent,
6 Haphazardly, 7 Amelia Earhart.
The central column reads: BAPTIZE

50

1 Vivaldi, 2 Judges, 3 Torah, 4 Adam,
5 Boa, 6 Fe, 7 L.
The character is: ISHMAEL

51

Cross=5, dove=3, key=8, star=6.

53

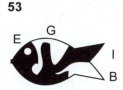

55

2E	2E	3S	2S	3S
1N	1N	1W	1W	1N
1N	1E		2W	1N
1E	1S	2W	2N	1S
2N	2E	2W	1N	2W

57

🍎

58

HEROD

60

1 On his forehead, 2 Psalm 119,
3 Mary Magdalene, 4 Joseph, 5 In
a burning bush, 6 Bleeding, 7 Joel,
8 King Jeroboam.

48

The correct spelling is c.

49

1 Dictionary, 2 Caligula, 3 Eisenhower,
4 Pakistan, 5 Destination, 6 Kettledrum,
7 Tangerine, 8 Flamingo, 9 California,
10 Strawberry.
The remaining letters form: HABAKKUK

52

A=19, B=1, C=12, D=23, E=4, F=20,
G=13, H=35, I=27, J=33, K=48, L=62,
M=81, N=110, O=191.

54

And he commanded the people to sit
down on the ground: and he took the
seven loaves, and gave thanks, and
brake, and gave to his disciples to set
before them; and they did set them
before the people.

56

A Stream, B Halo, C Fried, D Agony,
E Gloat, F Think, G Tinge, H Treat,
I Choir, J Cheese, K Theme, L Food,
M Indigo, N Offer, O Ornate, P Hoe,
Q Amount.
It is easier for a camel to go through the
eye of a needle, than for a rich man to
enter into the kingdom of God.
Matthew 19:24

59

Psalm 121:1 I will lift up mine eyes unto
the hills, from whence cometh my help.
Psalm 121:2 My help cometh from the
LORD, which made heaven and earth.
Psalm 121:3 He will not suffer thy foot to
be moved: he that keepeth thee will not
slumber.
Psalm 121:4 Behold, he that keepeth
Israel shall neither slumber nor sleep.

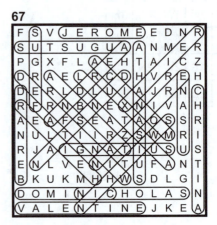
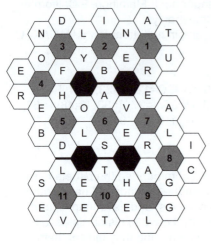

Solutions

61

SEEK, seed, feed, fend, FIND
(Other solutions may also exist)

63

The character is: AGABUS

65

The nine-letter name is: BATHSHEBA

66

62

For he that is dead is freed from sin.
Romans 6:7

64

And when she could not longer hide him, she took for him an ark of bulrushes, and daubed it with slime and with pitch, and put the child therein; and she laid it in the flags by the river's brink.
Exodus 2:3

67

68

Across: 3 Shapeless, 8 Iran, 9 Vermouth, 10 Emerge, 13 Throw, 14 Machete, 15 Pay, 16 Clapped, 17 Drama, 21 Alkali, 22 Greeting, 23 Yeti, 24 Essential.
Down: 1 Livestock, 2 Face cream, 4 Hover, 5 Portray, 6 Lion, 7 Seth, 11 Separated, 12 Hepatitis, 14 Mad, 15 Persist, 18 Magma, 19 Iris, 20 Gene.
Answer: CAESAREA

69

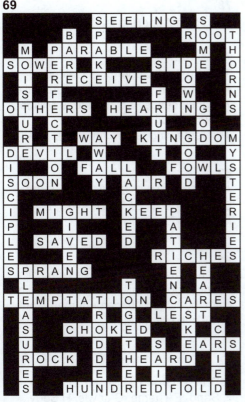

70

6	4	9	2	1	5	3	8	7
7	5	2	6	8	3	4	9	1
8	1	3	7	9	4	2	5	6
4	7	6	1	5	8	9	2	3
2	9	8	3	6	7	1	4	5
5	3	1	9	4	2	7	6	8
1	2	4	8	7	6	5	3	9
9	6	5	4	3	1	8	7	2
3	8	7	5	2	9	6	1	4

Name: ANANIAS

71

1 Abram, 2 Beersheba, 3 Mount Carmel, 4 Manna, 5 Jonathan, 6 Zephaniah, 7 The second, 8 Blindness.

72

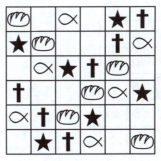

73

74

I	N	S	O	M
S	O	M	I	N
O	M	I	N	S
N	S	O	M	I
M	I	N	S	O

75

76

1 Mediator, 2 Abductor, 3 Recorder, 4 King Lear, 5 Metaphor, 6 Offender, 7 Reindeer, 8 December, 9 Educator, 10 Cape Fear, 11 Agitator, 12 Imposter.
The names are: MARK and MORDECAI

Solutions

77

2 Men, 3 Aisle, 4 Corsica, 5 Ho Chi Minh, 6 Brazzaville, 7 Straightening.
The central column reads: MESSIAH

80

1 Zealots, 2 Seraph, 3 Koala, 4 Siam, 5 Pig, 6 VA, 7 R.
The character is: SHAMGAR

81

Cross=27, dove=22, key=18, star=31.

83

85

3E	1S	2W	3S	2W
1S	3S	3S	3W	2W
2S	2N	■	2W	1N
2E	3E	1W	1S	3N
1N	3E	2N	2N	2N

87

88

JONAH

90

1 Abraham, 2 An east wind, 3 Daniel, 4 Sea of Galilee, 5 John's, 6 Rebekah, 7 Eight, 8 The sixth day.

78

The correct spelling is c.

79

1 Umbrella, 2 Superior, 3 Calendar, 4 Steamboat, 5 Overcoat, 6 Turquoise, 7 Frankincense, 8 Separate, 9 Milliner, 10 Revelation.
The remaining letters form: HAGGAI

82

A=27, B=11, C=2, D=13, E=16, F=38, G=13, H=15, I=29, J=51, K=28, L=44, M=79, N=72, O=151.

84

When I was a child, I spake as a child, I understood as a child, I thought as a child: but when I became a man, I put away childish things.

86

A Drift, B Groan, C Evoke, D Wither, E Sand, F Theme, G Jowls, H Body, I Hood, J Mighty, K Heated, L Ladder, M Hands, N Fourth, O Atone, P Sane, Q Living, R Done.
And whatsoever ye do in word or deed, do all in the name of the Lord Jesus, giving thanks to God and the Father by him.
Colossians 3:17

89

Revelation 10:1 And I saw another mighty angel come down from heaven, clothed with a cloud: and a rainbow was upon his head, and his face was as it were the sun, and his feet as pillars of fire:
Revelation 10:2 and he had in his hand a little book open: and he set his right foot upon the sea, and his left foot on the earth.

Solutions

91

RISE, rile, tile, tale, talk, WALK
(Other solutions may also exist)

93

The character is: LYDIA

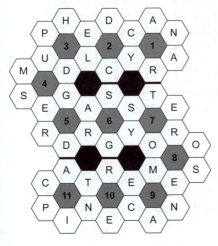

95

The Bible book is: LEVITICUS

96

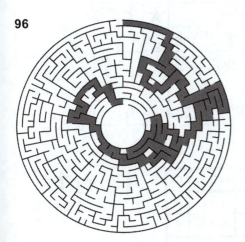

92

He that hath ears to hear, let him hear.
Mark 4:9

94

Though thou exalt thyself as the eagle, and though thou set thy nest among the stars, thence will I bring thee down, saith the Lord.
Obadiah 1:4

97

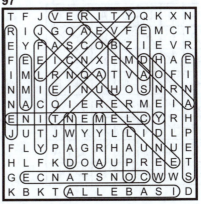

98

Across: 1 Agoraphobia, 9 Contour, 10 Idaho, 11 Trim, 12 Faintest, 14 Being, 15 Japan, 20 Carnival, 22 Aids, 24 Tonga, 25 Glacial, 26 Meteorology.
Down: 2 Genuine, 3 Room, 4 Pariah, 5 Oriental, 6 Image, 7 Acute, 8 Forty, 13 Indicate, 16 Abiding, 17 Scott, 18 Ranger, 19 Psalm, 21 Rinse, 23 Hail.
Answer: BETHLEHEM

99

|B|D|E|S|I|R|E|D| | | |W|A|Y|S|
|E| |E| |O| | | | | | |L| |O|M|
|L| |P| |R| |C|E|A|S|E|S| |G|E|
I		U		C			U		B		O	G	O	N	E
E		T		E	M		B		O				B	
V		Y		R	F	A	S	T	E	D			B	
E				E			N		I			D	E	
D	O	C	T	R	I	N	E		B	L	I	N	D	H	
		E						T			E		O	L
C	Y	R	E	N	E		A	W	A	Y		V		D
		T				H				C	H	I	L	D
H	E	A	R		I	S	L	E	S			L		
	I		S			E		R	E	M				
	I	N	T	E	R	P	R	E	T	A	T	I	O	N
P		N		A		U		S	N		I			
R	I	G	H	T		R	N	O			G			
O		A		A	S	T	O	N	I	S	H	E	D	
P	E	R	V	E	R	T		O			T			
H		E		E			L		E		E			
E				D	E	P	A	R	T	E	D			
T	U	R	N		P		A	N			N			
		J		H	A	N	D		T	H	E	E		
F	A	L	S	E		P		I			M	Y		
U			W	I	T	H	S	T	O	O	D			
L			S		O			C						
L	O	R	D		S	A	W		H	E	R	O	D	

100

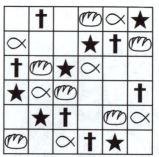

8	7	1	5	4	6	3	2	9
5	3	4	7	2	9	8	1	6
9	6	2	8	3	1	4	5	7
6	8	9	3	5	2	7	4	1
7	1	5	4	9	8	6	3	2
2	4	3	6	1	7	9	8	5
1	9	8	2	7	4	5	6	3
4	5	7	1	6	3	2	9	8
3	2	6	9	8	5	1	7	4

Name: HERODIAS

101

1 King Herod, 2 Rachel, 3 Lot's, 4 Gershom and Eliezer, 5 The angel Gabriel, 6 His daughters, 7 War, 8 He struck the river with his cloak.

102

103

P A U L U A R U
A P L A R U A N
L U P L A P L
A U A P A L U R
P L L U P N A L
U R L A L U A U
A U A U U P U A
P L A P L L P L

104

N	I	M	S	O
M	S	I	O	N
I	O	N	M	S
O	N	S	I	M
S	M	O	N	I

105

106

1 Horrible, 2 Embezzle, 3 Reveille, 4 Obsolete, 5 Dateline, 6 Encircle, 7 Zimbabwe, 8 Exchange, 9 Kamikaze, 10 Immobile, 11 Escalope, 12 Lacrosse.
The names are: HEROD and EZEKIEL

Solutions

107

2 Try, 3 China, 4 Clinton, 5 Vaccinate,
6 Philatelist, 7 Shirley Temple.
The central column reads: TRINITY

110

1 Amazing, 2 Voodoo, 3 Seoul, 4 Gobi,
5 Kea, 6 IT, 7 H.
The character is: GOLIATH

111

Cross=5, dove=3, key=2, star=4.

113

115

1S	1E	2S	3W	3S
1E	2S	2S	1N	1N
1E	2N	■	1S	1W
1N	1S	2W	2N	1N
3E	1E	3N	1E	3N

117

118

APPLE

120

1 Messenger, 2 King Herod, 3 Isaiah,
4 Shadrach, Meshach and Abednego,
5 Jeremiah, 6 The Second Coming of
Jesus, 7 The cow, 8 Salome.

108

The correct spelling is d.

109

1 Zimbabwe, 2 Tourniquet, 3 Restaurant,
4 November, 5 Distorted, 6 Talisman,
7 Mountain, 8 Incandescent,
9 Cigarettes, 10 Hospital.
The remaining letters form: JONAH

112

A=9, B=8, C=2, D=18, E=12, F=17,
G=10, H=20, I=30, J=27, K=30, L=50,
M=57, N=80, O=137.

114

And Ruth said, Entreat me not to leave
thee, or to return from following after
thee: for whither thou goest, I will go;
and where thou lodgest, I will lodge: thy
people shall be my people, and thy God
my God.

116

A South, B Wooden, C Brie, D Asking,
E Hobby, F Aim, G Sound, H Broke,
I Carve, J Own, K Lithe, L Served,
M Bush, N Arrive, O Agate, P Tail,
Q Yearly, R Mauve, S Eagle.
Be sober, be vigilant; because your
adversary, the Devil, as a roaring lion,
walketh about, seeking whom he may
devour.
1 Peter 5:8

119

Habakkuk 2:12 Woe to him that buildeth
a town with blood, and establisheth a
city by iniquity!
Habakkuk 2:13 Behold, is it not of the
Lord of hosts that the people shall labor
in the very fire, and the people shall
weary themselves for very vanity?
Habakkuk 2:14 For the earth shall be
filled with the knowledge of the glory of
the Lord, as the waters cover the sea.

Solutions

121

LORD, lore, more, mole, hole, HOLY
(Other solutions may also exist)

123

The character is: MATTHIAS

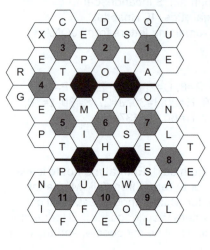

125

The nine-letter name is: CORNELIUS

126

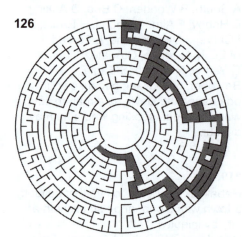

122

I have been a stranger in a strange land.
Exodus 2:22

124

O Lord, our Lord, how excellent is thy name in all the earth! Who hast set thy glory above the heavens.
Psalms 8:1

127

128

Across: 1 Arrows, 4 Rabies, 9 Reactor, 10 Omega, 11 Style, 12 Greater, 13 Sensational, 18 Hepburn, 20 Snake, 22 Scrub, 23 Narrate, 24 Shrank, 25 Nectar.
Down: 1 Across, 2 Ready, 3 Witness, 5 Above, 6 Inertia, 7 Stairs, 8 Frightening, 14 Emperor, 15 Observe, 16 Thesis, 17 Meteor, 19 Urban, 21 Apart.
Answer: EPHESUS

Solutions

129

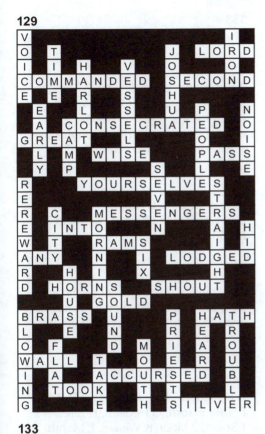

130

4	5	7	8	1	9	3	6	2
3	2	6	4	5	7	9	1	8
8	9	1	3	6	2	7	4	5
5	8	4	6	9	3	1	2	7
9	1	2	7	8	4	6	5	3
7	6	3	5	2	1	8	9	4
6	7	9	2	3	5	4	8	1
2	3	8	1	4	6	5	7	9
1	4	5	9	7	8	2	3	6

Name: SHISHAK

131

1 King Belshazzar, 2 Jezebel,
3 Philistines, 4 Ten, 5 Wolves, 6 Quail,
7 A golden calf, 8 Mount Nebo.

132

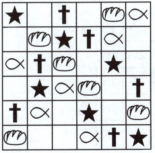

133

134

S	O	N	I	M
I	N	M	O	S
M	S	O	N	I
N	M	I	S	O
O	I	S	M	N

135

136

1 Captured, 2 Asteroid, 3 Icebound, 4 New World, 5 Banished, 6 Eclipsed, 7 Narrated,
8 Junk food, 9 Abridged, 10 Maligned, 11 Infected, 12 Neutered.
The names are: CAIN and BENJAMIN

Solutions

137
2 Opt, 3 Groom, 4 Presley, 5 Armstrong,
6 Bastille Day, 7 Liechtenstein.
The central column reads: APOSTLE

138
The correct spelling is c.

139
1 Explosion, 2 Mississippi, 3 Trapeze
artist, 4 Churchill, 5 Congregation,
6 Eiderdown, 7 Abbreviation,
8 Disappearing, 9 Arthur Conan Doyle.
The remaining letters form: MICAH

140
1 Abelard, 2 Lupine, 3 Jacob, 4 Logo,
5 Sir, 6 Ra, 7 H.
The character is: DEBORAH

141
Cross=4, dove=10, key=7, star=8.

142
A=7, B=3, C=8, D=26, E=10, F=10,
G=11, H=34, I=36, J=21, K=45, L=70,
M=66, N=115, O=181.

143

144
The hand of our God is upon all them
for good that seek him; but his power
and his wrath is against all them that
forsake him.

145

2E	2S	3S	2S	1S
2S	2S	2W	2W	2W
2N	1E	■	2S	1S
1N	3N	1E	2N	3N
2E	3E	1W	3W	2N

146
A Hunch, B Pluto, C Rhodes, D Root,
E Tee, F Torn, G Heaven, H Eire,
I Snout, J Moor, K Weave, L Month,
M Hotter, N Anthem, O Top, P Hoof,
Q Kansas, R Load, S Plenty.
Hath not the potter power over the clay,
of the same lump to make one vessel
unto honor, and another unto dishonor?
Romans 9:21

147

148
VICAR

149
Mark 7:32 And they bring unto him one
that was deaf, and had an impediment
in his speech; and they beseech him to
put his hand upon him.
Mark 7:33 And he took him aside from
the multitude, and put his fingers into
his ears, and he spit, and touched his
tongue;
Mark 7:34 and looking up to heaven, he
sighed, and saith unto him, Eph'phatha,
that is, Be opened.

150
1 Good fruit, 2 Conquest, War, Famine
and Death, 3 White, Red, Black and
Pale, 4 A balance, 5 The fruit is not
named, 6 Melchizedek, King of Salem,
7 Balaam, 8 Joshua.

Solutions

151
HEAL, seal, sell, sill, silk, SICK
(Other solutions may also exist)

153
The character is: RHODA

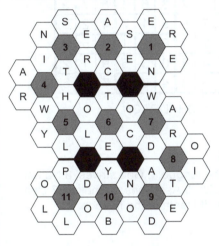

155
The nine-letter name is: THADDAEUS

156

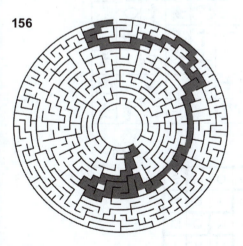

152

And Zilpah Leah's maid bare Jacob a son.
Genesis 30:10

154
I have compared thee, O my love, to a company of horses in Pharaoh's chariots. Thy cheeks are comely with rows of jewels, thy neck with chains of gold.
Song of Solomon 1:9-10

157

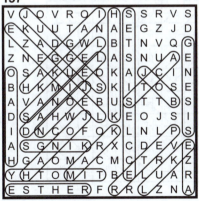

158
Across: 1 Envy, 3 Negative, 9 Collide, 10 Paste, 11 Personalized, 14 Elm, 16 Earth, 17 Dam, 18 Indira Gandhi, 21 Often, 22 Average, 23 Sorcerer, 24 Next.
Down: 1 Encipher, 2 Valor, 4 Ewe, 5 Amphitheater, 6 Instead, 7 Eden, 8 Disobedience, 12 Aorta, 13 Imminent, 15 Monitor, 19 Drake, 20 Boss, 22 Ate.
Answer: NINEVEH

159

					D	A	I	L	Y	
D	E	L	I	L	A	H		W			Y
				I			M	A	N		L	I	E	S
W	E	A	V	E	S	T		I		T		N
	N			H		S	T	R	E	N	G	T	H
	T	O	U	C	H	E	T	H		L
W		T			R		A	F	F	L	I	C	T
I		H			T		V		I			H
T	H	E	R	E	F	O	R	E		R	A	Z	O	R
H		R		A		N		E			E
S				S				G	R	E	A	T
	D	E	A	T	H			R			D
T		W			M		W	E	A	K
O		S	A	M	S	O	N		E			H
W	E	B		K		T		B	I	N	D	E
	R		E		H					B		A
	O		D	R	I	E	D		B	E	H	O	L	D
S	O	U	L		O		R			U
	G			P	A	S	S			N	O	T
T	H	R	E	E			U	R	G	E	D
	T		S	E	V	E	N			L
K		L		E				T	O	L	D	O	V
N		O		X			O			V
O	C	C	U	P	I	E	D		B	R	O	K	E	N
W		K		I		D			D
N		S		N			P	R	E	S	S	E	D

160

2	8	1	7	4	9	6	3	5
3	9	5	1	8	6	2	4	7
4	6	7	2	5	3	8	9	1
5	7	4	9	2	8	1	6	3
8	1	2	3	6	4	5	7	9
9	3	6	5	1	7	4	2	8
6	2	9	8	7	1	3	5	4
7	4	8	6	3	5	9	1	2
1	5	3	4	9	2	7	8	6

Name: SHADRACH

161

1 The tongue, 2 God strives, 3 Nathan, 4 Faith, 5 Assyrians, 6 Snakes, 7 Dead Sea, 8 Death of the firstborn.

162

163

R	L	A	U	A	P	L	P
P	A	U	P	L	U	U	A
A	A	P	L	L	A	A	U
U	A	U	L	U	P	P	L
U	L	P	P	A	U	L	P
U	L	L	U	L	P	U	A
L	A	P	A	P	A	U	A
P	A	U	L	U	L	P	L

164

I	N	O	M	S
M	O	I	S	N
S	I	N	O	M
O	S	M	N	I
N	M	S	I	O

165

166

1 Emmental, 2 Skeletal, 3 Terminal, 4 Hannibal, 5 External, 6 Reversal, 7 Scornful, 8 Approval, 9 Lacrimal, 10 Optional, 11 Marshall, 12 Eventful.
The names are: ESTHER and SALOME

Solutions

167

2 Bet, 3 Paris, 4 Denmark, 5 Anchorage, 6 Afghanistan, 7 Bedloe's Island.
The central column reads: SERMONS

170

1 Berlioz, 2 Wimple, 3 Climb, 4 Yule, 5 Aïd, 6 Me, 7 E.
The character is: ZEBEDEE

171

Cross=10, dove=9, key=8, star=11.

173

175

3E	1W	2E	3S	2S
3E	1S	1N	1E	3S
1S	1E		3W	1S
2E	3N	1S	1S	3W
3N	3N	2W	2N	3W

177

178

THOMAS

180

1 Twelve, 2 An angel caused his chains to fall off, 3 He broke the Sabbath, 4 Rehoboam, 5 Pontius Pilate, 6 Ishmaelites, 7 James, John and Peter, 8 Four days.

168

The correct spelling is a.

169

1 Breakfast, 2 Mixture, 3 Indigo, 4 Thunderstorm, 5 Mediterranean, 6 Nitrogen, 7 Earthquake, 8 Australia, 9 Rhinoceros, 10 Trepidation.
The remaining letters form: NUMBERS

172

A=11, B=20, C=6, D=1, E=5, F=31, G=26, H=7, I=6, J=57, K=33, L=13, M=90, N=46, O=136.

174

Wisdom is the principal thing; therefore get wisdom: and with all thy getting get understanding.

176

A Totter, B Happy, C East, D Mad, E Around, F Heel, G Shoal, H Gloom, I Dash, J Thread, K Vapor, L Habit, M Heed, N Haste, O Their, P Annoy, Q Den, R Hose, S Rob.
And the LORD said unto Moses, See, I have made thee a god to Pharaoh; and Aaron thy brother shall be thy prophet. Exodus 7:1

179

Luke 18:15 And they brought unto him also infants, that he would touch them: but when his disciples saw it, they rebuked them.
Luke 18:16 But Jesus called them unto him, and said, Suffer little children to come unto me, and forbid them not: for of such is the kingdom of God.
Luke 18:17 Verily I say unto you, Whosoever shall not receive the kingdom of God as a little child shall in no wise enter therein.

Solutions

181

PETER, meter, meted, mated, dated, dates, dames, JAMES
(Other solutions may also exist)

183

The character is: SILAS

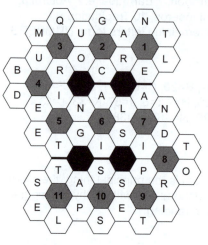

185

The Bible book is: ZEPHANIAH

186

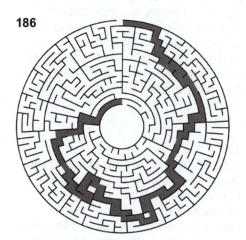

182

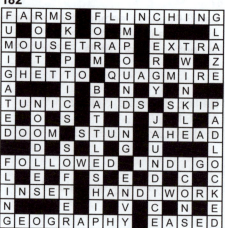

Love thy neighbor as thyself.
Leviticus 19:18

184

I cried by reason of mine affliction unto the Lord, and he heard me; out of the belly of hell cried I, and thou heardest my voice.
Jonah 2:2

187

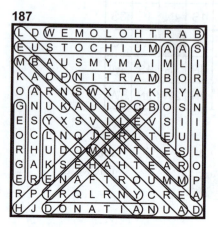

188

Across: 1 Chariot, 5 Desks, 8 Variation, 9 Era, 10 Rabbi, 12 Limited, 13 Spinning wheel, 15 Enhance, 17 Risky, 19 Tee, 20 Worshiper, 22 Rotor, 23 Regress.
Down: 1 Cover, 2 Air, 3 Italian, 4 Trial and error, 5 Denim, 6 Scentless, 7 Scandal, 11 Brightest, 13 Shelter, 14 Warthog, 16 Newer, 18 Yarns, 21 Pie.
Answer: KIDRON

Solutions

189

190

1	3	8	9	4	5	7	2	6
6	4	7	3	8	2	9	1	5
5	9	2	6	7	1	3	8	4
4	7	1	2	9	6	8	5	3
8	5	3	7	1	4	2	6	9
2	6	9	5	3	8	4	7	1
9	2	6	8	5	3	1	4	7
3	1	5	4	2	7	6	9	8
7	8	4	1	6	9	5	3	2

Name: NEHEMIAH

191

1 Jericho, 2 Gath, 3 Thirty-three, 4 The Ark of the Covenant, 5 Because of his jealousy at the relationship between David and Jonathan, 6 Hosea, 7 She was a prostitute, 8 God.

192

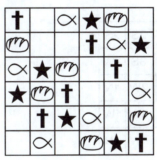

193

194

O	N	S	I	M
I	M	N	O	S
N	S	I	M	O
S	O	M	N	I
M	I	O	S	N

195

196

1 Magellan, 2 Aviation, 3 Talisman, 4 Tungsten, 5 Harridan, 6 Edmonton, 7 Watchman, 8 Scorpion, 9 Hawaiian, 10 Exertion, 11 Bulletin, 12 Al Jolson.
The names are: MATTHEW and SHEBA

Solutions

197
2 Arm, 3 Ivory, 4 Memphis, 5 Balthazar,
6 Purple Heart, 7 Herbert Hoover.
The central column reads: PROPHET

200
1 Aerosol, 2 Africa, 3 Waltz, 4 Agra,
5 Air, 6 Cu, 7 S.
The character is: LAZARUS

201
Cross=6, dove=9, key=5, star=2.

203

205

3E	3E	2W	2S	2S
3E	2S	2W	3S	2W
2E	1N	■	2W	1N
1S	3N	3N	3W	1W
2N	3E	1W	1W	1N

207

208
GABRIEL

210
1 Absalom, 2 Joab, 3 Samaritans,
4 Sennacherib, 5 Egypt, 6 Thirty,
7 John the Baptist, 8 Satan.

198
The correct spelling is d.

199
1 Underground, 2 Confectionery,
3 Announce, 4 Sculpture, 5 Counterfeit,
6 Understanding, 7 Washington,
8 Capricorn, 9 Everlasting,
10 Modernizing.
The remaining letters form: GALATIANS

202
A=21, B=9, C=27, D=15, E=19, F=30,
G=36, H=42, I=34, J=66, K=78, L=76,
M=144, N=154, O=298.

204
And Hannah answered and said, No,
my lord, I am a woman of a sorrowful
spirit: I have drunk neither wine nor
strong drink, but have poured out my
soul before the Lord.

206
A Waist, B Blow, C Here, D Beige,
E Thank, F Lotion, G Swear, H Many,
I Effect, J Listen, K Shady, L Wither,
M Noah, N Shear, O Eased, P Food,
Q Washes, R Ears, S Thin, T Green.
Now as he walked by the sea of Galilee,
he saw Simon and Andrew his brother
casting a net into the sea: for they were
fishers.
Mark 1:16

209
Isaiah 2:17 And the loftiness of man
shall be bowed down, and the haughtiness of men shall be made low; and the
LORD alone shall be exalted in that day.
Isaiah 2:18 And the idols he shall utterly
abolish.
Isaiah 2:19 And they shall go into the
holes of the rocks, and into the caves
of the earth, for fear of the Lord, and for
the glory of his majesty, when he ariseth
to shake terribly the earth.

Solutions

211

MARK, lark, lurk, lure, LUKE
(Other solutions may also exist)

213

The character is: PHILIP

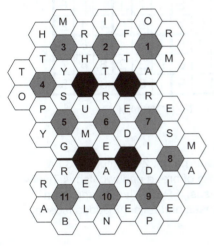

215

The nine-letter name is: ELIZABETH

216

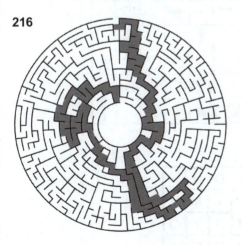

212

Man doth not live by bread only.
Deuteronomy 8:3

214

And ye shall eat in plenty, and be satisfied,
and praise the name of the Lord your God,
that hath dealt wondrously with you: and
my people shall never be ashamed.
Joel 2:26

217

218

Across: 1 Embarrassment, 7 Reasons, 8 Copra, 9 Mask, 10 Meetings, 12 Tether,
14 Tuxedo, 16 Hard copy, 17 Rage, 20 Elope, 21 Ezekiel, 23 Self-restraint.
Down: 1 Ear, 2 Beads, 3 Root, 4 Answer, 5 Expense, 6 Transpose, 8 Citrus,
9 Matchless, 11 Rescue, 13 Turmoil, 15 Speeds, 18 Alibi, 19 Pear, 22 Lit.
Answer: MEGIDDO

219

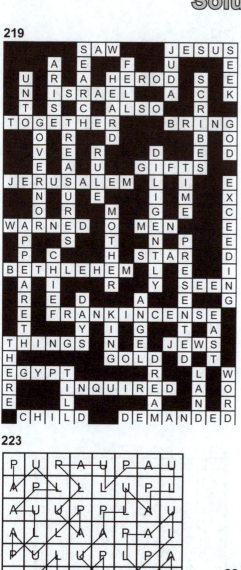

220

7	8	2	3	1	6	5	9	4
9	5	1	2	4	7	6	8	3
6	4	3	8	9	5	2	7	1
1	9	4	6	2	3	7	5	8
8	2	5	4	7	1	9	3	6
3	6	7	5	8	9	4	1	2
2	3	8	7	5	4	1	6	9
5	1	6	9	3	2	8	4	7
4	7	9	1	6	8	3	2	5

Name: REHOBOAM

221

1 Capernaum, 2 Beatitudes, 3 Five loaves of bread and two fish, 4 Twelve, 5 Jesus, 6 Peter, James and John, 7 Moses and Elijah, 8 Judas Iscariot.

222

223

224

M	S	O	N	I
S	O	I	M	N
N	M	S	I	O
I	N	M	O	S
O	I	N	S	M

225

226

1 Ravenous, 2 Atlantis, 3 Calculus, 4 Hittites, 5 Enormous, 6 Lifeless, 7 Arkansas, 8 Neurosis, 9 Daedalus, 10 Ruthless, 11 Epistles, 12 Westerns.
The names are: RACHEL and ANDREW

Solutions

227
2 Now, 3 Curie, 4 Hussein, 5 Hitchcock, 6 Coney Island, 7 Holy Sepulcher.
The central column reads: WORSHIP

228
The correct spelling is c.

229
1 Identical, 2 December, 3 Controversial, 4 Harbor, 5 Lactic, 6 Yellowstone, 7 Saturday, 8 Commercial, 9 Starboard, 10 Antiperspirant.
The remaining letters form: HEBREWS

230
1 Camelot, 2 Denali, 3 Psalm, 4 Nebo, 5 TNT, 6 pH, 7 Y.
The character is: TIMOTHY

231
Cross=25, dove=17, key=29, star=39.

232
A=33, B=10, C=19, D=15, E=18, F=43, G=29, H=34, I=33, J=72, K=63, L=67, M=135, N=130, O=265.

233

234
Behold, the days come, saith the Lord God, that I will send a famine in the land, not a famine of bread, nor a thirst for water, but of hearing the words of the Lord.

235

1E	2S	2E	1W	2S
3S	2E	1W	1S	2S
2N	1E	■	3W	1N
2N	1W	2N	1W	1S
3E	1N	1W	1N	2W

236
A Shadow, B Laughs, C Hook, D Sport, E Gander, F Booth, G Aches, H Fault, I Misty, J Baking, K Child, L Funny, M Nation, N Beaver, O Seeing, P Tames, Q Image, R Canon, S Mint.
Though I speak with the tongues of men and of angels, and have not charity, I am become as sounding brass, or a tinkling cymbal.
1 Corinthians 13:1

237

238
SAMSON

239
Ecclesiastes 3:1 To every thing there is a season, and a time to every purpose under the heaven:
Ecclesiastes 3:2 a time to be born, and a time to die; a time to plant, and a time to pluck up that which is planted;
Ecclesiastes 3:3 a time to kill, and a time to heal; a time to break down, and a time to build up.

240
1 Edom, 2 Methuselah, 3 One hundred and thirty, 4 Cyprus, 5 Elijah, 6 Samson, 7 The wicked, 8 Tax-collector.

241

PAUL, pall, poll, pole, role, ROME
(Other solutions may also exist)

243

The character is: PHOEBE

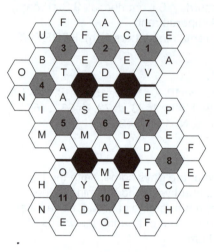

245

The nine-letter name is: NICODEMUS

246

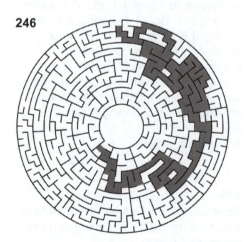

242

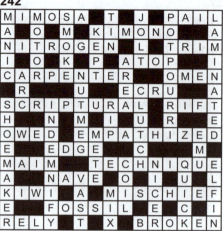

I am going the way of all the earth.
Joshua 23:14

244

For if we believe that Jesus died and rose again, even so them also which sleep in Jesus will God bring with him.
1 Thessalonians 4:14

247

248

Across: 1 Okra, 4 Software, 8 Parasite, 9 Gear, 10 Panda, 11 Cuisine, 14 Bronco, 16 Nearby, 18 Descent, 20 Cargo, 23 Mice, 24 Ice cream, 25 Shortens, 26 Most.
Down: 2 Koala, 3 Abandon, 4 Shin, 5 Frequent, 6 Wages, 7 Eerie, 12 Nib, 13 Coincide, 15 Roe, 17 Anagram, 18 Dumps, 19 Cheer, 21 Grass, 22 Less.
Answer: GOSHEN

Solutions

249

250

6	5	8	3	2	9	7	4	1
3	4	2	7	1	5	8	9	6
1	9	7	6	4	8	5	3	2
8	1	5	4	3	6	9	2	7
4	3	9	2	5	7	6	1	8
2	7	6	8	9	1	4	5	3
9	8	1	5	6	2	3	7	4
5	6	3	1	7	4	2	8	9
7	2	4	9	8	3	1	6	5

Name: ABISHAG

251

1 Deborah, 2 Baal, 3 Elijah, 4 Jesus, 5 Benjamin, 6 The son of, 7 Joshua, 8 Peter.

252

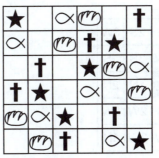

253

254

255

256

1 Duckling, 2 Aqualung, 3 Vitamin G, 4 Iron lung, 5 Daunting, 6 Ginsberg, 7 Overlong, 8 Locating, 9 Impeding, 10 Aborting, 11 Travelog, 12 Hong Kong.
The names are: DAVID and GOLIATH

Solutions

257

2 Why, 3 Grant, 4 Bahrain, 5 Swaziland, 6 Adriatic Sea, 7 Dorothy Parker.
The central column reads: CHARITY

260

1 Alabama, 2 Cherub, 3 Homer, 4 Rhea, 5 Mph, 6 Ma, 7 M.
The character is: ABRAHAM

261

Cross=4, dove=10, key=7, star=8.

263

265

3E	1E	2S	2S	3W
1S	3E	2W	3S	1S
2N	1N	■	1N	2N
3E	1N	1S	2W	2W
1N	3E	2W	2W	1N

267

268

SABBATH

270

1 Jealousy at God's acceptance of Abel's sacrifice, 2 Miriam, 3 Saul, 4 Hailstones, 5 Genesis, 6 Pharaoh, 7 Ten, 8 Five.

258

The correct spelling is b.

259

1 Carpenter, 2 Hippopotamus, 3 Connecting, 4 Disappointing, 5 Wedding, 6 Jerusalem, 7 Marsupial, 8 Disproportionate, 9 Atmosphere, 10 Fortunate.
The remaining letters form: JAMES

262

A=23, B=16, C=28, D=9, E=6, F=39, G=44, H=37, I=15, J=83, K=81, L=52, M=164, N=133, O=297.

264

Now the Lord had prepared a great fish to swallow up Jonah. And Jonah was in the belly of the fish three days and three nights.

266

A Pledge, B Chat, C Cycle, D June, E Ridge, F Spoon, G Rhyme, H Alarm, I Ditto, J Groom, K Mutter, L Action, M Lodge, N Sinner, O Leo, P Adjust, Q Doing, R Teeth, S Hiding, T Hiss.
The LORD shall judge the people: judge me, O LORD, according to my righteousness, and according to mine integrity that is in me.
Psalms 7:8

269

Zechariah 9:14 And the Lord shall be seen over them, and his arrow shall go forth as the lightning: and the Lord God shall blow the trumpet, and shall go with whirlwinds of the south.
Zechariah 9:15 The Lord of hosts shall defend them; and they shall devour, and subdue with sling stones; and they shall drink, and make a noise as through wine; and they shall be filled like bowls, and as the corners of the altar.

Solutions

271
RUTH, rush, rash, cash, case, care, core, CORN
(Other solutions may also exist)

273
The character is: ANANIAS

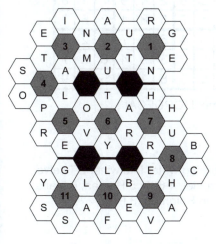

275
The nine-letter name is: DEMETRIUS

276

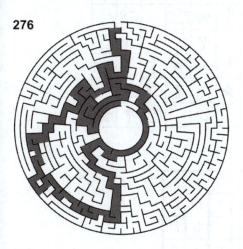

272

The truth shall make you free.
John 8:32

274
And the angels which kept not their first estate, but left their own habitation, he hath reserved in everlasting chains under darkness unto the judgment of the great day.
Jude 1:6

277

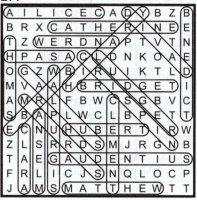

278
Across: 1 Clear up, 5 Stung, 8 Boredom, 9 April, 10 Serve, 11 Eremite, 12 Decade, 14 Freely, 17 Startle, 19 Sited, 22 Opera, 23 Malaria, 24 Truth, 25 Tuesday.
Down: 1 Cubes, 2 Error, 3 Redhead, 4 Pamper, 5 Stale, 6 Ukraine, 7 Gallery, 12 Distort, 13 Chateau, 15 Resolve, 16 Helmet, 18 Teach, 20 Tired, 21 Diary.
Answer: EMMAUS

Solutions

279

```
G A T H E R   A N D R E W   D
  H       E     L     A T   E
M O U N T A I N   O         P
  S       I   E Y E S       A
T A       N             L   R
H U N D R E D     P     I T E
A D       D I S T R I B U T E D
N   T     S     O   U   Y L
K N E W   C     V   Y     L
S   O   F I L L E D   J E W S
    W   P       O         B
S   O   L I K E W I S E   R
M I R A C L E     N     U E
A   L   S A T     F I V E A
L A D         K   F       D
L   A   G   P H I L I P   E
  N U M B E R     N   C
    O   A M O N G   I
    V   S         F E A S T
B A S K E T S     N       W
  E         M U L T I T U D E
  G A L I L E E         E L
    O   N I G H         N V
L O A V E S     F O R C E   E
      T R U T H
```

280

3	1	5	9	6	8	4	7	2
4	7	6	1	2	5	9	3	8
2	8	9	4	7	3	1	5	6
5	2	1	7	3	6	8	9	4
6	3	8	2	4	9	7	1	5
9	4	7	5	8	1	2	6	3
8	9	4	6	5	7	3	2	1
1	5	2	3	9	4	6	8	7
7	6	3	8	1	2	5	4	9

Name: MORDECAI

281

1 Turning water into wine, 2 Twelve,
3 Ezekiel, 4 666, 5 Haman, 6 Malta,
7 King Solomon, 8 Prey.

282

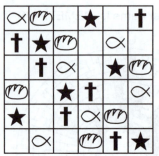

283

```
P A R L A P A P
P A U A L U L U
L U L L U A P L
U P U A P U A L
A A U R L R P N
A L P U L A A L
U P L A U L P U
L P A U P A U L
```

284

S	M	O	N	I
N	I	S	M	O
O	N	I	S	M
M	O	N	I	S
I	S	M	O	N

285

(dove, key, candle, star)

286

1 Gomorrah, 2 Infotech, 3 Demolish, 4 Eldritch, 5 Oligarch, 6 Nazareth, 7 Jeremiah,
8 Outmatch, 9 Savannah, 10 Encroach, 11 Pnom Penh, 12 Hannukah.
The names are: GIDEON and JOSEPH

Solutions

287

2 Lit, 3 Aaron, 4 Abraham, 5 Aconcagua,
6 Daniel Boone, 7 Champs Elysées.
The central column reads: MIRACLE

290

1 Lazarus, 2 El Paso, 3 Babel, 4 Oslo,
5 Ohm, 6 Io, 7 N.
The character is: SOLOMON

291

Cross=5, dove=7, key=8, star=9.

293

295

3S	2E	2E	1W	1S
1N	1E	3S	2W	1W
1E	2N		3W	2W
2E	2E	2E	1N	1N
3N	1N	2W	1E	3W

297

298

CASSOCK

300

1 The Land of Nod, 2 Frankincense, gold
and myrrh , 3 Amram, 4 Man and land
animals, 5 He quelled a storm on the Sea
of Galilee, 6 Tithe, 7 Adam, Eve, Jesus,
8 Solomon.

288

The correct spelling is c.

289

1 Conflagration, 2 Beginning,
3 Changeable, 4 Snowflake, 5 Anagram,
6 Bethlehem, 7 Seventeen, 8 Possession,
9 Extinguished, 10 Antarctica.
The remaining letters form: AMOS

292

A=15, B=7, C=5, D=28, E=8, F=22,
G=12, H=33, I=36, J=34, K=45, L=69,
M=79, N=114, O=193.

294

For the love of money is the root of all
evil: which while some coveted after,
they have erred from the faith, and
pierced themselves through with many
sorrows.

296

A Minute, B Floods, C Cooker, D Waits,
E Woman, F Odious, G Mouth,
H Shook, I Awake, J Wished, K Mowing,
L Flower, M Avenge, N Whines,
O Done, P Midget, Q Shiny, R How,
S Stands.
Who is a wise man and endued with
knowledge among you? Let him show
out of a good conversation his works
with meekness of wisdom.
James 3:13

299

Exodus 17:5 And the Lord said unto
Moses, Go on before the people, and
take with thee of the elders of Israel;
and thy rod, wherewith thou smotest the
river, take in thine hand, and go.
Exodus 17:6 Behold, I will stand before
thee there upon the rock in Horeb; and
thou shalt smite the rock, and there
shall come water out of it, that the
people may drink. And Moses did so in
the sight of the elders of Israel.

Solutions

301

LOAF, load, loud, lout, lost, list, fist, FISH
(Other solutions may also exist)

303

The character is: ELYMAS

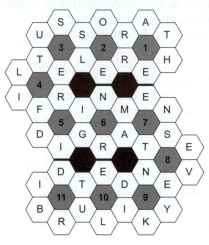

305

The nine-letter name is: DIONYSIUS

306

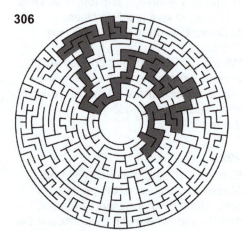

302

Q	A	C		H	Y	P	E	R	B	O	L	E
U	P	W	A	R	D			U	H	R		T
I		E		A		J	E	L	L	Y	F	I	S	H

How long halt ye between two opinions?
1 Kings 18:21

304

And he healed many that were sick of divers diseases, and cast out many devils; and suffered not the devils to speak, because they knew him.
Mark 1:34

307

308

Across: 1 Hen-coop, 5 Sushi, 8 Blini, 10 Ageless, 11 Sooty, 12 Rayon, 13 Mania, 15 Sailor, 16 Afloat, 18 Glass, 21 Sorry, 23 Title, 24 Inspect, 25 Ad lib, 27 Guest, 28 Miracle.
Down: 1 Hub, 2 Noisy, 3 Onion, 4 Prayer, 5 Steam, 6 Sheen, 7 Instantly, 9 Noodles, 12 Resigning, 14 All told, 17 Bottom, 19 Aisle, 20 Sweat, 21 Stair, 22 Relic, 26 Bee.
Answer: LACHISH

Solutions

309

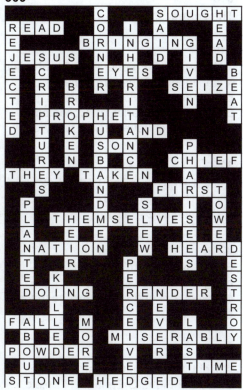

310

2	9	1	4	8	5	3	7	6
8	5	3	2	6	7	9	4	1
6	4	7	1	3	9	2	5	8
4	3	5	7	2	1	6	8	9
1	8	6	5	9	3	7	2	4
9	7	2	8	4	6	1	3	5
7	6	4	9	5	2	8	1	3
3	2	8	6	1	4	5	9	7
5	1	9	3	7	8	4	6	2

Name: ZEDEKIAH

311

1 Cain's murder of Abel, 2 Jerusalem,
3 Mephibosheth, 4 Elizabeth, 5 Jesus,
6 Love, 7 Ezekiel, 8 Capernaum.

312

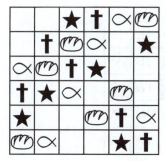

313

(word search grid with PAUL / ALPHA letters)

314

S	O	N	I	M
M	I	O	S	N
O	N	I	M	S
N	S	M	O	I
I	M	S	N	O

315

✦ (dove) † ☆ (bread)

316

1 Momentum, 2 Altruism, 3 Reaffirm, 4 Tristram (Tristan), 5 Headroom, 6 Actinium,
7 Cherubim, 8 Aluminum, 9 Satanism, 10 Pendulum, 11 Addendum, 12 Restroom.
The names are: MARTHA and CASPAR

377

Solutions

317

2 Cat, 3 Jesus, 4 Hershey, 5 Baffin Bay,
6 Beaufort Sea, 7 Alpha and Omega.
The central column reads: PASSION

320

1 Shepard, 2 Creole, 3 Ratel, 4 Fuji,
5 Eel, 6 LA, 7 H.
The character is: DELILAH

321

Cross=12, dove=10, key=18, star=13.

323

C   H

A   J

325

3E	1S	3S	1E	1S
1N	2E	1N	3S	2W
1E	3E		1W	1S
3E	3N	2W	1N	3W
3N	1W	2E	1W	3W

327

328

MANGER

330

1 A pillar of cloud, 2 Two, 3 Ravens,
4 A lake of fire, 5 The prodigal son,
6 Nebuchadnezzar II, 7 To attend a
census, 8 Canaan.

318

The correct spelling is d.

319

1 Roosevelt, 2 Frequently, 3 Disinherited,
4 Continuous, 5 Inappropriate,
6 Stethoscope, 7 Considerate,
8 Cockerel, 9 Scarlet, 10 Collected.
The remaining letters form: MALACHI

322

A=20, B=1, C=15, D=10, E=4, F=21,
G=16, H=25, I=14, J=37, K=41, L=39,
M=78, N=80, O=158.

324

For as by one man's disobedience
many were made sinners, so by the
obedience of one shall many be made
righteous.

326

A Tight, B Hearth, C Wash, D Vowel,
E Loud, F Fight, G Enough, H Shield,
I Reason, J Trial, K Dimmer, L Adore,
M Beaten, N Halted, O Sunday, P Noon,
Q Heath, R Titan, S Match.
And the angel came in unto her, and
said, Hail, thou that art highly favored,
the Lord is with thee: blessed art thou
among women.
Luke 1:28

329

Galatians 6:8 For he that soweth to his
flesh shall of the flesh reap corruption;
but he that soweth to the Spirit shall of
the Spirit reap life everlasting.
Galatians 6:9 And let us not be weary
in well doing: for in due season we shall
reap, if we faint not.
Galatians 6:10 As we have therefore
opportunity, let us do good unto all men,
especially unto them who are of the
household of faith.

Solutions

331

STAR, soar, boar, boat, coat, cost, cast, EAST
(Other solutions may also exist)

333

The character is: CLEOPAS

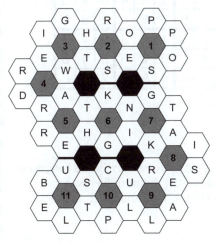

335

The nine-letter name is: SOSTHENES

336

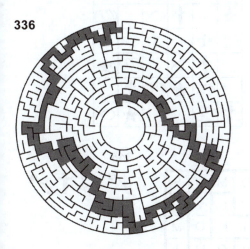

338

Across: 1 Fees, 4 Crossing, 8 Tactless, 9 Gown, 10 Serum, 11 Panther, 13 Escape, 15 Ladies, 18 Drastic, 20 Happy, 23 Glue, 24 Eloquent, 25 Isolated, 26 Ache.
Down: 2 Erase, 3 Satsuma, 4 Crew, 5 Obstacle, 6 Sight, 7 Nowhere, 10 She, 12 Penitent, 14 Surplus, 16 Dracula, 17 Say, 19 Shell, 21 Pinch, 22 Road.
Answer: HERMON

332

Weep not; she is not dead, but sleepeth.
Luke 8:52

334

I called for my lovers, but they deceived me: my priests and mine elders gave up the ghost in the city, while they sought their meat to relieve their souls.
Lamentations 1:19

337

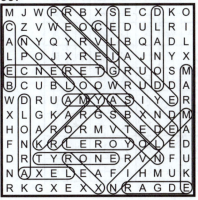

Solutions

339

M	A	K	E	R					K					H
	I				P	R	U	D	E	N	T			I
W	A	N	T		U				O		S			M
O		G		B	R	E	A	D		W		L	I	P
R		E			E				E	V	I	L		S
D		N					G	O	L	D		N		E
S	I	M	P	L	E				G			L		L
		E			S				G			O		F
G		S	C	O	R	N	E	R		T		R		S
R	S		O		N			T		L	E	N	D	E
A	N	F		N		G		T		N				R
C	O	R	R	E	C	T	I	O	N		B			V
E	E	A	E	G				R		L	I	O	N	A
	S	T	R	A	N	G	E			B				N
		F	O	O	L	I	S	H	N	E	S	S		T
		R	O	E	P			S	O	U	L			
		N	I	N	C	R	E	A	S	E		R		
C	E	A	S	E	H	R	D				R	E	L	Y
		P	O	O	R	T						L		
F		S	F	V								Y		
A	R	E	P	R	O	A	C	H		B				
S	I	L	V	E	R	N	I	E		O	U	N	D	
L		I	C		E	N				U				
		C	N		T	R	A	I	N		N	D		
	S	H	O	U	L	D	Y							

340

7	3	4	5	1	6	8	9	2
9	6	1	8	7	2	4	5	3
8	5	2	3	4	9	7	6	1
6	7	3	9	5	8	1	2	4
1	8	9	2	3	4	6	7	5
4	2	5	7	6	1	3	8	9
2	9	6	1	8	3	5	4	7
3	4	7	6	2	5	9	1	8
5	1	8	4	9	7	2	3	6

Name: ABIGAIL

341

1 Joshua, 2 Jeremiah, 3 The Kingdom of Heaven, 4 Jotham, 5 Hosea, 6 Delilah, 7 The Antichrist, 8 A ladder.

342

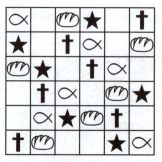

343

344

I	O	M	N	S
M	N	S	I	O
S	I	N	O	M
N	S	O	M	I
O	M	I	S	N

345

346

1 Alhambra, 2 Black Sea, 3 Estancia, 4 Leukemia, 5 Swastika, 6 Hiawatha, 7 Alopecia, 8 Dyslexia, 9 Rutabaga, 10 A capella, 11 Caligula, 12 Hysteria.
The names are: ABEL and SHADRACH

Solutions

347
2 Hen, 3 April, 4 Calvary, 5 Streisand, 6 Connecticut, 7 Vice President.
The central column reads: SERVICE

350
1 Abraham, 2 Utopia, 3 Frost, 4 Taft, 5 Ash, 6 Ye, 7 W.
The character is: MATTHEW

351
Cross=6, dove=8, key=3, star=4.

353

355

1S	3S	1W	1W	1S
2S	2E	1W	1N	1S
2N	1E	■	3W	2S
2E	2E	2N	1E	3N
1E	2N	2W	2N	2W

357

358
JERICHO

360
1 Gideon, 2 Bethlehem, 3 Joseph, 4 Joseph of Arimathea, 5 The Way of Grief, 6 Esau, 7 Samson, 8 Babylon.

348
The correct spelling is c.

349
1 Shipbuilding, 2 Portugal, 3 Astronomy, 4 Observing, 5 Astronaut, 6 Trepidation, 7 Remainder, 8 Honeycomb, 9 Circumference, 10 Everybody.
The remaining letters form: JUDE

352
A=10, B=16, C=29, D=19, E=4, F=26, G=45, H=48, I=23, J=71, K=93, L=71, M=164, N=164, N=328.

354
And God made two great lights; the greater light to rule the day, and the lesser light to rule the night: he made the stars also.

356
A Drove, B Theory, C Chant, D Having, E Lotion, F Joined, G Major, H Haunt, I Avenue, J Toe, K Flash, L Fading, M Tidied, N Shaken, O Tender, P Shine, Q Home, R Thigh.
And the LORD said unto Joshua, See, I have given into thine hand Jericho, and the king thereof, and the mighty men of valor.
Joshua 6:2

359
1 John 4:8 He that loveth not, knoweth not God; for God is love.
1 John 4:9 In this was manifested the love of God toward us, because that God sent his only begotten Son into the world, that we might live through him.
1 John 4:10 Herein is love, not that we loved God, but that he loved us, and sent his Son to be the propitiation for our sins.
1 John 4:11 Beloved, if God so loved us, we ought also to love one another.

Solutions

361

RUTH, rush, ruse, muse, mule, male, mall, maul, PAUL
(Other solutions may also exist)

363

The character is: PHILEMON

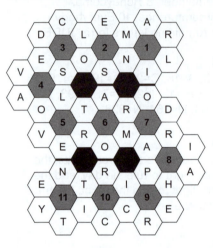

365

The nine-letter name is: ZACCHAEUS

366

362

Amend your ways and your doings.
Jeremiah 7:3

364

If I have told you earthly things, and ye believe not, how shall ye believe, if I tell you of heavenly things?
John 3:12

367

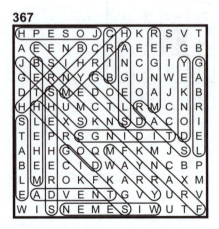

368

Across: 3 Destitute, 8 Reef, 9 Pancreas, 10 Beirut, 13 Scald, 14 Robbery, 15 Fan, 16 Iceberg, 17 Built, 21 Unseen, 22 Material, 23 Acne, 24 Recovered.
Down: 1 Proboscis, 2 Dedicated, 4 Empty, 5 Tension, 6 Tire, 7 Tray, 11 Residence, 12 Bystander, 14 Rag, 15 Fragile, 18 Bulge, 19 Cage, 20 Hero.
Answer: CAPERNAUM

Solutions

369

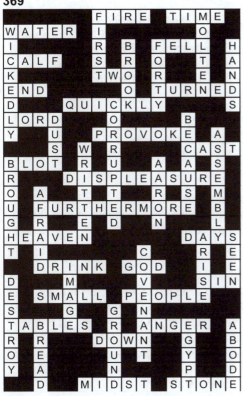

370

4	9	8	2	1	6	5	7	3
5	1	3	8	9	7	4	6	2
2	7	6	3	5	4	8	9	1
9	5	2	7	8	1	3	4	6
8	3	1	4	6	2	9	5	7
6	4	7	9	3	5	2	1	8
7	2	5	1	4	3	6	8	9
3	6	9	5	7	8	1	2	4
1	8	4	6	2	9	7	3	5

Name: SANBALLAT

371

1 What he sows, 2 The Tree of Life, 3 John, 4 Thou shalt not steal, 5 Noah and family, 6 Peter, 7 Thou shalt not kill, 8 Genesis.

372

373

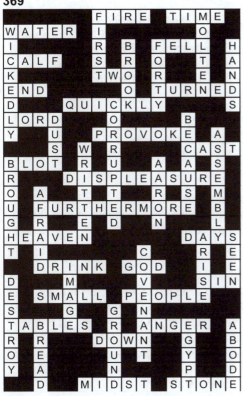

374

S	N	O	I	M
O	S	N	M	I
N	I	M	S	O
M	O	I	N	S
I	M	S	O	N

375

376

1 Poop deck, 2 Idle talk, 3 Limerick, 4 Asterisk, 5 Tomahawk, 6 Eggwhisk, 7 Songbook, 8 Habakkuk, 9 Aardvark, 10 Ragnarok, 11 Overlook, 12 Notebook.
The names are: PILATE and SHARON

377

2 Cry, 3 Adams, 4 Babylon, 5 Cleveland, 6 Deuteronomy, 7 Charles Wesley.
The central column reads: PRAYERS

Solutions

378

The correct spelling is a.

380

1 Apostle, 2 Nimitz, 3 Chile, 4 Dusk,
5 Koi, 6 We, 7 L.
The character is: EZEKIEL

381

Cross=10, dove=16, key=11, star=9.

383

G   D

B   E

385

1E	3S	2S	3W	2W
2E	3S	3S	1S	1N
1N	3E		3W	1N
1S	2N	2W	3N	1W
3E	2N	2E	3N	1N

379

1 Atlantic, 2 Hollywood, 3 Sauerkraut,
4 Disciple, 5 Venezuela,
6 Thermometer, 7 Representative,
8 Photography, 9 Aircraft carrier.
The remaining letters form: HOSEA

382

A=11, B=14, C=13, D=12, E=22, F=25,
G=27, H=25, I=34, J=52, K=52, L=59,
M=104, N=111, O=215.

384

For God so loved the world, that he gave his only
begotten Son, that whosoever believeth in him should
not perish, but have everlasting life.

386

A Office, B Ahead, C Plain, D Craved, E Amaze,
F Jeans, G Gloves, H Using, I Praise, J Rivet, K Whisk,
L Hush, M Honest, N Been, O Lion, P Vain, Q Hunt,
R Heater, S Thrust, T Edited.
Then Peter said, Silver and gold have I none; but such
as I have give I thee: In the name of Jesus Christ of
Nazareth rise up and walk.
Acts 3:6

387

388

GENESIS

389

Mark 14:23 And he took the cup, and
when he had given thanks, he gave it
to them: and they all drank of it.
Mark 14:24 And he said unto
them, This is my blood of the new
testament, which is shed for many.
Mark 14:25 Verily I say unto you, I will
drink no more of the fruit of the vine,
until that day that I drink it new in the
kingdom of God.

390

1 Thou shalt not commit adultery,
2 Miriam, 3 The Mount of Olives,
4 Puteoli, 5 Jesus, 6 Zechariah,
7 Gezer, 8 Thou shalt not covet.

391

CAIN, gain, grin, grid, arid, acid, aced,
abed, ABEL
(Other solutions may also exist)

392

Blessed are they that do his commandments, that they may have right to the tree of
life, and may enter in through the gates into the city.
Revelation 22:14